2nd Edition

# THE VARIABLE ANNUITY HANDBOOK

By Gary H. Snouffer, J.D., CLU

The National Underwriter Company
A Unit of Highline Media LLC

P.O. Box 14367 · Cincinnati, OH 45250-0367
**1-800-543-0874**
www.NationalUnderwriter.com

*This publication is designed to provide accurate and authoritative information in regard to the subject matter covered. It is sold with the understanding that the publisher is not engaged in rendering legal, accounting or other professional service. If legal advice or other expert assistance is required, the services of a competent professional should be sought.* – **From a Declaration of Principles jointly adopted by a Committee of the American Bar Association and a Committee of Publishers and Associations.**

ISBN: 0-87218-639-3

Library of Congress Control Number: 2004118368

2nd Edition


The National Underwriter Company
P.O. Box 14367, Cincinnati, Ohio 45250-0367



Printed in U. S. A.

# Acknowledgements

The sales and marketing of variable annuities encompass a great many disciplines within the insurance and investment business. For all of their help, I wish to thank my former colleagues at Union Central Insurance and Investments and its broker/dealer, Carillon Investments, Inc. Their expertise, insights and guidance were of immeasurable value in the writing of this book.

I also wish to thank the National Underwriter editors, especially Sonya E. King, J.D., LL.M., Deborah A. Miner, J.D., CLU, ChFC, and Joseph F. Stenken, J.D., CLU, ChFC, for their assistance in discussing the issues involved and in editing and checking the contents of the various chapters. Such high quality, professional backup provides a writer with considerable confidence.

# About the Author

In his over forty-five years in the insurance industry, Gary Snouffer has worked with annuities from both the sales and technical perspectives. While a vice president with a mutual life insurance company, he played an instrumental role in creating and marketing the company's first variable annuity.

Gary began his career as a life insurance agent, spending nearly a decade concentrating on personal financial and business needs sales. As an Assistant Editor for The National Underwriter Company, where he contributed to The *Advanced Sales Reference Service* and the *Agent's Reference Service,* Gary wrote about the sales process and developed training programs.

After leaving National Underwriter, Gary held various home office positions with Union Central Insurance and Investments, eventually becoming a vice president in the Marketing Department. With Union Central, Gary was responsible for the marketing aspects of product development for both life and annuity products as well as advanced underwriting support services and accumulation product marketing. Additionally, he was charged with the development of marketing and business plans.

Also while in the home office, Gary developed and conducted numerous seminars on life insurance and annuity product sales and technical concepts in the areas of business and estate planning. He designed seminars to introduce new products and explain the effective uses of sales and marketing materials and illustrations.

Gary received his undergraduate degree from Miami University of Ohio and his law degree from the Salmon P. Chase College of Law, Northern Kentucky University. He is a member of the Ohio bar and holds the Chartered Life Underwriter (CLU) designation.

Currently a consultant to several businesses, Gary resides in Cincinnati, Ohio.

# Table of Contents

Acknowledgements ............ iii
About the Author ............ iv

Chapter 1: Variable Annuities: A Staple for Investors and Savers ............ 1
Annuity Sales on the Increase ............ 1
Retirement Income is Up to Them ............ 3
Maintaining Purchasing Power ............ 4
A Measure of Safety ............ 5
Control of Investment Selection ............ 6
When to Pay Taxes ............ 7
Looking for Help ............ 7
Variable Annuities "Have It All" ............ 8
Convenient to Purchase ............ 8
Offer a Multitude of Choices to Maintain Buying Power ............ 9
Name Recognition ............ 10
Control of Investment Allocation ............ 11
Tax Paying Control ............ 11
Income Amount and Timing Control ............ 12
In the Following Chapters ............ 13

Chapter 2: Markets for Variable Annuities ............ 15
Building on Mutual Fund Awareness ............ 15
Inside the Variable Annuity Wrapper ............ 16
Composition of Households ............ 18
Changes in Retirement Income Composition ............ 20
Social Security ............ 20
Employer Retirement Plans ............ 21
One's Own Assets ............ 23
Not Saving What Is Needed ............ 24
Population Segments by Size ............ 26
Self-Employed: IRA and SEP ............ 27
Self-Employed with Employees ............ 28
Supplementing Employer Plans ............ 28
Timing the Tax ............ 29
Maximizing Income ............ 30
Receiving Large Sums ............ 32

Chapter 3: Approaching Markets ............ 35
Primary or Supplementary Market? ............ 35
Supplementary Marketing ............ 35
Primary Marketing ............ 36
Targeting Markets ............ 37
Characteristics in Common ............ 37
Market Research ............ 39
Survey Information ............ 40
Analyzing the Data ............ 42

As a Member of the Group ....................43
Other Markets ....................44
Smaller Employers ....................45
Tailoring the Sales Process ....................47
Tips on Seminar Selling ....................49
Invitation List ....................50
Sponsored Seminars ....................51
Keep Promotion Going ....................52
Designing the Seminar ....................53
Absolute Must: Response Card ....................54
Seminar Length and Speakers ....................55
On Building Your Sales Presentation ....................56
Need and Motivation to Act ....................56

Chapter 4: Selling Ideas ....................59
Finding the Dominant Appeal ....................59
Building Retirement Income ....................62
Variable Annuities as IRAs: Building Retirement Income with Efficiency ....................62
Children's Education ....................66
Variable Annuities as IRAs: More Help for Children's Education ....................66
Regular Saving and Investing ....................69
Importance of Regular Saving and Investing: Cost of Delay ....................69
Importance of Regular Saving and Investing: Dollar Cost Averaging ....................71
Tax Deferral ....................73
Maximizing Accumulation: Taking Advantage of Tax Deferral ....................73
Maintaining Control ....................74
Exercising and Maintaining Control: Having Many Choices ....................74
Exercising and Maintaining Control: Changing Investments ....................76
Exercising and Maintaining Control: Timing Income Taxes ....................77
Maintaining Purchasing Power ....................78
Maintaining Purchasing Power: Investing in Equities ....................78
Diversification ....................79
Dealing with Risk: Using Diversification to Advantage ....................79
Using Guarantees ....................80
Cementing Your Successes: Strategic Use of the Guaranteed Interest (or Money Market) Account ....................80
Cementing Your Successes: Availability of the Death Benefit and Optional Death Benefits ....................81
Cementing Your Successes: Availability of Guaranteed Living Benefits ....................82
Income Planning ....................83
Effective Income Planning: Defer, Withdraw, Annuitize ....................83
Penalty Tax Perspective ....................84

Keeping the Penalty Tax in Perspective: Don't Be Put Off by It ....84
Large, One-Time Amounts ....86
Handling Large, One-Time Amounts: Take the Pressure Off but Put the Money to Work ....86
Social Security Benefits Taxation ....87
Annuity Buildup Not Counted for Social Security Benefits Taxation ....87
Annuity Payouts and Life Insurance ....88
Annuity Payout and Life Insurance Combination ....88
Small Employer Retirement Planning ....89
IRAs for Smaller Employers ....89
Providing for Supplemental Retirement Income ....89
After the Sale ....90

Chapter 5: Marketing and Sales Support ....93
Achieving Customer Satisfaction ....93
Expectations for the Future ....94
Timing the Market ....95
Dollar Cost Averaging ....95
Asset Allocation ....97
Asset Allocation Model ....98
Performance Histories ....100
Third Party Sources ....100
Insurance Company Rating Services ....101
The Prospectus ....103
Risk Disclosure Document ....105
Sales Illustrations ....106
Account and Balance Summaries ....106
Periodic Reports ....108
Product Features ....108

Chapter 6: Licensing, Compliance and Ethics ....111
Federal and State Regulation ....111
Registered Products ....111
Broker/Dealer Products Only ....112
Federal-State Regulatory Matters ....112
Fund-Level Disclosure and Certification ....113
Securities Licenses ....114
Supervisor Licensing ....115
Registered Investment Advisor ....116
Compliance Meetings ....117
Continuing Education ....118
Supervision and Designated Offices ....118
Sales Presentations and Practices ....120
Sales Literature ....120
Suitability Statement ....121
Proposed Additional Suitability Rule ....122

Contract Exchanges and Bonus Annuities ..... 123
Market Timing Disclosure ..... 124
Contract Delivery ..... 125
Ethical Practices ..... 125
Customer Focused ..... 126
In-Office Documentation ..... 127
Remember—Something Will Go Wrong ..... 127

Chapter 7: Product Features and Characteristics ..... 129
Annuity Classifications ..... 129
Premiums ..... 130
Issue and Maturity Ages ..... 131
Accumulation Units ..... 131
Variety of Variable Accounts ..... 132
Choices Popular ..... 135
Guaranteed Interest Accounts ..... 136
Death Benefits ..... 138
Guaranteed Living Benefits ..... 139
Allocation to Accounts ..... 142
Transfers Among Accounts ..... 142
Automatic Rebalancing ..... 143
Dollar Cost Averaging Among Accounts ..... 143
Surrender Charges ..... 144
Charge-Free Withdrawals ..... 144
Periodic Withdrawal Program ..... 145
Waiving Surrender Charges ..... 145
Payout Options ..... 146
Fixed Amount Payout Option ..... 147
Fixed Period Payout Option ..... 147
Life Annuity Payout Option ..... 147
Life Income with Period Certain Payout Option ..... 148
Life Income with Refund Payout Option ..... 148
Joint and Survivor Annuity Payout Option ..... 148
Joint and Survivor with Period Certain Payout Option ..... 149
Changing the Payout Option ..... 149
Variable Payouts ..... 149
Immediate Variable Annuities ..... 150
Bonus Annuities ..... 150
Payments to Impaired Risks ..... 151
Market Value Adjustment ..... 151
Equity-Indexed Annuity ..... 152
Group Annuities ..... 154
Developing New Products ..... 154

Chapter 8: Charges and Fees: Pricing ..... 157
Good Value, Adequate Return ..... 157
Securities Markets Imrpovement Act ..... 158
Contract Fees ..... 160

Guaranteed Interest Account: Interest Margin ....160
Mortality and Expense Charge ....161
Investment Management Fees....162
Charges for Optional Benefits ....163
Proprietary Accounts....163
Transfer Fees ....164
Surrender Charges....164
Group Annuity Pricing....166
Operational Differences ....167
Comparisons and Customer Value....167

Chapter 9: Distribution of Products....171
Variety of Distribution Outlets ....171
Producer Compensation ....172
Paid to Other Distributors ....173
Percentages Paid ....173
Increasing Compensation ....174
Variable Annuity Replacements ....175
Making a Profit ....176

Chapter 10: Other Financial Services Products....179
Stocks and Bonds....179
Selecting Investments....181
Income Tax ....182
Derivative Investments....183
Mutual Funds....183
Variable Annuity Features....185
Wrap Accounts....186
Limited Partnerships, Unit Investment Trusts and Hedge Funds ....187
Real Estate ....188
Savings Accounts and Certificates of Deposit....189
In Conclusion ....190

Chapter 11: Variable Annuities in Business and Estate Planning ....191
Qualified Retirement Plans....191
Contribution Limitations ....192
Plan Requirements ....193
Required Minimum Distributions ....194
401(k) Plan ....196
SIMPLE 401(k) Plans....196
Using Variable Annuities in Qualified Plans....197
Individual Retirement Annuities ....198
Contributions ....198
Distributions....199
SIMPLE IRA ....200
Simplified Employee Pension ....201
Roth IRA....202

Tax Sheltered Annuities (403(b) Plans) ....... 202
457 Plans ....... 203
Nonqualified Retirement Plans ....... 204
Executive Equity Plans ....... 205
Education Funding ....... 206
From Personal Resources ....... 206
Tax Credits and Deductions ....... 207
Tax-Favored Education Savings ....... 207
Role of Annuities ....... 208
Gifts of Annuities ....... 210
Gifts to Charity ....... 210
Charitable Trusts ....... 211

Chapter 12: Taxation of Variable Annuities ....... 215
Federal Income Tax ....... 215
Withdrawals ....... 216
Premature Distributions ....... 218
Section 1035 Exchanges ....... 219
Complete and Partial Surrenders ....... 221
Sale of an Annuity ....... 221
Taxation of Payouts ....... 222
Fixed Payout ....... 222
Variable Payout ....... 223
Death of an Owner ....... 224
Federal Estate Tax ....... 226
Federal Gift Tax ....... 228
Annuities as Gifts ....... 230
Planning Considerations ....... 231

Appendix A: Actuarial Tables for Taxing Annuities ....... 235
Frequency of Payment Adjustment Table ....... 236
Table V—Ordinary Life Annuities—
One Life—Expected Return Multiples ....... 237
Table VI—Ordinary Joint Life and Last Survivor Annuities—
Two Lives—Expected Return Multiples ....... 237
Table VIA—Annuities for Joint Life Only—
Two Lives—Expected Return Multiples ....... 239
Table VII—Percent Value of Refund Feature
Duration of Guaranteed Amount ....... 241

Index ....... 243

# Chapter 1

# Variable Annuities: A Staple for Investors and Savers

## Annuity Sales on the Increase

Annuities, both fixed and variable, have been among the mainstays of the public's saving and investment choices for some years. Although they achieved their current high level of popularity in only the last ten to fifteen years, variable annuities have been around for over 60 years; fixed annuities have been available for far longer. Whether the public prefers fixed annuities or variable annuities at any particular time often has had much to do with interest rates, stock and bond prices, and how the economy is doing.

For many years in the 1980's and early 1990's, interest rates credited to fixed annuities were at or near historic highs. At the same time, the fixed annuity products that were developed contained attractive, new features and flexibility not previously available. There were few drawbacks to turning to these annuities, provided that they were issued by companies with solid financial underpinnings. Here was a relatively easy-to-understand product with high current interest rates, underlying interest guarantees, tax deferral, and results that were easy to track. What could be better? Maybe nothing could have been better, if these conditions had lasted forever.

But, of course, they did not. Market interest rates fell sharply in the early to mid 1990's, soon followed by credited current rates on fixed annuities. It also became an accepted opinion that fixed interest financial instruments have a more difficult time keeping pace with inflation than those with equity investments. Sales of fixed annuities slowed during that period. Variable annuities became the financial product of choice in ever-increasing numbers.

Since many of the premium dollars going into variable annuities were allocated to accounts that purchase stocks and bonds, product sales flourished as never before during the stock market run-up of the late 1990s. But then came the bear market that some analysts had begun to predict might never come again. According to *The* VARDS *Report*[1], the end of 2002 marked the longest consecutive bear market since 1941 and it continued before starting to turn around in early 2003.

What has been the effect on variable annuity sales of the downturn in the economy, the stock market, and market interest rates? As mentioned above, there had been a buildup of major proportions. In 2000, total premium flow was $137.5 billion.[2] This compares (roughly, because the method of calculating sales has changed somewhat) with figures for 1996, 1993, and 1990 of $74 billion, $46.6 billion, and $12 billion, respectively.[3] There had been massive increases. Then, total sales in 2001 fell to $112.8 billion, down 17.8% from 2000.[4] But in 2002, variable annuity sales held their ground with total premium flow of $113.7 billion.[5] And in 2003, a gain in sales of 11%, to $124.6 billion, was posted.[6]

There are good and compelling reasons to believe that variable annuities will continue to hold their ground and then some. Most of them are the same reasons that variable annuities became such a staple for investors and savers in the first place—reasons we will discuss first in this chapter and then add to in subsequent chapters. The fact is variable annuities are a must if one is to offer customers the opportunity to purchase the variety of financial products, which often are required to serve their needs. Any number of the customers' financial objectives can be addressed with variable annuities.

The needs that are addressed when people purchase variable annuities are much in evidence. For the most part, it does not take involved explanations to point them out and discuss them. Sometimes, it takes a certain level of sophistication to understand all of the ramifications and to adopt strategies, but the needs themselves are pretty straightforward.

## Retirement Income is Up to Them

Today, people know it is up to them to provide a substantial amount of their retirement incomes. Much has been written about the baby boomers, those born from 1946 through 1964, because there are so many of them. The oldest baby boomers are now in their upper 50's, and many others entering their 50's—those years when people begin to "get serious" about retirement. There are many reasons to believe it important to provide for yourself.

Faith in the solvency of the Social Security system has eroded. Proposals to make the system more sound are advanced; from time to time, one is implemented. But it is fair to say that a great many people wonder just how sound the system will be by the time they are ready to retire. Some of the proposed cures—such as making more of the income taxable, means testing, putting the retirement age off further, and using a less advantageous index for benefit increases—may improve the solvency of the system but may also have adverse effects on the beneficiaries of Social Security. Sometimes, people say they do not expect to get much from Social Security and feel the need to plan for a retirement without it.

Another reason people know they must do more for themselves is the change that has taken place involving working for only one or two employers during a business career. Employer retirement plans are likely to provide a lower percentage of needed income. Then, there are the widespread corporate reductions in workers (downsizing). Sometimes, the reduction in the number of workers is attributable to productivity increases—being able to do more with less; in this case fewer workers. Other times, it is because certain work can be done for considerably lower wages by workers living in foreign countries, euphemistically called "outsourcing." With competition from companies in other countries as well as from those located closer to home, businesses are under constant pressure to contain costs. And since the largest costs of many businesses are those connected with their workforces, cost containment must involve workers. This is evident to those affected, whether directly or indirectly. It is easy to see how comforting it would be to have one's own source of retirement income. No longer is it possible to assume a substantial employer-provided retirement income as a given in retirement planning.

Some people feel reasonably secure about the future of Social Security and their employer retirement plans. Nonetheless, many of these people realize the importance of supplementing these sources with retirement income they provide for themselves. As it is said, "You never have too much retirement income." A higher retirement income will afford greater choices of activities, travel destinations, and places to live. It can also create the opportunity to make gifts to family members and charities and, perhaps, even have an effect on the type and quality of health care available.

Notwithstanding the fact that many people realize that much of their retirement income adequacy is up to them, there often is a big gap between thought and action. A National Retirement Planning Coalition study shows that there is only limited awareness of the critical importance of comprehensive retirement planning. Key findings of the study include:

- *Long retirements expected* – The average respondent expects to spend at least 19 years in retirement. A long retirement requires a significant amount of savings, even if inflation remains modest over this extended period of time.

- *Retirement income needs underestimated* – Survey respondents indicate that they expect to need 60% of pre-retirement income to live comfortably, yet most retirement planning professionals recommend 75 to 90% for adequate retirement income.

- *Insufficient retirement savings* – Only one-third of respondents are very confident that they will be able to maintain the lifestyle they want through retirement years. Even many upper-income respondents, with earnings of at least $100,000 per year and nearing retirement, are behind track in accumulating the resources to generate retirement income needed to come anywhere close to meeting their current expenses.

- *Inadequate planning conducted* – Forty-one percent of respondents have not even attempted to determine how much retirement savings they will need to live comfortably in retirement. Another 41% who did attempt to calculate their required retirement savings could not complete the calculation, or could not determine the income they need to retire.[7]

## Maintaining Purchasing Power

Until the mid to late 1990s, people's ability to maintain their purchasing power in the future in light of the effect of inflation on the prices of the goods and services they buy was a constant concern. Many potential annuity buyers have vivid memories of the high inflation days of the late 1970s and early 1980s. Many are reminded of inflation each time they buy, especially with higher priced items such as cars or major appliances. Home prices in some areas have increased disproportionately. The cost of college has outpaced inflation at a time when a college education is more important than ever for financial success. During more recent years, the efforts of the Federal Reserve Board and others have brought about a lessening of the upward pressure on prices to a significant extent. Interestingly, almost amazingly, some people seem to forget that even modest inflation erodes the purchasing power of the assets that have been put aside for retirement.

Stocks and bonds as a group are seen as good hedges against inflation. Although it is not so true during a bear market and low interest rate period, it has been well documented over the years that the S&P 500 Index has increased faster, on average, than the Consumer Price Index (CPI). Twenty-year corporate bonds also have outpaced the CPI, though not by as much. Of course, not all stocks or all corporate bonds will serve to hedge inflation, because some will decrease in value. And during some periods, nearly all stocks and many bonds will decrease in value. But people recognize that they must be in a position to benefit from the capital appreciation of stocks and of bonds to some extent. They realize that they must put some significant portion of their retirement dollars into financial products that invest in stocks and/or bonds, or possibly other investments such as real estate investment trusts, if they are to have the income to cope with future inflation. But that does not necessarily mean that they wish or expect to become adept at selecting individual stocks and bonds.

## A Measure of Safety

Many people desire a certain measure of safety with respect to the funds they are saving or investing as well as with respect to the earnings that the funds will generate. They understand that fixed-rate products have an interest rate guarantee for some period but that renewal rates will not be known in advance and will depend on market conditions at the time of renewal. In some cases, there is a floor rate below which the renewal rate will not go, although the levels of floor rates have been lower in recent years than was the case previously. In addition, fixed-rate products often have a guarantee of principal. The companies issuing the products are able to offer guarantees because they diversify the investments which underlie those products. They diversify by type of instrument, time period, liquidity, and other factors needed to suit the requirements of the product. It is this diversification that brings safety.

The same principle holds true for financial products that invest in stocks and bonds, except that diversification is a joint effort which includes the buyer. The financial product, e.g., mutual fund or variable annuity separate account, will have diversification in keeping with the investment objective of the fund or account. However, the mutual fund or variable annuity buyer must attain this diversification by selecting those funds or accounts that provide the desired level of diversification when considered along with the buyer's other investments and savings.

So diversification is the key to safety. Either the buyer has it done by the product issuer or he participates in it to a significant extent. When the buyer participates by purchasing products that invest in stocks and bonds, he is in a position to enjoy the financial benefits of products which perform better, on average, than those where the product issuer has sole responsibility for diversification.

## Control of Investment Selection

Many people like to exercise a certain degree of control over where their money is invested but they do not necessarily want complete control. They may be willing to put some of their funds in products where the product issuer selects the investments and pays them a promised rate of interest. They may like the idea of having portfolio managers handling certain amounts of the money they are investing. But these people want to retain the ability to shift to other types of investments or to change the mix of the types of investments. They want to feel they are in control to the extent they want to be in control. At times, they will want to be relatively active in the management of their funds, and at other times, they will want to feel able to be relatively inactive with the knowledge that investment matters will proceed satisfactorily without their active intervention. To put it another way, many people like the idea of being able to exercise or not exercise control as they wish; often, these occasions are dictated by the amount of time and attention the people are willing and able to devote to their investments.

Beyond that, many people simply do not wish to select individual investments. They have neither the expertise nor the time to acquire the expertise. They may not have the self-confidence to assure peace of mind. In addition, they may not be able to achieve the level of investment diversification needed for the level of safety they would like. The fact that they will be subject to some relatively small fees for professional assistance appears to be a good bargain.

Maintaining control of investment selection also includes the desire to be able to pull substantial amounts of money out of equity investments when there is a bear market or a period of high volatility in equity markets. The funds then are placed in fixed investments, such as guaranteed funds, bond funds, or cash accounts such as money market funds. When the investment climate is right, money can be moved back into equities. And it may be that the equity accounts chosen then will be different from those invested in before. Sometimes, people prefer to leave already invested money where it is and to change investment selection only with respect to new money going into investments and savings.

As we will learn later, one of the great advantages to variable annuities is the fact that these types of changes can be made without closing out one account and starting another, thus incurring the attendant costs and possible income taxes. Changes may be made among variable annuity accounts quite easily and with little cost.

## When to Pay Taxes

When there are opportunities, people like to control when they pay taxes on various types of income and how much they pay. While it is not possible for most employees to do much about when they receive income, they can take some steps such as timing charitable contributions, medical expense payments, and real estate taxes as well as selecting when to take capital gains and losses and sell real property. They also can take advantage of all opportunities they have to participate in tax-qualified retirement plans and to borrow using home equity loans, so that interest is deductible.

Self-employed persons and professionals have more opportunities because, to a significant extent, they can control or, at least influence, when they receive income and when they pay business expenses. After all, customers usually will not pay until you bill them and suppliers will not object to being paid earlier, perhaps at a discount. Magazines and newspapers contain many articles on income tax tactics in the final quarter of each year. People never cease looking for ways to control how much they will pay in a particular year.

## Looking for Help

Thus far, in examining the reasons behind the high-level of popularity of the variable annuity, we have looked at people's recognition that they

1. need to take considerable responsibility for their retirement income;

2. need to maintain buying power in the face of inflation;

3. want a certain measure of safety obtainable by means of diversification;

4. like the idea of maintaining some control of their investments;

5. may not want to make individual investment selections; and

6. want to have some control over when and how much income tax they pay.

While it is true that people may realize that these are the things they want, many simply do not know "how to get there from here."

Many of these people want help and are willing to pay a reasonable amount for it so that they can have a chance to provide adequately for their futures. The help they need can come from qualified sales representatives and financial planners. It also can come from the purchase of financial products that feature professionally-managed portfolios that purchase a large enough number of stocks and/or bonds to achieve a desirable level of diversification. These products are convenient to purchase and offer the flexibility to accommodate any changes needed. As we will see next, variable annuities fall into this category of financial products and can be used to meet many financial needs.

## Variable Annuities "Have It All"

### *Convenient to Purchase*

One of the factors important to the success of implementing a plan to supplement retirement income is a financial product that can be purchased in convenient amounts, at convenient times, and on a convenient, systematic basis. With most companies, variable annuities may be purchased with low initial and continuing premiums, although there are products that require higher initial premiums. In most cases, flexible premiums are the rule so that a buyer may elect to make regular payments such as annually, semi-annually, quarterly, or monthly. Or buyers may make periodic or occasional payments according to their own schedule.

It often is said that the key to saving and investment success is consistent activity. The effect of compounding interest on earnings and the difficulty of "timing the market" with investments combine to make it difficult for intermittent activity to make up for that which has been lost because activity was not consistent. The company issuing a variable annuity will send a notice to remind the buyer to make another payment. This is much more convenient than expecting the buyer to remember to send a payment or to otherwise take the initiative to save or invest.

Of course, reports, which also offer opportunities to put additional money in, are sent with a number of other financial products, but the ease of buying variable annuities, coupled with their other features, makes systematic saving and investing very easy indeed.

### *Offer a Multitude of Choices to Maintain Buying Power*

Understanding that a financial program must invest in stocks and bonds if future buying power will be maintained in light of inflation, variable annuities have funds available which cover a wide range of investment approaches. Some of these types of funds may be described as

- growth;
- aggressive growth;
- growth and income;
- large capitalization stocks;
- small capitalization stocks;
- real estate;
- corporate bonds;
- government bonds;
- balanced;
- high-yield bonds;
- international stocks;

- international bonds;
- those using indexes such as the S&P 500 or NASDAQ; and
- those invested in market segments such as technology or health sciences

Add to this list, which is not a complete list, a guaranteed interest account, and the buyer has a multitude of choices.

Not all variable annuities have all of these funds but, on the other hand, they often have more than one of a particular type. These funds are managed by professionals and buyers merely allocate how much of their payments go into the funds selected. Buyers usually have no restrictions as to what percentage or amount may be allocated to what account. And they can change the allocation or move money from one fund to another as permitted by the variable annuity contract. As a result, buyers are able to allocate as much or as little as they wish to funds that offer the promise of maintaining future purchasing power. And, they can select from among funds which are as aggressive as they think desirable to accomplish the goals intended.

### *Name Recognition*

Some of the funds included in many variable annuities are proprietary; that is, they are provided by and managed by the investment managers of the issuer of the variable annuity. Other funds are provided and managed by other financial organizations, many of which have high name recognition in the marketplace. Having available for allocation of payments funds provided by familiar names can be attractive and a source of comfort for many variable annuity buyers. They may associate publicity with presumed good performance. This conclusion may or may not be justified because the favorable publicity may or may not pertain to the particular variable annuity fund, a fact which must be disclosed.

Publicity about the favorable performance of, for example, a mutual fund provided by the same organization as a variable annuity fund cannot be used to promote the variable annuity. That is because the two funds are different, usually have somewhat different objectives, may have different managers, and as a result, cannot be expected to perform in the same way in the future. All of that does not keep prospective annuity buyers from preferring names they have heard of over those they have not. It is important in these cases that a sales representative not allow the impression to remain with the buyer that information other than that pertaining to particular variable annuity funds may be relied on. Performance data on the fund under consideration is available from the issuer or from several independent sources discussed in Chapter 5.

### *Control of Investment Allocation*

Variable annuities make control of the allocation to investment accounts easy. When they make their first purchases, buyers allocate the payments among the various accounts. In many variable annuities, they also have a guaranteed interest account available. As time goes by, they can change this allocation of the payments. They also can reallocate current accumulated funds among the various accounts as provided by the contract. This means buyers can become more aggressive or less aggressive; they can resort to more or less money in guaranteed accounts. They can concentrate more on accounts which produce income. They can concentrate more on accounts which hold the expectation of capital appreciation. Then, when the buyers' needs for income become different, they can change the allocations or move money from one account to another.

Naturally, the various accounts perform differently from each other at different times. The result can be that a variable annuity buyer may find that the various accounts are not maintaining the balance among the various accounts that was originally intended. The buyer may rebalance the accounts by making transfers among them, subject to contract provisions. In some instances, the buyer can direct that automatic rebalancing be done on a periodic basis. All of these procedures make it possible for the variable annuity buyer to remain in control of the allocation to investment accounts, all without the necessity of selling some investments and buying others with resulting sales charges and tax consequences.

### *Tax Paying Control*

So long as premiums are paid into a variable annuity and no withdrawals are made, income taxes are not incurred by a variable annuity owner; rather, they are deferred until such time as money is withdrawn in some manner. What income tax is payable at the time of withdrawal depends on a number of factors, most notably how the money is withdrawn and how old the annuity owner is at the time of withdrawal. We will examine matters of taxation in other chapters and more completely in Chapter 12, but the general rule is that any money taken out is subject to tax.

This means that until money is withdrawn, it is not subject to current income tax. To the extent the buyer controls when withdrawals are made from a variable annuity, he controls income taxation with respect to it. Many savings and investment products cause the owner to incur income taxes even though all earnings are left in the product and the purchaser receives no actual income or other earnings. To be sure, the income and earnings serve to increase the value of the other products and any income taxes paid increase the taxpayer's basis for the future, but the purchaser is not in a position to control how much will be considered distributed and when the taxes are incurred. With variable annuities, the owner is in a better position.

### *Income Amount and Timing Control*

A person buys a variable annuity with the intention to take income from it at some time in the future. Although there may be percentage or amount restrictions for some years or tax consequences, including tax penalties until age 59½, eventually the buyer can take what is wanted from an annuity. Even during the early years of restrictions, substantial amounts can be withdrawn. This kind of freedom gives the buyer considerable control of the timing of income. And again, these actions can be taken without selling one financial product and buying another. It is all part of the full sequence of events expected in the life of a variable annuity.

There is one more important factor with respect to the amount of income. It is one unique to annuities. An owner may elect to have annuity proceeds paid over a period of years or even for life. The payout can be either a fixed amount or it can be variable. That is, with a variable payout, the amount that is paid each time will vary according to the performance of the investments in the accounts from which they are withdrawn. The variable payout allows the annuitant to continue the participation in equity investments.

The income is made up of both principal and interest and, for that reason, is a larger amount than would be the case if only interest or earnings were distributed. When a life income is elected and the annuitant is, for example, in the upper sixties or older, the income is considerably higher than interest or earnings alone would be and it will last as long as the annuitant lives. For lower income annuitants, this can be of major benefit. Still again, this is the same financial product that was used for other purposes earlier in the owner's life. Material changes need not have been made.

## In the Following Chapters

We will examine all important aspects of variable annuities in the chapters that follow. In Chapter 2 we will look at potential buyers, including those who want adequate retirement, entrepreneurs and other self-employed persons, those who want to be able to postpone taxes with flexibility, those who need to maximize income that will last forever, and those who need to put to work some large proceeds they have realized. Next, in Chapter 3, we will talk about approaching markets, the need for many transactions, target marketing, seminar selling, approaching employers with and without tax-qualified retirement plans, contacts as a regular part of servicing customers, and building your sales story and sales presentation.

Selling ideas are in Chapter 4. Among these are maintaining buying power, the confidence of having many choices, maintaining and changing the investment mix, getting in and out of guarantees, controlling when you pay income tax, drawing income when you want it, making maximum use of IRAs, including the new ones, dealing with large amounts of money, and long-term gifts to children and grandchildren. Chapter 5 addresses marketing and sales support topics such as performance histories, dollar cost averaging, asset allocation, third party information sources, rebalancing accounts, and using the prospectus. Variable annuities are registered products and SEC, NASD, state insurance department, and broker/dealer compliance requirement discussions are in Chapter 6.

Product features and characteristics of variable annuities are found in Chapter 7. Here we look at both common and less common features. Charges and fees are considered in Chapter 8, in the context of how variable annuities are priced. Pricing is an important subject when comparing products and the comparison must consider all of the elements if it will be accurate. Factors having to do with the distribution of variable annuity products, including the compensation of the various parties, are taken up in Chapter 9. These matters also have a material bearing when making product comparisons. Of course, comparisons also extend to products other than variable annuities. Those other financial products used for saving and investment are discussed in Chapter 10.

Variable annuities have significant uses in business and estate planning as we will see in Chapter 11. A very important one is in tax-qualified retirement plans as well as plans to supplement qualified plans. In addition we will consider IRAs, TDAs, and 457 plans, gifts to charities and individuals, and structured settlements. In Chapter 12, we will conclude with the important taxation and ownership provisions affecting variable annuities. Included are income tax aspects applicable to the accumulation period and to withdrawals, exchanges under Internal Revenue Code section 1035, and periodic payments, as well as federal estate and gift tax considerations. Ownership and beneficiary aspects also are covered.

Variable annuities are versatile and exciting financial products to market and sell. They can be a solution to many customers' financial needs. Understanding them and accurately portraying their benefits and features in the context of customers' financial needs can be rewarding to your customer and to you.

## Chapter Endnotes

1. Rick Carey, "VA Products Clawed By The Bear," *National Underwriter*, L&H/Financial Services Edition, Cincinnati, OH, February 24, 2003.
2. Rick Carey, "VA Sales In 2000 Felt The Waves From The Slide In Equities," *National Underwriter*, L&H/Financial Services Edition, Cincinnati, OH, March 12, 2001.
3. "Special Report, Year-End (12/31/96) Sales and Asset Survey," *The Variable Annuity and Data Service (VARDS)*, Financial Planning Resources, Inc.
4. Rick Carey, "Variable Annuity Sales Fell 17.8% To $113 Billion Last Year," *National Underwriter*, L&H/Financial Services Edition, Cincinnati, OH, March 11, 2002.
5. Rick Carey, "VA Products Clawed By The Bear," *National Underwriter*, L&H/Financial Services Edition, Cincinnati, OH, February 24, 2003.
6. Rick Carey, "Variable Annuity Sales Climbed 11% In 2003," *National Underwriter*, L&H/Financial Services Edition, Cincinnati, OH, March 5, 2004.
7. National Retirement Planning Coalition Study, Press Release, November 19, 2002, National Association for Variable Annuities (NAVA).

# Chapter 2

# Markets for Variable Annuities

## Building on Mutual Fund Awareness

Though the prominence of variable annuities is rather recent, the public has been well aware of mutual funds for a far longer time. The first mutual fund in the United States was established in 1924. The Investment Company Act of 1940 defined and classified investment companies, established minimum capital requirements, and provided for other requirements. The Investment Company Amendments Act of 1970 made refinements. The result has been that the mutual fund industry is among the most highly disclosed and publicized of the financial services industries.

Because so much information is readily available, nearly every issue of financial papers such as *Barron's* or the *Wall Street Journal*, and of monthly financial or financial planning magazines has articles on mutual funds. Financial programs on television and websites dealing with financial matters or financial markets feature mutual funds with great regularity. It seems there is always something going on with purchase trends, performance of certain sectors, changes in investment managers, and other news. When editors have nothing else to report, they can always put out a ranking of the top 10, 25, or 50 funds of a certain type over certain periods of time. And they usually follow that with the bottom rankings in the same category. Since readers and viewers seem to like such scorecards, the stories attract attention.

A report by the Investment Company Institute[1] indicates that some 53.9 million U.S. households owned mutual funds, including mutual funds held in variable annuities, in 2004 (up from 53.3 million in 2003 after two years of market declines but still less than the all time high in 2001 of 56.3 million). The number of individual owners was 92.3 million. An estimated 36.4 million households (32.5 percent of the total number of households) held the funds in employer-sponsored retirement plans. The number owning mutual funds outside these plans was 39.3 million (35.1 percent of households). As would be expected, mutual fund ownership increases with household income. Twenty-seven percent of all households with incomes less than $50,000 owned mutual funds, while 72 percent of those with incomes of $50,000 or more owned funds.

Incidence of mutual fund ownership continues to be greatest among households headed by individuals age 35 to 64. Fund ownership in 2004 declined among households headed by individuals younger than age 25, age 45 to 54, and age 55 to 64. Fund ownership increased among households headed by individuals age 35 to 44 and 65 and older.

The reasons cited in numerous studies for the high acceptance level of mutual funds are diversification, professional money management, and liquidity. An investor with virtually any size account can have these advantages. Most individual investors do not have the time, the money, or, in many cases, the desire to select individual securities, diversify widely enough to achieve an acceptable level of safety, and learn and stay abreast of financial, industrial, and worldwide developments that could affect the performance of their investments. And, although mutual funds offer professional money management, individual investors can make their own changes by taking money from one mutual fund and putting it into another.

## Inside the Variable Annuity Wrapper

In most respects, a variable annuity is a package of mutual funds in a unified wrapper, which also may contain a guaranteed account. (As was said earlier and will be discussed in more detail in Chapter 10, the variable accounts in a variable annuity have some differences from mutual funds.)

A variable annuity has some distinct advantages over a collection of mutual funds. First in importance is income tax deferral. While funds are accumulating in a variable annuity, there is no current income tax to be reported. Income tax is paid when money is withdrawn or paid out from the annuity. There is a price for the tax deferral, of course. Unless one of the exceptions (discussed in Chapter 11) applies, there is a 10% penalty on any taxable distributions prior to age 59½.[2] Further, except for periodic payouts, all taxable interest and earnings must be taken before the previously taxed investment or principal can be withdrawn.[3]

Many mutual funds benefit from special provisions applicable to dividends from stocks. If income passed from the fund to investors is "qualified dividend income" in the hands of the fund and not short-term capital gains or interest from bonds, special tax treatment is given such income (until the special provisions expire at the end of 2008). And some annual mutual fund income is reported as capital gains, which is generally taxed more favorably than at ordinary income rates. All variable annuity distributions receive ordinary income tax treatment. This current treatment offsets some of the advantage of complete deferral enjoyed by variable annuities. Comparisons between variable annuities and mutual funds are discussed more in Chapter 10.

The tax deferral wrapper of a variable annuity offers yet another advantage. Funds may be moved from one account to another without the necessity of having to buy and sell shares. This means there is no tax reporting when money is transferred as is the case with mutual funds.

In addition, a variable annuity has a death benefit. That is, in the event of the death of the annuitant, there is a guaranteed minimum amount that will be paid to a beneficiary. What the minimum is varies (as discussed in Chapter 7), but it will never be less than the amount of money put into the contract. No such guarantees are available with mutual funds.

Another advantage of a variable annuity is the availability of payout options, including those which pay for the life of the annuitant. This enhances the value of the variable annuity as a financial product for retirement considerably.

And, after all, most people are investing for retirement. There may be some shorter range goals, particularly the education of children, but retirement is at or near the top of every list of financial objectives. The biggest group of people interested in saving and investing for retirement is the baby boomers. Born from 1946 through 1964, the baby boomers number some 78 million and they are at their peak earning years and moving toward retirement age.

## Composition of Households

Let us take some looks at incomes of the various segments of the population and at the composition of households. First we will look at household incomes and family make-up and then we will turn to individuals, particularly identifying which of them are the affluent and near-affluent.

According to Census Bureau figures for 2003, the mean income for all households was $59,067. The median income (the median is the point half way between the top and the bottom of the range) was $43,318. For householders ages 35-44, the median was $55,044. For those ages 45-54, the median figure was $60,242. At ages 55-64, the median was lower at $49,215. The median for those 65 and over was $23,787.[4] Although there have been slight dips in the median income in recent years, the overall trend has been upward although not by very much in many cases. Though some of the increase is due to modest inflation, more of them seem to be because of the tendency for both heads of families headed by two persons to be working.

To subdivide household incomes a bit, the Census Bureau figures show that among all of the 112 million households, the upper limit of income for the third fifth of them in 2003 was $54,453. The upper limit for the fourth fifth was $86,867. The lower limit for the top 5% was $154,120.[5]

A look at the types of households in 2003 is of interest. Some 68% of them were family households and the remaining 32% were non-family. In the family categories, 51.5% of the overall total were married-couple families, 12.3% were headed by females with no husband present, and 4.2% were headed by males with no female present. In the non-family categories, 17.5% of the overall household total were female householders and 11.2% were male householders.

The households with the highest incomes in 2003 were ones with married couples. Their mean income was $78,434, compared with the all families mean income of $69,507. Families with a male householder had a mean income of $53,766 while female householder families had a mean income of $37,507. Non-family households had lower incomes, with male income households exceeding those of female income households.[6]

Of considerable interest and discussion is how individuals fared during the decade of the 1990s, a particularly dynamic time. According to a study by American Demographics magazine, "while most Americans were doing better at the end of the 1990s than they were at the beginning, the demographic breakdown of each income group stayed remarkably stable. For instance, despite all the hype about twentysomethings' raking in six-figure incomes from the Internet boom, the share of households headed by a person under the age of 25 who earned more than $100,000 a year was about the same in 2000 as it had been a decade before." It was not this group that made the big incomes but those older; "Nearly 6 in 10 households with an income in six figures (or higher) are headed by a person between the ages of 35 and 54, roughly the same as it was in 1990.

"On the other hand, racial and ethnic minorities appear to have made some gains in income throughout the 1990s. Although the data is not exactly comparable, due to a change in census methodology, there was slightly more diversity at the top of the income ladder in 2000 than there was at the start of the 1990s."[7]

Looking more at the segments, those age 25 to 34 are overrepresented in the middle to upper-middle class. As they get older, some will move up and out of this income category, and many will find a perch in the upper class. People 35 to 54 now account for 58% of the near-affluent (incomes between $75,000 and $99,999). Over the coming years, as baby boomers age and hang onto their jobs, expect to see a larger share of people age 55 and older in this category.[8]

The 50's are the real golden years. Half of all households with incomes of $100,000 to $199,999 are headed by someone who is 45 to 64 years old. Only 12% headed by a person under age 35 are affluent. The super-affluent are in the peak earning years. Nearly one-third of households in which income is $200,000 a year or more are headed by a person between the ages of 45 and 54, the older segment of the baby boom generation.[9]

Whether the households are family or non-family and whether they are high income, moderate income, or lower income, the people who make them up have a clear-cut interest in improving their retirement incomes and resultant lifestyles. They sometimes feel that they have little extra to put aside or that they have little knowledge of just where to put their money when they do. But there is little doubt of the level of interest that the people have. Not surprisingly, it often is the case that when an attractive and easy to understand and implement method of accumulating extra retirement income is presented, people find that they can manage to find a way to take advantage.

## Changes in Retirement Income Composition

According to the *Income of the Aged Chartbook*,[10] in 2001, the latest figures available, some 39% of the aggregate income of those 65 or over was from social security. Twenty-four percent came from earnings, 18% from retirement plans, 16% from asset income, and 3% from other sources. Of course, the percentages vary markedly when comparing the incomes of those in the highest 20% of income with those in the lowest 20%. In the highest income group, 36% comes from earnings, 23% from asset income, 20% from retirement plans, and 19% from social security.

For those in the lowest 20% income group, 82% of their income came from social security, and other sources were far lower. In fact, public assistance was the second largest source at 9%. Income from assets and retirement plans were less than 4% each. Obviously, the people with significant accumulated assets and retirement benefits and willing and able to work were better off and less reliant on social security benefits as their chief source of income. Clearly, people are better off if they have saved and accumulated assets of their own and have employer retirement plans, IRAs, and other retirement plans.

### *Social Security*

A much publicized change is the one affecting social security. Today, those over age 65 represent 12.4% of the U.S. population;11 by 2030, when the youngest of the baby boomers will have reached age 65, the 65 and over population will be 20%. The progression is 13.2% in 2010 and 16.5% in 2020. Women outnumber men, as expected. Of the total in 2030, about 55 of those 65 and over are projected to be women and 45% men.[12] What is more telling is the comparison of retirement beneficiaries with the number of workers paying into the social security program. In 2002, there were about 3.3 workers for each social security beneficiary. It is projected that by 2030 there will be just 2.2 workers for each social security beneficiary.[13]

The gravity of the situation is discussed almost constantly and various proposals are talked about and put forth for evaluation. One that already has been put in place is a gradual increase in the normal retirement age for social security purposes. That will be all well and good, given the fact that it may be possible, even likely, that baby boomers will be able to work to a later age because of improved health and longevity. One required ingredient in this formula is that valuable and pleasing employment must remain available for those in their sixties and beyond. The employment atmosphere today, affecting workers in their late fifties and early sixties, would seem to suggest that not to be an entirely dependable prospect.

People's confidence in social security being there at retirement is very important because it affects, at least in some ways, their actions with respect to saving and investing. Twenty-five years ago, surveys showed that about 60% described themselves as confident or very confident in the social security system. The two confidence figures have gone down, more some years than others, until the percentages in current years are about 50%. When asked how important a source social security benefits would be, 27 or 28% of those surveyed in recent years have said they would be a major source, 56 or 57% have said they would be a minor source, and 15 or 16% have indicated social security would not be a source at all.[14]

Interestingly, according to the most recent Retirement Confidence Survey, the majority of today's workers are unaware of the change in social security calling for an increase in the normal retirement age for social security from 65 to 67. Half expect to reach full eligibility sooner than they actually will. Many of these incorrectly expect to be eligible for full retirement benefits at age 65, but some believe they will be eligible even before age 65.[15]

### *Employer Retirement Plans*

The retirement income that workers receive from their employers' retirement plans is very important to them but many do not receive those benefits. In 2001, among individuals age 65 or older, 34.9% received income from an employer-based retirement plan or a retirement annuity. The median annual amount the people received was $8,136, and the average was $12,187.[16]

Gender is a particularly strong factor in these retirement amounts. In 2001, 44.7% of men age 65 or older received income from these plans, compared with 27.6% of women. The median annual income for men was $10,500 and the average was $15,201. For women, the median annual income was $5,760 and the average was $8,599. A woman age 65 or older was only 62% as likely to receive a pension payment as her male counterpart. When she did receive one, her average benefit was 57% of that received by a man in the same age group.[17] Of course, these figures reflect the employment situation of those already age 65. With the increases in employment of women in higher paid positions in more recent years, the discrepancy should diminish to a considerable extent.

The amount of retirement income one is apt to receive from an employer retirement plan is changing for other reasons. First, there has been a shift from defined benefit plans, where coverage of eligible employees is compulsory and the employer made most of the contributions and virtually all of the investment decisions, to defined contribution plans, 401(k) plans, and other profit sharing plans.

While more workers are covered today and vesting periods are shorter, employers often are contributing less per employee, and the employer contributions more often are dependent on contributions from employees. Defined contribution plans work fine for young employees but are not as rewarding for older employees. Whether employees participate in 401(k) plans often is affected materially by how much, if anything, the employer provides as a matching contribution. The recent trend has been for employers to reduce or sometimes eliminate their matches. As a result, employees who need to consider retirement needs sometimes pass up opportunities to participate in tax-advantaged plans or do not avail themselves of the opportunity to select the types of investment accounts that may be best for them.

Retirement income from an employer plan can be affected even more when the worker does not remain employed long enough to produce a significant benefit. Because of today's shorter vesting schedules, it is more likely that the worker will qualify for some benefit at retirement. But the benefit may not be very large. Further, any period the worker spends working for an employer who does not have a plan, or working as a self-employed person before starting a plan, will not add to it. More and more people are changing employers or going to work for themselves, sometimes voluntarily and sometimes not. There can be many advantages to changing jobs or going into business for one's self under the right conditions, but building a retirement income from an employer plan is not one of them.

The significance of one family having benefits from two retirement plans available should be mentioned. As stated above, many households will have both parents working and presumably qualifying for employer retirement plans. This may or may not turn out to be the case, of course. One parent or the other may take time out for child rearing; one may work for an employer who does not have employee benefits or be self-employed. And then, there is the fact that divorce can alter all of the plans made beforehand.

These same dual-benefit considerations apply to social security benefits. The retirement benefit paid to the spouse who has not worked continuously probably will be less than it would have been otherwise, but it may be greater than it would have been as only the spouse of a retired worker.

The facts and figures with respect to the impact of changes in employer retirement plans are not as well understood as those having to do with social security. One of the reasons is that employer plans vary a great deal and are not publicized outside the employer company. Sometimes, they are not well understood inside the company either because they are somewhat complicated or because the employer does not want the information disseminated widely for competitive reasons. In these days when employers are making changes to their plans in order to contain or reduce the costs of the plans, they are careful to announce that the changes have been made. But the overall impact on employees' benefits is sometimes hard to gauge. It is natural for employers not to want to be criticized for what they consider to be necessary changes because, after all, they are providing retirement benefits to their employees. For that reason, they do not make a point of emphasizing the cuts that have been made in anticipated benefits. Of course, social security does not suffer from any lack of publicity. It has a number of political aspects and becomes the subject of many speeches and statements, often quite superficial and providing more heat than light.

### *One's Own Assets*

The third major source of retirement income is one's own assets, for the most part the money an individual has saved and invested in savings accounts and CDs; stocks, bonds, and mutual funds; annuities; and real estate. There is a multitude of choices and options; in fact, there may be too many for a considerable number of people to deal with. And in any period where a bear market in stocks combines with low market interest rates, many of the most popular choices and options are unattractive, at least for the short run. Many people find it difficult to put money in savings or investments that promise good future results but hold limited promise for the short run. This tends to discourage many people from even attempting to increase the amount of money they put aside for their retirements. As is well known, the longer one waits to put money aside, the harder it is to accumulate the amount of money needed at the time of retirement; the road leading to achieving the retirement assets goal just keeps getting steeper and steeper.

One of the more recent changes that has impacted on the need for retirement income is the future availability and cost of retiree health insurance benefits. Many private-sector employers have been overhauling their retiree health benefit programs by limiting contributions or eligibility, or dropping the benefit for future or even current retirees. These changes have been driven by rapidly rising health costs, coupled with accounting rule changes that forced private-sector employers to recognize the long-term liability of the benefits. Very few employees are expected to be eligible for retiree health benefits in the future. Retiree health coverage generally is offered only by large employers, as very few small employers ever offered the benefit in the first place, and more than half of private-sector workers are in firms with fewer than 500 employees. Long term care is another matter and usually not a part of retiree health coverage.[18]

The cost of prescription drugs has become a major factor affecting retired persons as drug prices have risen dramatically in recent years. As is well known, prescription drugs were not covered by Medicare when it was created in the 1960s. In 2003, a Medicare prescription drug law was enacted to take full effect in 2006. Prior to that, drug discount cards are available during a transition period. The new law has received anything but complete support because of provisions for a deductible, co-payments, and most of all for a benefit gap of $2,850 (between $2,250 and $5,100 in annual drug costs). Nonetheless, it is coverage where none existed before. Though the Medicare coverage includes incentives for companies now providing drug coverage to retired employees to continue to do so, a big issue remains the future of such employer-provided plans. As it is now, companies have been increasing employee co-payments each year for some time. And some plans are imposing deductibles of $150 or more, or employees must pay one-half the retail cost of the drugs. Still other plans are paying for certain expensive drugs only if a doctor first tries a less expensive treatment and then petitions the health plan for approval.[19] The cost of prescription drugs is likely to remain an issue of concern for those planning for retirement.

### *Not Saving What Is Needed*

Whether or not people are saving what they will need to retire often depends on what they think they will need. According to the Retirement Confidence Survey, slightly more than 20% of workers say they are very confident of having enough money to live comfortably throughout their retirement years, and another 45% say they feel somewhat confident. A good question is do the people in the survey know what it will take?

Only some 37% of working people indicated that they had tried to calculate how much money they will need to have saved by retirement time. When couples are taken together, the percentage is higher at 43%. Of those who have tried to figure out what would be needed, 15% indicated the amount to be less than $250,000; about 7% said it should be between $250,000 and $499,999; some 9%

thought they needed to save between $500,000 and $999,999; and 17% thought $1,000,000 or more would be needed. Not surprisingly, 36% could not provide the result of their calculation and another 3% were unable to do the calculation.[20]

Workers appear to underestimate the proportion of their pre-retirement income they will need to live comfortably in retirement. Half of workers expect that they will need less than 70% of their pre-retirement income. Only 16% anticipate needing 70% to 79%, and fewer than 2 in 10 anticipate needing 80% or more of their pre-retirement income to live comfortably.

Part of the underestimation comes from workers' views of working after retirement. Seven in 10 say they think they will work for pay after they retire, almost three times the proportion of today's retirees who indicate they actually worked for pay in retirement. Moreover, 7 in 10 workers indicate they expect full-time or part-time employment to be a major (20%) or minor (50%) source of income in their retirement. This contrasts with the experience of retirees, 3 in 10 of whom report that employment is a major (8%) or minor (20%) source of retirement income.[21] It appears that people's knowledge that they probably will enjoy good health later into their retirement years is overshadowing the fact that many of the jobs they will want to turn to and that will be available to them will have rewards other than high compensation. Couple this with that the fact that the number of retirees interested in working will rise markedly as the many baby boomers retire, and one may conclude that planning for employment to be a substantial source of retirement income may be unwise.

It is clear from all of this that many, if not most, of today's workers are ideal prospective customers for variable annuities. Those who are not saving and investing enough now can benefit from the convenience and ease of purchasing variable annuities, which are most appropriate for retirement planning because of their long-term and tax-deferred nature. Those who do not know where to put their money can benefit from professional money management, diversification, and the flexibility inherent in being able to make changes and reallocations later. Those who need to have some of their funds in guaranteed accounts can do that. Those whose savings and investment actions eventually fall short of their plans can benefit from the availability of annuity payout options that maximize the income that can be produced from the capital available. It is as if variable annuities were created for people with the characteristics of baby boomers.

## Population Segments by Size

Earlier in this chapter, we looked at segments of the population as they pertained to income levels. In this portion of the chapter, let us look at the size of the segments. It goes without saying that much has been written about the baby boomer segment, those born between 1946 and 1964. That is because this is the largest segment at 28.2% of the population, or about 76 million people, according to the breakdown done by *American Demographics*.[22] Since the retirement of the oldest members of this group is imminent and the retirement of the rest of the group is coming into view, and since the incomes of many of these people are such that they can save and invest in variable annuities, they have to be considered among the best prospective customers around. All of the publicity surrounding the potential shortfalls in social security funding and related issues on account of the large number of baby boomers retiring and all of the changes in retirement plans and retiree health insurance benefits have to make an impression.

The segment that follows baby boomers has been labeled Generation X, people born between 1965 and 1976. It is smaller at 16.4% of the population or about 44 million people. It sometimes is said that Generation X members are in the shadow of the baby boomers. By that, it is meant that because so many baby boomers remain in influential positions, the opportunities for members of Generation X are more limited than they would be if there were not so many baby boomers in place. Lately, articles have begun to appear to the effect that some baby boomers are finding their opportunities being squeezed a bit by members of Generation X on account of the fact that younger people are less expensive to employ. But Generation X must be on the lookout for Generation Y, people born between 1977 and 1994. This is another sizable segment at 25.8% of the population, or about 70 million people.

People older than baby boomers are sometimes referred to as the Eisenhower Generation although *American Demographic* refers to this generation in two segments. One is called War Babies and consists of people born between 1940 and 1945; they make up 5.7% of the population or 15 million people. The other is labeled Depression Babies, people born between 1930 and 1939. This segment has 6.5% of the population or 17.5 million people. The final segment, the GI Generation, those born in 1929 or before, makes up 9.1% or 24.5 million people. Many of the people in these final segments are already retired.

Variable annuities can be a valuable savings and investment vehicle for many in these final three segments. For those already saving and investing for retirement, there is less need to convince them of the desirability of doing so. The ease of purchase, the value of tax deferral, the benefits of diversification and professional money management, the availability of guaranteed accounts, and the efficiency of annuity payout options all advance their savings and investing goals. Control over withdrawals after retirement which might enable these individuals to do the extra traveling and other spending they want adds to the worth of variable annuities. For those who have already retired, variable annuities offer places for their existing funds that can reduce their worries and concerns and even enhance what they are able to do with the funds they have.

## Self-Employed: IRA and SEP

Self-employed individuals may use Individual Retirement Accounts or Annuities (IRAs) or Simplified Employee Pensions (SEPs) to accumulate for retirement. The contributions to these plans are income tax deductible, and the interest and earnings are tax deferred while they remain inside the plans. Both of these plans have contribution limits, as discussed in more detail in Chapter 11. Some individuals have been self-employed for most of their working lives. Long ago, they decided that working for themselves had many advantages, notwithstanding the disadvantages such as no employer retirement plan or other fringe benefit programs.

In recent years, more and more people have become self-employed who heretofore would not necessarily have chosen that route. This is the result of reductions in the employee force (downsizing) in some companies and of the greater use of part-time and/or temporary employees by many companies. These cost-cutting measures are taken so that the companies can remain competitive in industries which are ever-expanding, and more often include competitors from outside the United States. The workers who now are part-time or temporary workers often are among the newly self-employed who must find additional work to fill their work weeks and continue saving and investing for retirement on their own.

Variable annuities are particularly good financial products to fund IRAs and SEPs because they can be purchased with flexible deposits to fit permissible contribution limits as they change year by year. They also free the self-employed person from active investment management so that more time can be devoted to build the business and produce current income. The variable annuity advantages of diversification, professional money management, availability of equity and bond accounts, ability to make allocation changes, availability of guaranteed accounts and annuity death benefits, and a variety of payout options, including annuitization for life, are all together in one place.

## Self-Employed with Employees

Self-employed persons who have employees, that is, small employers, have more complex considerations. Many are not in a position to make retirement plan contributions on behalf of their employees. This means that they cannot contribute for themselves except for IRAs (which have been expanded from what they once were, as discussed in Chapter 11). The employer can assist employees in purchasing IRAs on their own by providing payroll deduction for that purpose.

There is a full range of qualified retirement plans. However, smaller employers, in a position to make contributions for employees or to offer matching of employee contributions, usually will want to stay away from plans that require the expense of extensive administration. Conventional SEPs and Savings Incentive Match Plan for Employees (SIMPLE) IRA plans can be used. There also are SIMPLE 401(k) plans, which are easier to administer than conventional 401(k) plans.

Using variable annuities in these plans makes it possible for the plans to have the same advantages that larger employer plans, such as conventional 401(k) plans, have. There is the full range of investment choices, managed by professional managers, that many participants like; there is the ability to allocate investments and change allocations from time to time; guaranteed interest accounts usually are available; when payout time comes, there is the full range of withdrawal and income options at retirement; and there is the death benefit guarantee. It is hard to see how there could be a better package for the smaller plan.

## Supplementing Employer Plans

It is argued that higher paid employees of employers with retirement plans are discriminated against because the combination of the retirement plan benefit and the social security retirement benefit is a smaller percentage of the employees' compensation before retiring than that of lower paid employees. The reason is that the higher paid employee's social security benefits are capped due to contribution maximums applicable each year. To have the same percentage of income at retirement, the higher paid employee needs to take other measures.

The employer may have a supplemental retirement plan or deferred compensation arrangement. These are nonqualified plans with no plan contribution tax deductions available, although the employer may deduct benefit payments at the time they are made.

Not all employers are in a position to make contributions to nonqualified retirement plans and higher paid workers often need to save on their own. This is also frequently the case with respect to self-employed persons whether or not they have employees. Qualified retirement plans have contribution limits and if the self-employed person has employees, his or her participation is further limited. Sometimes, saving and investing on their own has appeal and logic to self-employed persons and smaller employers. Even though contributions to qualified retirement plans are income tax deductible, generally all of the income received is taxable.

On the other hand, personal savings and investment payments are not deductible but some of the money coming back will not be taxable. Generally, only the interest and earnings are subject to tax. And when variable annuities are used to provide periodic income payments, the nontaxable amount is spread over the income period, thereby subjecting only a portion of the income each year to tax, as explained further in Chapter 12. Not having to pay tax on part of your retirement income can allow the money to go farther. Again, the variable annuity advantages are there: convenience of purchase, diversification, professional fund managers, ability to change investment allocations, deferral of tax on interest and earnings, guaranteed interest accounts, death benefits, and fixed and variable annuitization options.

## Timing the Tax

We have been discussing a number of different segments and types of people interested in saving and investing primarily for retirement. Some people, although highly interested in solidifying their retirement income, are also quite interested in postponing all the income tax liability they can as long as they do not hamstring their ability to receive and use the income they need when they need it. Some of the tax havens of some years back, while certainly able to generate tax savings, turned out to be so inflexible that some people could not get to the income when they needed it for unexpected expenses. That is not what most people want.

Successful people assume that their highest marginal income tax rate during their working years will be higher than their highest marginal rate after retirement. That is because they expect to have a relatively lower income after retirement, notwithstanding all their efforts to accumulate for retirement, and because indexing in the tax law gradually will move the rates upward to apply to higher numbers, plus the availability of extra exemptions at age 65 and other factors. So, waiting to take income, and the income tax that goes with it, until after retirement is a simple and straight-forward strategy. But people must not allow this approach to limit their options. They must be able to get to the income before retirement if it is needed, even though tax will need to be paid on the income at that time.

Variable annuities have these abilities built in. While you are in the accumulation period prior to the time you begin to receive payouts on a regular basis, interest, earnings, and gains in value of the investments held by the sub-accounts are deferred for tax purposes. But if you need to withdraw money prior to payout time, you pay income tax on what you withdraw, to the extent of interest and earnings. If you are over age 59½, or if you qualify for one of the other exceptions to the 10% penalty,[23] there are no other income tax costs (although in the early years of an annuity a surrender charge may apply) and no need for any product redemptions or reconfigurations. The variable annuity goes on as before.

## Maximizing Income

Many people will enter their retirement years without having accumulated as much as they need or had planned to have. Although the reason often is that they did not or could not save or invest enough during their working years, there are other reasons. Financial emergencies, particularly those related to serious medical problems and disabilities, can both cause additional outlays of cash and limit people's income-earning capabilities. In some cases, investments have been affected by a prolonged bear market or unfortunate investment decisions will have been made; or it could be that unwise major purchases will have been made. Sometimes, large, and not adequately insured, losses to property occur. The result is that the people have not accumulated enough to derive an adequate income from interest and earnings on the amounts accumulated. Yet, to start digging into principal amounts can be worrisome. That can be "a slippery slope." As principal is used up, the interest and earnings from the remainder are less. And with life expectancies increasing, who knows how long the income will be needed or how long people will live? A long life should be a positive thing, but it cannot be if income dwindles to below a reasonable standard of enjoyment.

While most people prefer to dwell on how much they can accumulate and how much income can be produced from it, the fact is, some will have a nagging concern over whether things will work out as well as they anticipate. It may be the case that these people will want to know, in some detail, how it is possible for the money they have accumulated to provide a maximum income that will last as long as they live. Annuities, especially variable annuities, offer solutions to this problem unlike any other type of financial services product.

The values in a variable annuity can be annuitized essentially at any time. The annuity payment is calculated by combining the principal and any expected interest or earnings, for the time considered, and spreading them out so that each periodic payment consists of some of each. These payments can be calculated to last for a certain period of time or for the life of the annuitant. The longer the payment period, the less each payment is; the reverse also is true. This life income feature is what makes annuities so valuable to people in their retirement years.

Once people reach a certain age and start a lifetime payout, the amount of income that an annuity will pay each month or each year for life far surpasses what could have been paid out each period in interest or earnings. People whose saving and investing have fallen short of what they would have liked are materially aided by the ability to have these larger income amounts. To be sure, since the periodic payments include principal as well as interest or earnings, the principal will be used up at the end of the period. That would not have been the case if only interest or earnings were paid out and principal were retained. However, if the income is paid for the life of the annuitant, there may be no overriding necessity for the principal to be retained. And the possibility of death soon after annuity payments begin can be ameliorated by use of guarantee periods and joint annuity payments. (See Chapter 7 for more details.)

To this point, the life income discussion has been cast in the framework of a fixed payout. Variable annuities also have the option of variable payouts. Periodic payments are recalculated from time to time using the values in the variable subaccounts. Thus the periodic payments rise or fall with those values, making the annuitant able to continue a strategy of using variable accounts to track with inflation to the extent possible as time goes by. Either variable or fixed payouts may be used and the choice does not have to be made until it is time to start taking income.

## Receiving Large Sums

There are a number of people who will receive a large amount of money and will want and need to save and invest it for retirement and other needs. An obvious starting point is people who have inherited a significant sum of money. Then, some people will sell a house or other real or personal property of significant value; sometimes, it is the sale of the family home with a move into a retirement community or, perhaps, assisted living where housing is rented.

Additionally, a number of workers will receive severance package settlements, due to their agreement to retire early or due to their requirement to do so. While these people will need to use some of the money for living expenses, they may have a sizable amount that needs to be saved and invested for the future, once they have other employment or have decided to become self-employed.

Some people participating in employer retirement plans will determine that a lump sum is the best way to take their retirement proceeds. Most of the time, rolling the proceeds into an IRA, so that their tax position is preserved, should be considered. However, there may be some proceeds which should be taken on an after-tax basis and saved and invested. (More details are in Chapter 11.) People in business will sell their interests to others. Many of these arrangements will call for installments to be paid to the seller. Others will be subject to bank loans providing lump sums or relatively large amounts over a short period of time to the seller.

Many of the people who receive these large amounts of money are not in a position to select individual investments. However, they are likely to be interested in diversification for safety and professional investment management while retaining the option to adjust the investment mix. In addition, these individuals may wish for some guarantees and appreciate the fact that the income tax on interest and earnings can be deferred to the time when proceeds are actually used and enjoyed. In short, variable annuities are excellent places for this money.

Of course, it usually is not possible to find whole groups of people who have recently received large sums of money to form a market for you, with the possible exception of participants in retirement plans or those being offered severance arrangements. But when talking with people about their future plans, it is a good idea to ask whether any of these events have taken place or will in the near future.

In addition to the employer retirement plans, especially plans of smaller employers, supplemental income plans, and the sale of business interests mentioned above, there are other considerations for variable annuities in business and estate planning and also the specialized area of structured settlements. These subjects are taken up in Chapter 11.

## Chapter Endnotes


1. "U.S. Household Ownership of Mutual Funds in 2004," *Fundamentals*, Investment Company Institute, Washington, D.C., October 2004.
2. IRC Section 72(q).
3. IRC Section 72(e).
4. "Money Income and Earnings Summary Measures by Selected Characteristics: 2002 and 2003," *Income, Poverty, and Health Insurance Coverage in the United States:* 2003, U.S. Census Bureau, U. S. Government Printing Office, Washington, D.C., p. 4.
5. Table H-1, "Income Limits for Each Fifth and Top 5 Percent of Households, All Races: 1967-2003," U. S. Census Bureau, U. S. Department of Commerce, Washington, D.C., 20233-8500.
6. Table H-9, "Race of Head of Household—All Races by Median and Mean Income: 1980-2003, U. S. Census Bureau, U. S. Department of Commerce, Washington, D.C., 20233-8500.
7. Alison Stein Wellnes, "The Wealth Effect, *American Demographics*, December 2002/January 2003.
8. *Ibid.*
9. *Ibid.*
10. *Income of the Aged Chartbook 2001*, (released May, 2003), Social Security Administration, Office of Policy, Office of Research, Evaluation and Statistics.
11. *Profiles of General Demographic Characteristics*, Table DP-1, U. S. Census Bureau, Census 2000.
12. *Projections of the Total Resident Population*, NP-T3-F, Population Projections Program, Population Division, U. S. Census Bureau.
13. *The 2003 Annual Report of the Board of Trustees of the Federal Old-Age and Survivors Insurance and Disability Insurance Trust Funds*, U.S. Government Printing Office, Washington: 2003.
14. Karlyn Bowman, "Attitudes About Social Security Reform," (Updated February 20, 2003), *AEI Studies in Public Opinion*, American Enterprise Institute, Washington, D.C.
15. "The 2003 Retirement Confidence Survey Summary of Findings," Employee Benefit Research Institute, American Savings Education Council, Mathew Greenwald & Associates, Inc., Washington, D.C.
16. "Retirement Annuity and Employment-based Pension Income," *Notes*, EBRI Retirement Income Research: 2003 Findings, January 2003.
17. *Ibid.*
18. "Retiree Health Benefits: Savings Needed to Fund Health Care in Retirement," EBRI Issue Brief Executive Summary, February 2003, No. 254.
19. Milt Freudenheim, "Workers Paying a Larger Share for Drug Plans," *The New York Times*, June 12, 2003.
20. "The 2003 Retirement Confidence Survey Summary of Findings," *Op. cit.*
21. *Ibid.*
22. "Comparing the Breakdown," *American Demographics*, October, 2000.
23. IRC Sec. 72(q).

# Chapter 3

# Approaching Markets

## Primary or Supplementary Market?

When considering how you will go about marketing variable annuities, one of your early decisions involves the level of intensity of the marketing you will be doing. Will variable annuities be one of a fairly large number of products you will be offering as a part of a customer's overall plan? Or will annuities, including variable annuities, be lead products and major sources of earnings for you?

### *Supplementary Marketing*

The practices of many variable annuity marketers result in a marketing approach where accumulation products (variable annuities, fixed annuities, mutual funds, and perhaps other investments) play a significant role in their customers' future income plans but a relatively minor role in providing earnings to the sales representative on a year-to-year basis. That is, the sales representative may market life insurance and disability income to individuals and businesses as his primary business activity. He then markets accumulation products to those same individuals and businesses in order to provide a more complete service to them. When one of these sales representatives considers new people to approach, an important consideration is that these people be potential buyers of life insurance and disability income at some point in the not-too-distant future.

There is no mystery to the concentration on life insurance and disability income in these cases. The compensation to be earned, as a percentage of the premiums paid, especially in the first year, is far higher than is the case for accumulation products such as variable annuities. On the other hand, variable annuities are a good bit easier to sell, usually taking less time to accomplish, and sales are made many times more frequently. Consequently, many sales representatives prefer to concentrate on marketing variable annuities and other accumulation products.

Variable annuities are marketed by many persons who perform financial planning services for their customers. In many of these cases, the performance of the financial planning services is uppermost in the relationship with the customer. The services often are provided for a fee. The person performing the planning services may be compensated for the sale of financial products as well, or the planner's total compensation may be from sales of financial products. There are variations among the states with respect to permissible compensation arrangements involving financial planning services and purchases of financial products where both are provided.

In the two types of circumstances above – where the sales representative markets variable annuities as additional products accompanying life insurance and disability income purchases, and where the person provides financial planning services and markets variable annuities as part of the services provided – the variable annuities can be considered supplementary marketing. No additional or focused marketing is undertaken for the variable annuities; they are a part of the regular sales process taking place with the customer.

### *Primary Marketing*

When, on the other hand, it is intended that variable annuities, as well as fixed annuities, mutual funds, and other investment products, will be major sources of earnings, things are quite different. It is necessary to reach a greater number of people, have many more transactions with people, and make many more sales. The reason is the relatively lower level of compensation for variable annuity and other investment product sales. We will look at variable annuity compensation levels in more detail in Chapter 9, but it is well known that the level of compensation per sale is such that it takes a great deal of premium to produce significant earnings.

As we have seen earlier, there are reasons this should be so. The public is much more interested in variable annuities than in life insurance and disability income.

People are apt to see purchasing variable annuities more in terms of an opportunity than in terms of a duty. People know they need to accumulate for the future whereas they frequently have only a vague notion about insurance, no matter how often they may have had the subject discussed with them. As a result, there is a much higher likelihood of a discussion under favorable circumstances when the subject is variable annuities.

Following the more favorable hearing, variable annuities are much easier to put into effect. Although there is a need to determine that the variable annuity is suitable for the proposed purchaser, there is no underwriting in the insurance sense. Consequently, there are no physical histories or examinations, no attending physician reports, no blood drawn, or other tests. There is no wait for approval of the business. On the contrary, there is a need to get the business submitted immediately and for the contract to be delivered promptly after it is issued.

### *Targeting Markets*

In order for you to make the greater number of sales needed, it is necessary that you have enough good people to see and have reason to see them. We have discussed reasons to see various classes of people, but here we are referring to having reasons to see particular people, or better, particular groups of people. When there is a group of people, which is accessible to you, with some characteristics in common and needs that can be addressed by the products you have for sale, that is a market for you. It is even better if the people in the group communicate with each other because your favorable reputation can precede you and pave the way. A group of people you have targeted for attention is referred to as a target market.

### *Characteristics in Common*

*Money to Save or Invest* – One of the characteristics that is desirable for people to have in common is some money that can be put in financial products for the future. For most, this is in the form of disposable income. For others, it is a sum of money from a non-recurring source, such as the sale of property or other asset, or from another financial product with which they are no longer satisfied, such as a product with a history of below average earnings or one that does not have enough potential for capital appreciation. So, to start you will want to look for people with money available. An obvious starting point is among those whom you have reason to believe are earning enough to be in that position, or who otherwise show signs of relative affluence such as their home or neighborhood, or the recreational and other activities in which they engage.

*In the Same Age Group* – Another characteristic in common is age. The people might be within a particular range of ages. When people are within a fairly small age range, their financial interests may be similar. Middle-aged people are more interested in planning for a retirement that is coming ever closer than are younger people. Older people usually are beyond the accumulation stage and are looking for ways of handling what they have accumulated. Younger people may be more interested in ways to maximize what little accumulation ability they have. Your approach to each of the various age groups can be different, emphasizing what is important to that particular group.

*Common Place of Employment* – Those employed by the same employer have that characteristic in common. By learning about a company, you are in a position to know relative earnings of various groups, the fringe benefits available, and what opportunities the employees have for saving and investing through their employer. In time, you can learn who the more influential people are and, at least, something of what people's expectations for their future with the employer are. If you can become favorably considered by people employed by the same employer, you will have a powerful target market. This is all apart from whatever financial work you may be able to do with the employer. If you can work with the employer, either on a company basis or on a personal basis, your target market will be even more fruitful because of the prestige you will have built.

*Type of Work* – Another characteristic in common is the type of work the people do. People who do the same type of work tend to find each other and get together either formally or informally. Those doing the same work at a particular employer usually associate closely with each other. Those with different employers tend to get together through associations or less formal organizations. It often is the case that people doing the same type of work have other interests in common. Frequently, those of similar ages tend to associate more with each other than with others in the group. By learning about some of the people in a group, you can infer correctly about other people in many cases. You cannot rely entirely on these inferences but you can be in a much better position of understanding than you would have been with someone not a part of the group.

*Principals of Businesses* – Similarly, principals of businesses find each other in business organizations. The organizations may be for the purpose of sharing or exchanging information among the members or bringing in outside sources of information for education or consulting with members. It may be to promote the purposes of the member organizations by concerted public relations or marketing endeavors or by bringing political issues to the attention of members of local, state, and national governments. In such business organizations, it is not unusual to find principals of businesses of similar sizes or of complementary enterprises working closely with each other. These common characteristics attract people to each other. When you learn about some of those who are principals of businesses, the knowledge will be useful with others who are similarly situated.

*Common Interests and Hobbies* – Social and service organizations can be targeted as well. People who have such things in common as hobbies and sports, and high degrees of interest in music, literature, art, drama, good health, and religion tend to want to be together so they can discuss and enjoy their interests. The same is true of graduates of a college who belong to a local organization and of former members of college fraternities and sororities who belong to alumni and alumnae associations or chapters. Of course, these interests do not necessarily carry over so that the people have similar financial characteristics but those in the organizations tend to know more about most aspects of the lives of the people they associate with regularly than of other people. The common interests and knowledge of each other can provide a connection that can be the beginning of a target market for you. Then, if enough of the people have the financial characteristics and needs for your products, the organization can be a full-fledged target market for you. Service organizations can become target markets in much the same way.

*Communicating with Each Other* – In our definition of a target market, we mentioned the desirability of the people communicating with each other. This is because any favorable attitudes about financial products or the person(s) marketing the products will be communicated, thus lowering barriers for a marketing approach as well as increasing the likelihood that people in the group will take some of the initiative in seeking out information on the products. Where group members are situated near each other and have regular contact, the communication among them can help make the group be a very strong target market. Where the members do not communicate regularly, because they do not see or talk with each other on a regular basis, the group still is far better than marketing to the public at large because of the persuasiveness of the fact that members of the group with similar characteristics have become customers. Members of the group are aware they are in a position to seek opinions from members they do not know, though they do not make such contacts very often.

## Market Research

A logical question is, how do you find out about the characteristics in common and the needs in common that the members of a group may have? The answer is by doing research. Much of the research we have in mind would be done by surveying some persons you already know who are in a group you want to consider a target group. If the persons you survey are your customers already, so much the better. They will know about the products and services you have available and you will not need to gain their confidence. And although some customers may have some reluctance about referring you to people with whom they work or with whom they socialize, their reservations usually can be overcome or their fears assuaged. Clearly, your customers among potential target groups are the best sources for your research.

People you know who are not customers are next best. They usually will be agreeable to listening to what you have to say. But it is important that you not leave out any of the steps you would use in approaching someone you do not know for information. That is, when you approach someone you do not know, you will want to have a well organized presentation that is brief, easily understood, and leads to a definite course of action. The course of action usually consists of the person supplying you with information about the potential target group.

You can survey people you do not know, but that is harder because of the barriers that are placed in the way of seeing them under favorable conditions. If you can get referred to them by someone you know that is a big help. If you cannot, you still can survey them, of course, but your percentage of success in approaching and interviewing them will be lower than with those you know.

### Survey Information

The survey should be designed to gather information on the group for your analysis so that it can be used to determine which groups will make the best target markets for you. The types of information you want will: (1) define the group; (2) list the common characteristics of the group members; (3) list the presumed financial needs of the members; (4) describe the extent and nature of the communication among the members; and (5) identify usable sources of member information, as discussed in more detail below.

1. *Define the group* – They can be described as employees of XYZ Company; owners of particular types of businesses or of businesses of a particular size; particular occupations or professions, such as accountants, account executives for advertising firms or pharmaceutical houses; or members of golf or tennis clubs, or of social or religious

groups. The location of the people is important; they should be in your target area. An important part of the definition is the number of people involved. There must be enough people in the group to be a viable market, especially considering the need for a large number of sales transactions.

2. *List the common characteristics of the group members* – Some of the possible characteristics were mentioned above: they have above average incomes; their ages are in the accumulation of assets years; the majority have children ten or more years from college; they are close to the point of taking distribution of their assets; they work for the same employer or at the same location.

3. *List the presumed financial needs of the members* – From what you have been told of the group and of common characteristics, what are the major financial needs to anticipate? Candidates are accumulation for retirement years, help with selection of financial products for saving and investment, efficient and effective distribution of assets they have or will have, business planning involving financial products, planned charitable giving, and tax planning.

4. *Describe the extent and nature of the communication among the members* – Frequent and significant communication is the best, but even occasional communication is better than little or none, assuming the people know each other by name and know some of the basic information about each other. When people know each other to some extent, they are more apt to accept another person's recommendation or referral. When you hold a meeting involving more than one, there is comfort and validation among them that the meeting will be of value.

5. *Identify usable sources of member information* – You must have names, addresses, telephone numbers, e-mail addresses, and even fax numbers where appropriate. Membership and company directories are the best if they are available. Remember that such items must be used discreetly if distribution of them is not public. Telephone and street directories, CD ROM's, and Internet websites can be helpful when needed. Names, addresses, and telephone numbers are starting points. Information on a company's employee benefits is available from the literature distributed to employees when members of your target group are employees of a particular employer. More and more

employee benefit information is on websites, especially those used to provide information to employees or assist in tracking claims. Information of a more personal nature usually is available only from the members themselves or from those who know them.

### *Analyzing the Data*

The data you gather by means of surveys of as many members as possible of the potential target group can be supplemented with information that may have been published locally or included on the company's website. Any materials published by the organization will help fill in missing information. The Chamber of Commerce will have some other information that has been published. The public library will have whatever newspaper and local magazine accounts there are, as will files on the websites of the newspapers and magazines. More and more companies and organizations have web sites of their own containing background and other helpful information. The idea is to get as much information as practicable on which to base your decision on whether to adopt the group as a target market.

Our definition of a target market began by saying the group is one that is accessible to the person doing the marketing. Obviously, you must be able to contact the members of the group, preferably with relative ease. Naturally, you can contact by mail or e-mail anyone whose address you have. If you expect that they will take the initiative of coming to a meeting or otherwise contacting you, that may be sufficient, although many recommend following up meeting invitations with telephone calls to improve attendance. You can contact by telephone anyone whose telephone number you have. However, telephoning is becoming ever more problematic with the prevalence of answering machines and voice mail. And, of course, you must be cognizant of the National (and possibly state) Do Not Call registry. If the people you plan to call have their home phones registered with a Do Not Call registry, the contacts should be made at work if at all possible.

Sometimes, asking the person you are contacting for a reply by e-mail works. If you can have an introduction or referral from a friend or associate, or from an employer, you stand a much better chance of getting through, getting your call returned, or receiving an e-mail response. Accessibility to members of the group is an important aspect in your analysis. Without sufficient accessibility, you may not be able to put the other information you have to good use.

You can never have too much information about whether a group can become a target market for you, but there is a limit to the amount of time and money you are able to spend collecting it. Once you have gathered the information with which to make a decision, it is time to analyze it:

- Can you gain sufficient access to enough people?
- Are there characteristics in common?
- Do the members appear to have needs that can be filled by the financial products you have to market?
- Do the members communicate sufficiently with each other?
- Can you get data on the members at a reasonable cost in time and money?

Having considered all of these things, are there enough people in the group to constitute a target market for you? Rarely will the viability of a target market be a completely obvious decision. There will be certain factors about which you are uncertain. You will have to make some assumptions subject to further developments and insights. Some of the assumptions will turn out to be accurate and some will not. Your analytical prowess will improve with experience.

Although a few sales representatives or sales organizations are able to concentrate primarily on one group of people, because it is large enough and continues to add new members, most representatives and organizations believe they must have several target markets at a time. This is particularly true when you are marketing variable annuities and related financial products as lead products. You must have enough people to whom to market that the larger number of transactions and sales you need can take place.

### *As a Member of the Group*

Getting involved yourself in one or more organizations has proved to be effective in developing target markets. Then, you can be your own source of data on the members and you can become known by them under favorable conditions. There is little problem with access to the members. Of course, these must be organizations of which you can be a contributing member. When these endeavors have been successful, several principles were observed.

Never become a member of an organization primarily to market your products. The members will recognize it quickly and will not like it. Become a member of an organization that has a purpose you truly believe in and want to support actively. Service organizations fit this definition but so do others, such as those devoted to literature, music, good health, certain hobbies, and the like. Purely social organizations may or may not.

What we are referring to are organizations that require you to work on worthwhile projects with other members. This will give you the opportunity to become well acquainted with people in a setting different from your usual setting. In many cases, these will be people you might have difficulty getting to see through a direct approach. After all, people of all sorts take part in projects for the good of others and to further their interests outside of their work.

Sales representatives often can take advantage of their people skills by working on committees to which some other members are not attracted. Most organizations always need more members and need to raise money. Working on those committees automatically brings you into consistent contact with many members of the organization and, because the work is important to the vitality of the group, it usually is appreciated.

When you work with other members, one of the things you want to accomplish is to learn about them and their businesses or professions and personal affairs, and for them to learn about you. One of the especially good things about marketing variable annuities and related financial products is that the ups and downs of the stock market and economic news are always of interest and become topics of conversation. In fact, once people learn that you have some knowledge of these matters, you almost cannot avoid talking about them. The people will bring them up time and again. This means there will be ample opportunities to discuss topics associated with your work and to offer assistance. This is all to the good since contacting many people is the only way to have many sales transactions, which can result in a substantial number of variable annuity contracts sold.

## Other Markets

Some sales representatives build lists of potential customers without utilizing a target marketing process as such. One way is to collect names in certain categories. Many have found success in keeping track of the maturity dates of the certificates of deposit their customers and potential customers have. During periods when CD rates are low, people are willing to listen to an explanation involving products with the long-term potential for higher returns. They also are willing to listen to an explanation involving products that offer the opportunity for a reasonable level of participation in the stock and bond markets in order to retain purchasing power. Contacting the people on the list a few weeks before their CD's mature has resulted in moving the money to variable annuities in many cases.

In a similar vein, some sales representatives have found it profitable to keep track of the surrender charge period on the fixed annuities their customers and potential customers have. This is especially true of single premium fixed annuities, which often are considered by them to be similar to CD's in many ways. Once the surrender charge period has run, a transfer to a variable annuity may be made. And it usually can be made without recognizing any gain for income tax purposes. (All relevant tax aspects of the transfer should be considered. See the discussion of Internal Revenue Code section 1035 transfers in Chapter 12.) Exchanges to variable annuities can offer the opportunity for participation in the stock and bond markets in order to retain purchasing power and the opportunity for higher returns.

But observe this caution. An individual who exchanges a fixed annuity for a new annuity, fixed or variable, incurs a new surrender charge period during which withdrawals are limited. The ramifications of this must be disclosed. Also, it is the position of the securities industry that an exchange of one variable annuity for another often is not warranted.

## Smaller Employers

A number of sales representatives have found success concentrating on smaller employers with whom they use variable annuities as a backbone of their retirement plans. As mentioned in Chapter 2, smaller employers know they need to have some sort of retirement plan for their regular employees, including themselves in many instances, in order to be competitive in attracting and retaining good workers. Labor markets go through cycles but any time unemployment is relatively low, competition for good people can be intense. On top of that, many smaller employers feel a responsibility toward their employees that includes at least some opportunity to participate in the tax advantages of qualified retirement plans to the extent possible.

A small employer may facilitate employees contributing to Individual Retirement Accounts or Annuities (IRAs). The amount that an employee may contribute on a tax-deductible basis has been increased in recent years and catch-up provisions, applicable to those age 50 and over, also are available. In addition,

Roth IRAs, on which contributions are not tax-deductible but payouts may be income-tax free, have appeal to some employees.

If the employer is in a position to make contributions on behalf of employees or offer matching, there are conventional SEPs or Savings Incentive Match Plan for Employees (SIMPLE) IRA plans. There also are SIMPLE 401(k) plans that are easier for a small employer to administer. The amounts that may be contributed to these plans also have been increased in recent years. (More discussion of these plans is in Chapter 11.) Of course, the full range of pension and profit sharing plans is available, especially to larger employers.

One of the things that makes variable annuities so appealing in these smaller employer plans is the fact that employees can have the range of investment choices that are so popular with conventional 401(k) plans. Yet, the employer is not burdened with the administration costs. Only a variable annuity can bring all of these choices and options in one convenient package.

This range of choices available to employees also makes variable annuities appealing with plans designed to supplement the employer's retirement plan. An employer may have a basic or modest retirement plan that many employees may need to supplement in order to build additional income for retirement. Employees can purchase variable annuities on a regular and consistent basis. The premiums for the supplemental variable annuities are not income-tax deductible but the income when paid will be only partially taxable. For certain employees, the employer can increase compensation providing the means for making the additional purchases. Generally, it is better for the employer not to own and pay for the annuities directly as a supplementary income plan. (There is more discussion of these tax aspects in Chapter 11.) Where the types of choices available in the variable annuity resemble those available in the employer's basic plan, especially when it is a 401(k) plan, a certain degree of coordination and thinking in common are possible.

Before leaving the subject of small employers, mention should be made of the increased popularity of what are called voluntary benefits programs. Here, we are referring to individual life insurance and disability income insurance, as well as medical expense and related coverages paid for entirely or almost entirely by the employees themselves. Smaller employers can make these plans available by handling premiums for them and permitting employees to discuss them with representatives of the insurance providers. If participation among the employer's employees is sufficient, there also may be some pricing advantages and simplified underwriting available. Variable annuities can be made a part of an employer's voluntary benefit program so that retirement or supplementary retirement can be addressed.

When considering whether to attempt to market voluntary benefits to a particular employer, there are several criteria to consider:

1. The employer should be of such a size that there are enough employees to be worth the effort of setting up procedures but not so many that it would be overwhelming.

2. The more employees in one employer location the better.

3. The employer's existing benefit plans are limited enough that the voluntary benefits that are presented will make a difference.

4. Employee incomes are adequate to be able to afford voluntary benefits but not necessarily so high that the employees will not see the need for them.

5. There must be access to the employees for at least a brief period of time while they are at work.

Perhaps, it goes without saying that it is important that employees have sufficient trust in their employer to be open minded about discussing the benefits being offered. And it is very helpful when the employer endorses the program, at least to some significant degree, and is supportive of your efforts to establish administrative and payroll procedures.[1]

## Tailoring the Sales Process

After you have decided on your marketing targets, it is time to tailor the sales process you will be using. Whether you use individual contacts, seminars, or other types of meetings as the initial contacts with members of your target market, the steps of the sales process are similar, even when they are executed in different ways:

1. The pre-approach by mail, e-mail, telephone, or in person.

2. The approach by telephone, in person, or at a meeting.

3. The gathering of customer financial information.

4. Analysis of the information gathered.

5. A presentation of needs identified and proposed solutions.

6. Implementation of solutions agreed to by the customer.

7. Any necessary follow-up and service after the sale.

8. Continuing service, follow-up, and consideration of additional needs and solutions.

When you are approaching potential customers for variable annuities and related financial products one-at-a-time, the pre-approach and approach are similar to those used with other financial products. When you are using seminars or group meetings, they are different. The pre-approach is the invitation to attend the meeting, whether it is an open invitation or an individual invitation by mail, e-mail, or telephone. The approach is in two parts. First there is the invitation at the meeting (usually extended more than once) to complete a response card that requests a contact by one of the financial counselors or sales representatives present. Then, when the representative calls to schedule the appointment, the approach is completed. In these cases, assurance usually has been given to those attending the seminar that there is no obligation; for that reason, contacting people who have not come forward by responding may not be appropriate, although it is done some of the time. A different tactic is to invite those not responding to another seminar as a way of determining their level of interest.

The rest of the sales process, whether the potential customer has been contacted individually or has come to a meeting, is handled on a one-to-one basis. There may be some differences, however. A person who has asked to be contacted may have a definite idea of what he is interested in pursuing. Or he may be wary of a sales representative who attempts to go far afield of the potential customer's immediate interests and become involved in many additional financial considerations. When you sense that may be the case, it is best to continue along the path of the potential customer's interest and, after determining suitability, sell the product the person is interested in buying. Once you have gained your new customer's confidence, then you can go back and offer additional financial services and products. This is in keeping with the idea of having many sales transactions in order to produce a sufficient level of variable annuity premiums. (Of course, if it is your intention to perform more complete planning services before making any product recommendations, you will proceed differently.)

We also need to remember that the person who completes a form requesting a contact may have no idea of what he should be considering, notwithstanding the information provided at the seminar or meeting. Such a person probably will welcome an offer to do some financial analysis, including determining interests and risk tolerance, in order to get an idea of what sorts of products he should consider.

## Tips on Seminar Selling

Selling by using seminars to approach potential customers has become very popular and is in wide use. This is particularly true for selling financial products that have a certain degree of built-in demand such as variable annuities. Seminars involving retirement planning or accumulating for the future seem to have appeal for a large number of people. Seminars on estate planning or financial planning usually have not drawn as well although sometimes those attending are more affluent and, in some cases, better potential customers. Even though people probably should be interested in insurance planning, that is not a popular subject for seminars.

*Committed to the Steps* – Those successful at seminar selling make the point that a person can do well only by being committed, persistent, patient, and dedicated. The person must be committed to following the steps faithfully and not yielding to the temptation to take short cuts. He must have a system for keeping track of people who have been invited to seminars and who have attended. Since, for a variety of reasons, it may take several invitations to get the acceptance of some good potential customers, the system must provide for sending somewhat different invitations to the same people at proper intervals. The commitment must extend to planning and implementing a seminar or seminars that are worthwhile, suited to the knowledge level of the potential audience, and presented in a non-threatening atmosphere by qualified speakers.

*Be Persistent* – The giver of seminars must be persistent. One of the major reasons for not achieving anticipated results through seminar selling is that the person stopped giving the seminars too soon. Many times this was a lack of patience and the expectation that results would come more quickly than they did. In retrospect, the seminars contained good enough information, the speakers were adequate, there were at least some good potential customers there (although often fewer than the seminar givers had hoped), and some sales contacts resulted. What was needed for success was more of everything. If the list of people mailed was a good one, things very likely would have been better after additional seminars.

*Be Patient* – Patience is not a word usually associated with many sales representatives of financial products. Yet, seminar selling requires it. If the representative short cuts the process, for example, by contacting people who attended and did not respond, it can poison the atmosphere if the group of people invited know each other. If those attending do not know each other, there may be less damage but, as was mentioned above, it often is better to invite people to other seminars. When someone has attended more than one seminar, it might be more appropriate at that time to contact this individual directly to offer additional services. Obviously, the person has more than a little interest in the subjects being discussed. Of course, you can only be sure a person has attended if you have a system for tracking attendance and any follow up mailing you might have done.

### *Invitation List*

Perhaps the most important key to the success of seminar selling is the list of persons you invite to attend. Who attends probably is more important than what is presented, although you will want to offer the best content and speakers you can. The more the people on the list fit in with those who are in your target markets, the better. After all, you would have designed the seminar for those types of people. When seminar givers are disappointed with the results of the seminars, it is most often the case that not enough of the right kind of people, or just not enough people, attended.

Lists of people to invite can come from a variety of sources. The closer you are to the people on the list, the more likely you are to be able to predict whether they will attend and how effective seminars will be. If you have a membership list of a target group, it will be a better list than one where you have only superficial knowledge of the people on it. Sometimes, sales representatives have success with lists of people they have contacted in the past but have never interviewed, assuming there had been good reasons to retain their names in the prospective customer files.

The business of developing lists from public sources using database management techniques has become more refined than ever. You can purchase a list with nearly any profile. When selecting a company from whom to purchase a list, there are several things to keep in mind. First, look for a track record. You not only want to see the proof presented by the company, but will want to check out their references. If you know someone who has used the company, ask that person. Or you can begin with a referral to a company someone else has used with success.

Second, work diligently at giving a detailed definition to the type of people you want to appear on the list. Database management techniques today allow for multiple search categories. It is far better to get a smallish list of people who fit your target well than a large list of people who do not fit your target. This is especially true if you anticipate sending repeat invitations to people on the list, as many seminar givers recommend.

Third, expect to pay a fee commensurate with the value of the list. Sophisticated searches take more computer time and cost more. But the cost of the list is low compared to the time and energy you will devote to the seminars and you will want to have as much success as possible. A last point is that the information on these lists comes from public sources for the most part. These sources sometimes are not refreshed as often as they might be, and some of the information may be out of date. To an extent, that cannot be prevented. Here again, the selection of the list-providing company is very important.

Some sales representatives have success with inviting people by newspaper advertisements, e-mail, and similar approaches. The people responding call a telephone number, mail, or e-mail a reply to the address shown in the ad or message, or respond to a web site or e-mail address. Although this approach has been successful for some, it usually is relatively expensive for the number of people who respond and finally attend. It also violates the principle of targeting your markets, since the invitation is extended to "the world at large." Many feel that is not the place to start with seminar selling.

### *Sponsored Seminars*

There are variations on seminar selling that have proved to be more successful, for the time, energy, and money invested, than the types of seminars we have been discussing. One of these is sponsored seminars. For example, a company with whom you or one of your associates has done business might be willing to sponsor a retirement planning or asset accumulation seminar for its employees, or for certain of its employees. In order to get company sponsorship, you will have to convince the employer that the information is worthwhile and needed by the employees and that it will be a positive experience for both employer and employee. What employers fear most is thinly disguised direct sales solicitations masquerading as seminars. It should be easy to assure the employer that there is no reason to fear aggressive tactics by explaining how the seminar is conducted and under what conditions employees are contacted following the seminar.

Sponsored seminars usually can be conducted at or near the employer's place of business. It is unusual for the employer to allow for time away from work for those attending, but seminars can operate successfully just following the close of work. Another approach is to have a series of shorter seminars at lunch time, with a box lunch provided. Here you are in a position to track attendance as an indication of interest in the topics discussed.

Earlier, we discussed the fact that seminar selling often is abandoned before it has had a reasonable chance for success. Sponsored seminars need to be repeated from time to time and new ones, perhaps including some parts of old ones, presented. You must continue your presence in your target markets. Different people will be interested the next time; some of the same people will return, perhaps with more resolve this time to take action. If the seminar has been a positive experience for both the employer and the employees who attend, it will not be difficult to schedule another after a reasonable period of time.

Some sales representatives have found the social, special interest, or service groups to which they belong receptive to seminars on some aspects of financial planning or explanations of various financial products. Many of these groups have regular educational programs and welcome the active participation of the members in one or more of them. Here again, there is the fact that these subjects are of interest to nearly everyone and are more likely than not to be well received. Obviously, the seminars or programs have to be conducted with the realization that those attending have not overtly expressed an interest in the subject. For that reason, your follow-up activities must be a bit more subtle. But there is no question you will have established your identity and shown some of your expertise among people in the group. Those factors are likely to prove to be invaluable.

### *Keep Promotion Going*

With respect to any groups where you have presented sponsored seminars, workshops, or group programs, it is important that you keep promotion going afterward. If the employer or organization has a regular publication or newsletter, whether it is on paper or by e-mail, it usually will welcome well-written articles. When there is a tie-in to a recent seminar, it is even better, especially if some enthusiasm has been built among some of the people who attended. Those responsible for the publication may want to take advantage of the positive atmosphere concerning the seminar. If you feel able to write such articles, there is an abundance of ideas in the financial and trade press to inspire you. If you do not, distributors of variable annuities and other financial products produce a wealth of appropriate pieces that they will give permission to publish. What you are attempting to do is to keep the subjects discussed in the seminar in front of potential customers who then may take the initiative to approach you directly or indirectly. The articles also can pave the way when you approach them. Before we leave this subject, we should point out that sometimes it is possible to publish articles before the seminar takes place. This may improve attendance and establish some familiarity with you in advance of the seminar.

### *Designing the Seminar*

When designing a seminar for the first time, there is a great temptation to "tell everything you know" about the subject in order to establish your expertise as the reason to want to contact you for assistance and guidance. That usually is the wrong thing to do.

There are two primary purposes for the seminar. The first is to give enough useful information to those attending so that they will consider the time well spent. This is not necessarily complex information. In fact, it is likely that it will not be. You want those attending to be able to go away remembering some of what was said. Relatively simple concepts and ideas are easier to comprehend and remember. One must keep in mind that, for the most part, it is people who have relatively unsophisticated knowledge of financial planning and financial products who respond to seminar invitations. Those who are well-versed or who have financial advisors usually do not consider that the time will be well spent. It is not a positive experience for most people to find themselves at sea trying to understand what is being said. Their minds will wander quickly.

The second purpose of the seminar is to make it easy for a person attending to sign a response card requesting a contact, or to ask individual questions of speakers or others or give opinions during breaks in the seminar program. In order to ask questions or give opinions, the people must feel comfortable that they understand what is being said. When people hear something said with which they already are familiar, there is a validation of what is said based on previous information. That is a very positive thing so long as there is not so much previously known information that the presentation appears to be trite. Considering these two purposes, the scope of the information provided in the seminar probably needs to be relatively limited.

The ideas that are presented can be of the same type you would use in sales interviews, for example. information about why it is necessary to accumulate for the future, especially retirement, investment earnings and interest rate trends, the need for diversification, and the like. Some of the ideas in Chapter 4 can be adapted for this use. Other professionals, such as attorneys, can present information on estate planning, trusts, and advanced directives such as durable powers of attorney and living wills. The other professionals also are looking for opportunities to attract new clients and customers. Naturally, you will want what others say to be consistent with what you or your associates present. There must be good coordination so that things go smoothly. As we said, the problem usually is in limiting what is presented to what can be absorbed, rather than being concerned with filling the time available.

### *Absolute Must: Response Card*

There is one absolute must with respect to the content of the seminar. On several occasions during the various presentations, the speaker must call the attention of those attending to the cards that request information or an individual consultation or both. Logically, when a speaker has concluded discussion of a subject, he can invite, "If you would like to know more about this or would like to see how it applies to your own circumstances, note that on the response card (which is then held up) to receive an individual consultation."

It usually is better to make this suggestion at several strategic points in the program than to wait until the end. A seminar attender who is hesitant to complete a card, even though he knows there can be a benefit, can build momentum (or is it courage) to take action with the series of invitations. Of course, it is possible to overdo it resulting in resistance stiffening instead of softening.

Seminar information should be reinforced with a few, simple handouts, which also contain the name, address, and phone number of the person or organization presenting the seminar. Not only do the handouts illuminate the points discussed, but they supply the names of contacts for more information.

Sometimes, a simple, fill-in outline of the entire seminar is used. This is not to say you should or should not hand out elaborate outlines or summaries of the entire seminar; some seminar givers do and others do not. The more elaborate handouts can distract the listeners from what the speakers are saying, robbing speakers of the opportunity to develop points in a systematic and sometimes dramatic and even entertaining fashion.

On the other hand, if you want listeners to acquire a substantial amount of information or to become acquainted with a procedure or process, such as a planning process, it might be preferable to use the more elaborate approach. With either approach, you will want to use an agenda indicating what subjects will be discussed during designated times.

### *Seminar Length and Speakers*

The length of the seminar is an important consideration. Again, there is the temptation to try to cram too much information into one seminar and the time needed grows longer and longer. Remembering the two purposes of the seminar, the time should be limited, and there should be breaks built into the total time allotment. Many seminar givers believe that two to three hours, including breaks, is about the limit. At the end, there should be time for those who want to linger to ask additional questions; this can be extremely valuable time for gently promoting contact with those presenting the seminar. Of course, if there are special circumstances, the time must be different. When you are presenting at lunch time or after work, the content and time must be adjusted to fit. And programs for organizations usually are expected to be shorter.

It seems pretty basic to say but seminar speakers should be good presenters and able to answer questions without undue hesitation. You, as the seminar giver, should have a prominent presence but that does not mean necessarily that you need to be a major presenter. If you have the credentials and are at ease presenting, you can do so, of course. However, you can achieve a prominent position by introducing and credentializing the other speakers, handling question and answer portions, and the like. The audience must depart knowing who you and your business associates are and what you do, but there is nothing wrong with your having imported "outside experts" for the seminar. In subsequent interviews, you can refer to what certain speakers said even though you have said the same things in interviews all along. These ideas will carry more weight having come from a seminar which your potential customer attended.

We have referred to the other business associates who may be present during the seminar. Some seminar givers conduct the program with only the help of any outside speakers and a person to handle the arrangements and logistics of the meeting. Others have business associates present, especially if more than ten or fifteen people will be attending. The other associates are introduced in their capacity to answer questions and listen to comments, and they have easily recognizable name badges. The people attending want to have easy access to someone to talk with when they are inclined to do so, which may be during a break; they dislike waiting in line for too long. And any conversation is apt to improve chances that the person will ask to be seen individually. Besides, the associate who talked with this individual will have a reason to talk with him again later in the program or afterward.

## On Building Your Sales Presentation

Whatever the method of marketing, the sale takes place during one or more individual discussions with the potential customer. Earlier, we referred to the sales process which applies to the sale of variable annuities just as it does to most financial products. We also referred to the facts that there is a perception among many people of the need to accumulate for the future, especially retirement, and that products such as variable annuities have some level of built-in receptivity. The result is that some people are more willing to discuss these matters than others; you are able to get interviews with them more often. But they still will resist buying, and they will resist buying now in particular. It is not easy to agree to part with money, to make a financial commitment. If it were easy, the person being interviewed might have no money available by this time.

In building your sales presentation, you will want to take advantage of the built-in receptivity by coming to agreement with the potential customer about an interest in accumulating for the future. You may not need to prove that it is needed but you may have to give the customer some data on how much it might take. You may not need to prove that it is a good strategy to put some of the customer's dollars in products that invest in stocks and bonds as well as in guaranteed interest accounts, if desired, but you may need to provide some pertinent data on how to go about doing it and how you can be of assistance.

Perhaps the most important thing you need to learn is: what is the potential customer's motivation for considering the purchase of financial products? Is he interested in "having the good life" or in not being poor? Are there specific financial goals? What is the relative importance of providing for the potential customer's spouse, children, or grandchildren? How important is tax planning? Then, you will want to know about the customer's risk tolerance and need for access to the money that is saved and invested. In short, what are the potential customer's needs that can be satisfied with variable annuities and related financial products.

## Need and Motivation to Act

You will want your approach presentation to hit the high points of the process you intend to follow to gather information and come to agreement on needs.

When you have gathered the information, you need to do an analysis; then, you will be in a position to identify needs and solutions to the needs. This can be a structured process extending over two or more interviews or it can be short, often concluding in the same interview because the needs are agreed to easily and the solutions readily apparent.

When the process will be a short one, the establishing of a need that your product can fill should not be short-circuited. Unless there is a need that must be filled, there is no motivation to act. Without the firm establishment of a need, the variable annuity purchase becomes akin to a commodity purchase. It is just something to consider along with a number of other things going on in the potential customer's life. If there is no motivation to act, then clearly there is no reason to act now, which so many times is the essence of the sale.

When the potential customer feels the motivation to fill a need, it is much more likely that he will want to act on it and remove at least one of his worries or concerns. There are other reasons to act now, such as the fact that investment markets are volatile or interest rates appear to be moving one way or the other. But the one that often proves to be the most powerful is the ability to resolve a problem or concern the potential customer has so that he can go on to other things.

The concept of packaging together funds, such as mutual funds, is an easy one for most people to understand but they sometimes do not have such an understanding of variable annuities. When presenting a variable annuity as the solution to one or more of the potential customer's needs, it is easy to get bogged down in detailed explanations of the product, leaving unsaid why the details are important to the potential customer.

When all is said and done, the customer should understand, as fully as he would like to, the variable annuity he is purchasing. However, a sales representative must be careful that the discussion is not just of the product's features. The benefits that the customer derives from the features are what matter. You never want the potential customer to conclude that what he saw was a wonderful and flexible product for someone but not be able to see why he should be the one to buy it. It is a long established principle of selling that people buy benefits; they do not buy features.

## Chapter Endnotes

1. Barthelman, Alan F., "What Factors Make a Good Prospect for Worksite Products?" *National Underwriter*, Life and Health/Financial Services edition, September 27, 2004, p. 14.

# Chapter 4

## Selling Ideas

### Finding the Dominant Appeal

Effective sales ideas are ideas that sell. An idea sells because it strikes a responsive chord with a customer; sometimes these are called customer "hot buttons." There may be a number of points that appeal to a customer, but there usually are just a couple that are dominant. Once you find one or more of these dominant ideas that appeal to a customer, you will want to concentrate on what you have found. You will need to cover other matters during the interview but it is important that you continue to emphasize the thoughts that appeal most to the customer.

Of course, finding the dominant ideas usually is anything but like "falling off a log." A customer will not volunteer that the point you have just made is important enough that he is apt to take action. It will be up to you to discern that from the customer's reactions and, perhaps, the intensity of the questions asked about the idea. Sometimes, you will misread a customer and concentrate on a minor issue for too long. Selling is an art, not a science; people frequently surprise you by saying or acting out things you do not expect. Dealing with people is not dull, to be sure. The good thing is that as long as you remain on positive terms with the prospective customer, you will be able to change directions and move to different sales points.

Research done among would-be financial services product customers has shown that people want information about products, services, and procedures. But they want the information provided in a convenient way. That is, they do not want to know "everything." In other words—they want to know what they want to know. And they do not want to feel they are being manipulated as they are receiving the information. We can take advantage of this understanding by being straight-forward, reasonably succinct, and by concentrating on what they find most helpful and appealing. And we should neither "talk down" to them, try to impress them with our "superior knowledge" of products and services, nor use manipulative interview techniques.

Would-be customers want to be in control and to engage in self direction with respect to the products and services they buy. Often, these can be exercised particularly when people have a number of choices available to them. There are many opportunities for the variable annuity owner to exercise control and self direction; there are many choices that continue well beyond the initial choices at the time of purchase. A number of examples can be made known to the customer who wants to exercise such self direction and control.

Financial services product customers want to be able to trust the representative with whom they are dealing and the companies from which they are buying. Conducting yourself in a straight-forward, non-manipulative manner, concentrating on those things that are most important to the customer builds trust. Follow-up and follow-through add to it. Good and timely service from the issuing company builds trust with the company. Customer surveys have shown that most customers value highly a company which handles transactions accurately and in a timely fashion, and which is responsive to customer questions and requests.

Finally, customers are said to want fulfillment; that is, they want to feel they have accomplished what they have set out to accomplish. With variable annuities, there are ample opportunities for people to realize their ambitions for accumulating money for the future. There are numerous choices available that fit the risk tolerance of a particular customer. There also are ample occasions to exercise control and self direction with respect to the premiums they pay, the accounts they choose, the internal transfers they make, the withdrawals they use, and the payout provisions they employ.

In this chapter, we will put forward a number of sales ideas. We will do so by, first, stating the essence of the idea and, then, using some sample language in most instances. We will not attempt to fashion "complete sales tracks," for that would be a waste of space. Most registered representatives of even limited experience are happy to have a new idea, a notion of how the idea works, and something of how to say it. But they will take what has been provided and convert it into their own language and methods of showing and discussing it.

More complete presentations are not shown here for another, perhaps even more important, reason. Materials shown to a potential variable annuity customer must be approved in advance by the broker/dealer distributing the variable annuity. It is one thing to discuss general concepts; it is something else to show materials that are more particular to a specific variable annuity product. Compliance matters are discussed in more detail in Chapter 6.

The twenty sales ideas presented in this chapter include:

1. Variable Annuities as IRAs: Building Retirement Income with Efficiency;
2. Variable Annuities as IRAs: More Help for Children's Education;
3. Importance of Regular Saving and Investing: Cost of Delay;
4. Importance of Regular Saving and Investing: Dollar Cost Averaging;
5. Maximizing Accumulation: Taking Advantage of Tax Deferral;
6. Exercising and Maintaining Control: Having Many Choices;
7. Exercising and Maintaining Control: Changing Investments;
8. Exercising and Maintaining Control: Timing Income Taxes;
9. Maintaining Purchasing Power: Investing in Equities;
10. Dealing with Risk: Using Diversification to Advantage;
11. Cementing Your Successes: Strategic Use of the Guaranteed Interest (or Money Market) Account;
12. Cementing Your Successes: Availability of the Death Benefit and Optional Death Benefits;

13. Cementing Your Successes: Availability of Guaranteed Living Benefits;

14. Effective Income Planning: Defer, Withdraw, Annuitize

15. Keeping the Tax Penalty in Perspective: Don't Be Put Off by It

16. Handling Large, One-Time Amounts: Take the Pressure Off but Put the Money to Work;

17. Annuity Buildup not Counted for Social Security Benefits Taxation;

18. Annuity Payout and Life Insurance Combination;

19. IRAs for Smaller Employers; and

20. Providing for Supplemental Retirement Income.

## Building Retirement Income

Virtually all people are interested in hearing about, and perhaps acting on, ideas involving tax benefits to them. Few subjects are discussed more than taxes and any opportunity to pay lower taxes should be explored. Recent tax laws have enhanced some existing provisions and added important new ones in the areas of retirement and children's education – two areas of high interest to most prospective variable annuity customers. Let us look first at retirement.

### *Variable Annuities as IRAs: Building Retirement Income with Efficiency*

What makes traditional IRAs so popular, and a very efficient way to build retirement income, is the fact that an individual may be able to take an income tax deduction on the contribution made. An individual, under age 70½ who has compensation of at least the amount contributed, may be able to deduct up to $4,000 per year (in 2005-2007; $3,000 in 2004). The same amount may be made for a non-working spouse; thus, the two spouses can contribute and deduct $8,000 (in 2005-2007; $6,000 in 2004). When both spouses are working, the same $8,000 may be contributed. In addition, there is a catch-up provision, of up to $500 per year (in 2004 and 2005; $1,000 after 2005), which applies to those age 50 and over.[1]

Not everyone can take these deductions or take them in full but many people can. The deduction may be reduced or eliminated if the contributing person or spouse is an "active participant" in a qualified retirement plan. In 2005 and after, a phase-out of the deduction begins at $50,000 of adjusted gross income (AGI) for a single person and is completed at $60,000. (In 2004, the phase-out began at $45,000 and was phased out at $55,000.) For a married couple filing jointly, where both spouses participate in retirement plans, the 2005 phase-out begins at $70,000 and is completed at $80,000 (the 2004 phase-out began at $65,000 and ended at $75,000). These amounts increase by $5,000 per year until 2007 when the phase-out begins at $80,000 and is completed at $90,000. In the case of married taxpayers, filing a joint return, where only one is an "active participant" in a qualified retirement plan, the phase-out begins at $150,000.[2] Clearly, although a number of people will not be able to deduct contributions to traditional IRAs, a great many people will be able to. And the usefulness of deductible IRAs is further enhanced by the fact that the 10% penalty for premature distributions does not apply to distributions used for certain education expenses.[3] (More on that shortly and in Chapter 11.)

For those who cannot or, for some reason, do not want to deduct contributions, there is the Roth IRA. Contributions are not deductible but interest and earnings accumulate on a tax-deferred basis and when the proceeds are distributed, they are tax-free if the Roth IRA has been held for five years and the taxpayer is at least 59½ years of age.[4] Contributions made to Roth IRAs may be removed without tax for college expenses even when the taxpayer is under age 59½.[5] That is, it is considered that the first amounts distributed are contributions on which tax already has been paid. Only after all contributions have been removed will there be taxable distributions of interest and earnings. (More on these provisions in Chapter 11.)

Generally, people want all the deductions they can get in order to reduce their current taxes. They will be attracted to being able to take current deductions – the "a bird in the hand is worth two in the bush" philosophy. But, under some circumstances, tax-free income can be even better in the long run.

To illustrate, let us consider contributing $4,000 per year at 5% interest to an IRA. At the end of 20 years, the amount accumulated is $138,877. With a deductible IRA, the person's cost is less because of the deduction ($4,000 less a 25% tax bracket deduction is $3,000), but the income is all taxable when it is distributed. (For comparison purposes, we will put the annual $1,000 tax deduction in a side fund.) With a nondeductible Roth IRA, the person's cost is the full $4,000 per year but the distribution is not taxed.

| | Regular IRA | Roth IRA |
|---|---|---|
| 20 Year IRA Accumulation | $138,877 | $138,877 |
| 25% Tax on Distribution | - 34,719 | - 0 |
| Net Proceeds | $104,158 | $138,877 |
| Less Net Cost after Deduction | - 60,000 | - 80,000 |
| Net IRA Interest | $ 44,158 | $ 58,877 |
| Side Fund Accumulation | $ 34,719 | |
| Less Net Cost | - 20,000 | |
| Net Side Fund Interest | $ 14,719 | |
| Total Net Interest | $ 58,877 | $ 58,877 |

Figures are derived from a compound interest table, the sum to which one dollar per annum, paid at the beginning of each year, will increase.

To be sure, these are simplistic comparisons. It is assumed that all distributions are taxed at 25%, which may not be the case; in fact, many would argue that the tax rate at retirement will be lower. We have placed the annual $1,000 tax deduction in a side fund to accumulate at 5%. If the side fund is not taxable and tax rates stay the same, as shown, the regular IRA and side fund combination equals the Roth IRA. A decrease in tax rates from time of contribution to time of distribution works to the benefit of the regular IRA and side fund combination. An increase in tax rates from time of contribution to time of distribution works to the benefit of the Roth IRA. Any tax on the side fund works to the disadvantage of the regular IRA and side fund combination. However, the plain fact is that both tax deductions and tax-free distributions are worth a great deal. The overriding conclusion is that people should take advantage of these two types of IRAs to the extent they are permitted. Whether deductible or nondeductible, each spouse is limited to putting $4,000 into one type of IRA or another. Because of human nature, they usually will want to maximize what can be deducted first and then consider the other method of accumulating for the future.

Some sample language to use in presenting retirement planning ideas follows.

*M/M Customer, I am sure you are aware of IRAs, where a deductible contribution may be made to help you accumulate more for your retirement. You also probably are aware that because you participate in your employer's retirement plan, and* *because your family income is as high as it is, you cannot take an IRA deduction, even though the income limits have been increased. But do you know that because your spouse is not a participant in an employer plan, a deductible IRA can be set up for him/her? There is a joint income limitation for that, too, but it is $150,000. Most of us are able to qualify with that kind of limit.*

*Deductible contributions are great because when you send $4,000 to your IRA, you have to take only $3,000 out of your pocket if you are in a 25% tax bracket. The other $1,000 comes from a reduction in your income taxes. Or to put it another way, if you want to put $4,000 into savings or investments after taxes, you would need to earn $5,333 to have the $4,000 left after taxes.*

*Now, sometimes people tell me that this is all well and good but $4,000 a year isn't going to do much when it comes to retirement. These people are happy to be reminded of the Roth IRA and the fact that both you and your spouse can make $4,000 contributions. What is remarkable about the Roth IRA is the fact that though the contributions are not deductible, the income at retirement is tax-free – not a lower rate of tax, not part of it taxed. All of it is tax-free. That means when you take a $10,000 distribution, for example, you get to spend all $10,000 of it, not what is left after paying taxes, such as $7,500 in a 25% bracket. In your specific situation you can't have both a deductible IRA and a Roth IRA, but you have your choice for your spouse and the Roth IRA is available for you. Putting $8,000 each year into IRAs can be a big assist to your retirement income. Let me show you an example of how the two types of IRAs work.* (Show an illustration similar to the one above.)

There is another valuable option for a self-employed person who does not have employees, perhaps a sales agent or representative or other independent contractor who essentially works alone. It is a Simplified Employee Pension (SEP), which allows for contributions of 25% (net of the contribution) up to a maximum amount of $42,000 (in 2005 indexed; $41,000 in 2004).[6] Employees must be included in SEPs; hence, we are suggesting their use here for those without employees. Variable annuities may be used to fund SEPs. (See the discussion in Chapter 11.)

Employees of public schools and other non-profit organizations are eligible to participate in tax sheltered annuities (sometimes referred to as tax deferred annuities) on a salary reduction basis. They can put substantial amounts into these plans ($14,000 in 2005 and $15,000 in 2006 ($13,000 in 2004) with substantial catch-up provisions for those age 50 and over).[7] Sales representatives who specialize in this area often service large plans in large school districts or large institutions, such as colleges or hospitals. In addition, employees of state and local governments are eligible for IRC Section 457 plans of salary deferral that also permit contributions of up to $14,000 in 2005 and $15,000 in 2006 ($13,000 in 2004) with catch-up provisions for those age 50 and over and those in their final three years before retiring.[8] (There is further discussion of these plans in Chapter 11.)

## Children's Education

### *Variable Annuities as IRAs: More Help for Children's Education*

Paying for the education of children is one of most potential customers' highest priorities. Funds that have been saved in advance are the best because there have few strings attached and, for the most part, they can be used at any time. But there is an array of other potential sources of education, some that most people can use, and others that only people with limited resources are able to use. Much of the available education aid is in the form of loans, credits, and deductions and provisions are complex. Other educational aid is a matter of using available saving and investment vehicles in the most efficient ways possible. Because there are so many provisions, the potential customer is confronted with what may be too many choices, a situation that often leads to inaction rather than action. People want choices but not so many that they have trouble taking them all in. Briefly, let us look at the options available (more thorough discussions are in Chapter 11):

1. **Financial Aid and Loans** – Since qualifying for *financial aid* is not easy, it should be considered a fall-back position when other education financing is not at hand. *Student loans* are much easier to get but they are loans that the student must pay back. They can be a significant drag on the new graduate's financial start in life, lasting for many years. Still, they are better than not being able to pay for higher education at all.

2. **Tax Credits and Deductions** – The *Hope Scholarship Credit*, which can provide a tax credit of as much as $1,500 during each of the first two years of college, and the *Lifetime Learning Credit*, which can provide a tax credit for 20% of up to $10,000 of qualifying education expenses during later college years, including post graduate education. The Hope Credit applies per student and the Lifetime Learning Credit applies per taxpayer. The credit amounts are indexed for inflation.[9] Interest on student loans is deductible from income. The deduction is available from gross income so that it is not an itemized deduction

(and therefore can be taken even though the taxpayer is using the standard deduction). It is for up to $2,500 of interest paid for qualified higher education expenses. Income phase-outs apply.[10] Another education expense deduction of up to $4,000 applies but is set to expire at the end of 2005.[11]

3. **Tax-Favored Education Savings** – Contributions to *Coverdell Education Savings Accounts*[12] are not tax deductible but earnings in the accounts are not taxed. Up to $2,000 may be placed in the accounts each year and may be distributed to pay qualified education expenses. In this case, these expenses include those of elementary and secondary schools as well as post-secondary. There are phase-out provisions applicable to permitted contribution amounts. Generally, all funds must be distributed by the beneficiary's age 30 or the earnings are taxable. *Section 529 plans* are state-sponsored or privately-sponsored arrangements where the taxpayer purchases prepaid tuition credits or certificates or makes contributions to educational savings accounts. As might be expected, these plans differ from each other. Contributions or credits available are limited in some way, e.g., five years of expenses or a stated dollar amount. Contributions or purchases are not tax deductible but earnings are deferred and payments for qualifying expenses are not taxed. Distributions not used for qualifying expenses are subject to a 10% penalty on the earnings distributed.

4. **Distributions from IRAs and Other Plans** – Distributions from *traditional IRAs* used for qualified higher education expenses for the taxpayer, the taxpayer's spouse, or the child or grandchild of either spouse, are not subject to the 10% penalty for premature distributions, even if made prior to age 59½.[13] Since the contributions had been deductible and the interest and earnings deferred, the distribution is subject to income tax, however. In general, the same treatment is given to distributions for educational expenses from *SIMPLE IRAs, SEPs, SIMPLE 401(k) plans, tax sheltered annuities* and *IRC Section 457 plans. Roth IRA* earnings used for educational expenses are taxable but not subject to the 10% penalty, while contributions that are distributed have already have been taxed and will not be taxed again. (These plans are discussed in Chapter 11.)

As mentioned, there may be too many choices for many people. And it is important to remember that the situation in 10 or 15 years may be different from today. We all have seen tax provisions enacted, then modified in one way or another, and even eliminated or offset by another provision. Since credits are used during the college years, they must be available then. Having interest deductions for student loan interest is good but it is better if there are no loans for the graduating student or parents to contend with. State tuition programs may be useful and should be considered.

What seems clear is that IRAs and other plans, funded with variable annuities, can be very effective in addressing education expenses. While provisions affecting IRAs may be changed in the future, the usual practice is not to take away tax benefits on amounts already contributed and accumulated. Add to that the fact that the same IRA used for retirement can be used for education to a significant extent. This means that if, for one reason or another, some of the funds intended for education are not needed, they can remain in the IRA for retirement. And the decisions about using the money do not have to be made until college time arrives.

Following is sample language to use in talking about education funding.

*M/M Customer, one of the financial concerns you have expressed is that your child (or grandchild) have the money to go to college, and even to graduate or professional school, if possible. I think you are right to have that in mind as something you would like to address. The latest studies*[14] *I have seen show clearly that college graduates have many more career options, have better promotion opportunities, have higher earnings ,and are less frequently faced with unemployment. Whether your first concern is that your children (or grandchildren) find a good job in the first place, with solid possibilities for advancement, have the ability to earn an above average income, or are less apt to need to deal with unemployment, a college education puts them in the best position. And graduate or professional school improves the situation.*

*There are a number of ways to accumulate money for college. One of them is tax deductible. Since your spouse is not participating in a qualified retirement plan as you are, he/she can set up an IRA for $4,000 per year and deduct it on your joint return. Money can be taken out for education. Then, you, or both of you if you decide not to use the deductible IRA, can put aside $4,000 each to set up nondeductible IRAs that provide for income at retirement that is totally tax-free. Obviously, tax-free income will go farther than income that will be reduced by tax. Let me show you an illustration of the difference. (Show the illustration of the two IRAs as above.)*

*With the deductible IRA, you can take money out at college time to pay for tuition, books, academic fees, supplies, and equipment. The money will be taxable but there is no penalty for taking the money out early; this is an exception to the usual rule. With the nondeductible IRA, you can take out the money you have put in without paying any tax. If you take more than that, you will have some tax consequences so you may want to leave the rest in, to be taken tax-free at retirement.*

*With these IRAs, the same plans you are using for retirement can be used for many of the education costs you will have. You have flexibility because you don't have to dedicate certain contributions for retirement and certain others for education. Of course, you can make dedicated contributions but you don't have to.*

## Regular Saving and Investing

Most of the selling ideas used in the remainder of this chapter are designed to apply to variable annuities not used in IRAs although the principles apply equally well when they are used for IRA funding.

### *Importance of Regular Saving and Investing: Cost of Delay*

People have all kinds of reasons for putting off the saving and investing they should be doing. One of the most common is no reason at all; it is just not getting around to it. Sometimes, the lack of action is aided by too high or too low stock prices or by interest rates that are too low. An important point is that most people are better off when they do something, not when they do nothing. One way to dramatize the need to act is by showing the effect of the loss of interest compounding when saving or investing is delayed. The following is some sample language to use in presenting this sales idea.

*M/M Customer, you would not be unusual if you sometimes delayed saving and investing the money you wanted to. It's pretty easy to want to wait for stock prices to go down some, or for interest rates to rise, before making a commitment to save or invest. But financial experts tell us that delaying action can be very costly. The reason for that is the effect of the compounding of interest or earnings on investments over time. And delay costs us the time. Let me illustrate; I am not using any particular product, just illustrating a principle.* (Refer to the chart in Figure 4.01.)

FIGURE 4.1

## THE COST OF DELAYING IMPLEMENTATION OF AN INVESTMENT PROGRAM

SCENARIO ONE: An individual begins investing $3,000 per year today and continues for 20 years.

| | |
|---|---|
| Amount Invested Annually | $3,000 |
| Number of Years Invested | 20 |
| Total Investment | $60,000 ** |
| | |
| Accumulation at 5% at Year 20 | $104,158 |
| Amount of Interest Earned | |
| ($104,158 - $60,000) | $44,158 |
| | |
| Accumulation at 6% at Year 20 | $116,978 |
| Amount of Interest Earned | |
| ($116,978 - $60,000) | $56,978 |

SCENARIO TWO: Instead of beginning to invest today, the individual waits five years and then begins investing $3,000 per year and continues for 15 years.

| | |
|---|---|
| Amount Invested Annually | $3,000 |
| Number of Years Invested | 15 |
| Total Investment | $45,000 ** |
| | |
| Accumulation at 5% at Year 15 | $67,972 |
| Amount of Interest Earned | |
| ($67,972 - $45,000) | $22,972 |
| | |
| Accumulation at 6% at Year 15 | $74,018 |
| Amount of Interest Earned | |
| ($74,018 - $45,000) | $29,018 |

** NOTE: Investing an extra $15,000 by beginning to invest $3,000 annually now instead of waiting five years produces an additional $36,186 assuming a 5% return ($104,158 - $67,972) and an additional $42,960 assuming a 6% return ($116,978 - $74,018).

*Let us assume you want to put aside $3,000 each year for 20 years and can earn 5% on the money in some product or another. In 20 years, you would have put aside $60,000 but your account would be worth $104,158. The extra $44,158 came from the compounding of earnings and interest.*

*But now let us assume that you waited 5 years before starting to invest. At the end of 15 years, you would have invested $45,000 and your account would be worth $67,972. The extra $15,000, invested at $3,000 per year for the first 5 years, produced an additional $36,186. Looking at it another way, if you decided you wanted to have the same $104,158 by the end of 15 years, you would need to put approximately $4,600 per year in; that's 53% more. It's pretty clear that the sooner you invest and save with those products you choose the better off you will be. As I said, this is not an illustration of any particular product and is not guaranteed. Your results will vary according to the performance of the accounts you choose.*

For additional emphasis, a higher interest rate also may be illustrated in the belief that investments, which include a substantial equities component, have done better in the past than 6%. The figure for $3,000 per year at 7% over 20 years is $131,596; in 15 years, the figure is $80,664. Thus, the extra $15,000 produces $50,932. Larger amounts are more dramatic, of course.

### *Importance of Regular Saving and Investing: Dollar Cost Averaging*

A major reason for delaying putting money into investments is waiting for the right time. The right time can arrive when higher stock or bond prices have dropped or when low prices have started to show signs of increasing. People attempt to "time the market" even though, many times, they deny that is what they are attempting. Yet, the fact is that if most people would begin investing, using dollar cost averaging, they would come out much better than if they waited for the right time, which often does not occur very soon.

Below is some sample language to use in discussing dollar cost averaging. (In this discussion, we will use the dollar cost averaging example shown in Figure 4.02. This same example is also discussed in Chapter 5.)

FIGURE 4.2

## DOLLAR COST AVERAGING*

| Time | Premium | Unit Value | Units Purchased |
|---|---|---|---|
| 1 | $200 | $10.00 | 20.00 |
| 2 | $200 | $12.00 | 16.67 |
| 3 | $200 | $ 9.00 | 22.22 |
| 4 | $200 | $ 7.00 | 28.57 |
| 5 | $200 | $10.00 | 20.00 |
| Totals | $1000 | $ 9.60 Average | 107.46 |

* Charges against premiums, if any, have been disregarded in this example.

*M/M Customer, many of the people I talk with tell me they are tempted to put off making investments, waiting for an opportunity when the price has gone down a bit. What they often find is that they end up waiting for quite some time, and the money they intended to invest is left uninvested in the meantime. Many of these people have been happy to hear about the concept of dollar cost averaging and find that it makes a great deal of sense.*

*The concept is this: you decide to make continuing investments of a specific amount at regular intervals. The result is that the equal dollar amounts buy relatively fewer investment units when the unit values are higher and relatively more units when the unit values are lower. In this example of investing $200 at each interval, we see that 20 units are purchased the first time when the unit value is $10. The second regular investment is made when the unit value has risen to $12 and so fewer units are purchased. By the time of the third investment, the unit value has fallen to $9 so that more units are bought. By the end of the five purchases in this example, 107.46 units have been purchased. With the unit value back at $10, the account is worth $1,074.60, more than would have been the case if an equal number of units had been purchased each time.*

*One other point. The average unit value during the period was $9.60, but the average price paid was $9.31 ($1,000 payments divided by 107.46 units). This means the cost paid was $.29 per unit less than the average price, an added benefit of using dollar cost averaging.*

*As you might imagine, the success of dollar cost averaging is dependent in the long run on the performance of the investment purchased. But it can take some of the stress out of deciding when the right time to make investments is. The truth is the right time is regularly. Regular investing using dollar cost averaging has been successful for many investors.*

When a customer has a relatively large amount of money to invest, he still may want to use dollar cost averaging over an upcoming period of time and not invest all of the money in particular variable accounts now. Many variable annuities offer a provision for putting the large amount into a money market or other account and then making regular transfers to other designated accounts on a dollar cost averaging basis.

## Tax Deferral

### *Maximizing Accumulation: Taking Advantage of Tax Deferral*

Earnings and interest in a variable annuity's accounts accumulate on a tax-deferred basis until they are withdrawn. This has the effect of paying a higher rate of return or increased earnings. The amounts accumulated are much more than would have been the case if the interest and earnings were subject to current income tax. When the interest and earnings are withdrawn, they are taxed and that must be taken into account when making the comparison between currently taxed and tax-deferred accumulations. And in order to present a complete comparison, the penalty for premature distributions should be mentioned. (We use earnings rates after taxes, a table of tax-exempt equivalents and a compound interest table to calculate the figures.)

*M/M Customer, many of my customers tell me that one of the things they like most about their variable annuities is the fact that the interest and earnings credited to their accounts each year are tax-deferred; the customers don't have to pay a tax until they withdraw money, some time in the future. This means all of the yearly earnings are credited and the people don't have to increase the taxes they are paying on account of it.*

*As you think about it, when you pay a yearly tax, as you must do with nearly all other savings and investments, it is as if the rate credited has been reduced by the amount of the tax. If you get 6% on your money, but are in the 25% income tax bracket, it is as if you actually received 4.5%. Now, 25% is not the highest bracket, and you are or will be in a higher bracket, but let's look at that one as an example:*

$3,000 PER YEAR

| 6% | After Tax | 4.5% | Difference | |
|---|---|---|---|---|
| 15 Years | $ 74,018 | $ 66,763 | $ 65,158 | $1,605 |
| 20 Years | 116,978 | 102,733 | 98,349 | 4,384 |
| 25 Years | 174,469 | 149,602 | 139,712 | 9,890 |

*By the end of 15 years we see a difference of just over $1,600. In 20 years, the difference is almost $4,400 and growing. In 25 years, the difference has grown to nearly $9,900, quite a large amount. Let's use the 25 year figure of $174,469. Of that, $99,469 hasn't been taxed yet. At 25%, the tax would be $24,867, leaving a balance of $149,602, still quite a lot more than the $139,712. And if your tax rate is less than 25% at retirement time, which many people say is likely, the difference would be greater. The reason is that there have, in effect, been interest and earnings on tax savings during the 25 year period.*

*I should add a few notes to this. We have used a 25% tax bracket as an example; this may or may not be valid, we don't know. We do know that most people gradually move into higher brackets during their investing years and then go to a lower bracket during their retirement years, as we suggested. So, chances are, we are being rather conservative here. Another note is that we have assumed you would terminate the annuity at one time and pay the tax. That is not necessarily what you will do. In fact, most people plan to take income each year after retirement; the tax isn't paid all at once, and is deferred on the amount not yet received. Another option used by many people is to elect to receive income systematically over a period of years or for life; in that event, the tax can be spread over the period of payments. The final note is that we have assumed you would take your money after you are age 59½, a sensible assumption since we are discussing retirement. Any withdrawals you make before that age may be subject to an additional tax of 10% to make up for the tax deferral you enjoyed while the money was accumulated.*

## Maintaining Control

### *Exercising and Maintaining Control: Having Many Choices*

As discussed above, people like to be in control of their financial activities and in a position to exercise self direction. Perhaps one of the best ways to have control and self direction is for there to be many choices. Some people will make use of the many choices by being active in making changes and exercising options;

others will be content not to do that, secure in the feeling that their affairs are managed in their best interests. A way to dramatize the control that customers have is to speak of the benefits that the choices make available to them.

*M/M Customer, many of my customers tell me that one of the things they like best about using variable annuities in their investment programs is the fact that they can maintain control over how often they invest and in what investments. While financial experts point out how important it is for people to invest regularly, if they are to accomplish their objectives, it is comforting to know you are not locked in to investing a particular amount each month or each year. You may begin paying into the contract, and then stop for a period of time if there is a need for you to; then, you may begin again or you may begin paying a different amount. It's all up to you. As I said, you're not locked in.*

*When you start paying into the contract, you choose from among all of these accounts where your money should go.* (Here you present the information on the guaranteed and variable accounts.) *As you see, there is a growth account, an aggressive growth account, a bond account, and a balanced account with an allocation of stocks, bonds, and other securities,* (and whatever other accounts you want to highlight as examples of the accounts available). *This contract also has a guaranteed interest account which pays a stated rate of interest each year. Something else: all of these accounts are managed by professional managers; you can choose the managers who have the kind of experience you are looking for.*

*These choices are yours to make. And the nice thing is you're not locked in here either. You are free to make changes in the allocation of the money you are paying. More than that, you can move money already invested into different accounts; and this happens without your having to pay taxes on sales, as would be the case with many other investments. Another option that is completely up to you is when to start taking income from the contract. I should point out here that there are some tax ramifications surrounding when you take income and you will want to take those into consideration.*

*There is another option that has been important to many of my customers. You have the option not to be so involved in making changes, as many people do who do not have the time or inclination to involve themselves more actively. You can "let things ride" pretty much as they are and feel content that the professional investment managers will do their best to maximize the returns on the accounts they are managing. After all, their performance records are important to everyone involved.*

### *Exercising and Maintaining Control: Changing Investments*

When control is less of having choices and more of fixing things when they do not go according to plan, the ease of making changes in the allocation of premiums and among the accounts is important to bring out. Sometimes, the automatic rebalancing feature (see Chapter 7) can be of comfort to those who do not want to be in a position to actively participate in making changes. The fact that all of the adjustments can be made without recognizing taxes on sales also is of importance.

*M/M Customer, some of my customers like to watch their accounts closely and then make changes in them when they think it is time to go another route for a while. They are happy that they can make the changes without incurring any income taxes as long as they don't take any of the money out of the contract. Perhaps, you realize that with most types of investments, if you want to change from one fund to a different one, you can do that, of course. But you will have to do so by selling your interest in the one account and buying an interest in another. This means there will be taxes to pay on any gains during that year.*

*What my customers like is the fact that they can move money from one account in the variable annuity to another without any tax consequence. In fact, the deferral of tax, as the values in the accounts continue to accumulate, goes merrily on. There may be some fees to pay but a certain number of these internal changes can be made each year without any fee. This moving of money makes it possible for these people to go that different route for a while with a minimum of fuss.*

*Naturally not all people like to be so active in making changes. Some like to pretty much "let things ride," content that the professional investment managers will do a good job. However, what some of these people find is that, over time, some accounts perform better than others because of economic conditions at the time. The result is that more of their investments than they intended are in particular accounts, whereas they had intended for the mix to remain pretty much as it was when they last made account allocations. These customers take advantage of our automatic rebalancing feature. What happens is that as often as you direct, money automatically is taken from one account and placed in others you have designated so that the allocations in the accounts you have selected are maintained. This rebalancing feature is yours to use as you wish; you can discontinue it at any time and resume it later. And note here, too, the rebalancing occurs without current income tax.*

### *Exercising and Maintaining Control: Timing Income Taxes*

Most people are not given much control over when they pay taxes. Yet, a variable annuity affords such an opportunity through the tax deferral during the accumulation period and taxes payable only on withdrawals and payouts when they are taken. This is no small point in the "scheme of things" for many people. To point it out in the context of control over what is happening is a good tactic.

*M/M Customer, I am sure you have noticed that, each year in the late fall, articles appear in all the newspapers and magazines describing tax planning tactics. So many of the tactics can be used only by a few people, especially those with businesses of their own. The rest of the readers can only wish they had more opportunities. A variable annuity gives you at least one more opportunity. The money you put into the variable annuity accounts accumulates earnings and interest each year. But you do not pay income tax on the accumulated earnings each year so long as they are not taken out of the contract.*

*Someday, and certainly at retirement since a variable annuity is a long-term product particularly suited to supplementing retirement income, you will want to start taking money out. The years you will want to take the most out are the years when your other income is the least. This means that you will be paying income tax at a lower rate than if you took the money out when your other income was higher. In fact, you may choose to take little or none out in the years when your other income is particularly high. And what you don't take out continues to accumulate on a tax-deferred basis. I haven't seen that tactic mentioned in those articles on tax planning very often, but I think you will agree it is a good one and one you can use yourself. I need to point out that I have focused on retirement since there usually are some tax consequences if you withdraw money before age 59½.*

*Retirement also affords you another tax tactic. When you reach retirement age, one of your options is to take an income for life; with that option, less of the income you receive each year is subject to tax; more of it is yours to keep. When and if you decide to use this option is completely up to you. When the time comes, you will want to look at the figures for the various ways of taking income and make the decision that suits you best.*

# Maintaining Purchasing Power

## *Maintaining Purchasing Power: Investing in Equities*

Everyone agrees that a saving and investment program must take account of inflation. Sometimes, it is less known that in order to have returns greater than inflation, some of the investing must be in equities or bonds; this means there will be some element of risk. Younger people are not especially averse to risk; they become more concerned as they get older when there will be less time to recover from an unfortunate investment. People can purchase variable accounts with investments in stocks and bonds with varying risk profiles; they also can purchase less risky accounts.

*M/M Customer, inflation has been mild over the past few years but I am sure you remember or know about the late 1970s and early 1980s when it was much higher. And you know that inflation is a major concern of financial markets and of regulatory bodies such as the Federal Reserve Board. Whether inflation is rising or falling, its effect over the years has been substantial. It is estimated that it takes nearly five times as much money today to have the same purchasing power as thirty years ago. As you contemplate your saving and investment plans, no doubt you want to factor in some consideration of which kinds of investments have done well compared to inflation.*

*Generally speaking, over the past 50 years small company stocks have far outstripped inflation; large company stocks, those usually referred to as "blue chip" stocks, have done almost as well. Even long-term government bonds are somewhat ahead. Treasury bills have run about parallel to inflation. What this tells us is that in order to run ahead of inflation, you must invest some of your money in stocks, such as the ones in many of the accounts in our variable annuity.*

*As you know, past performance is no assurance of how accounts will perform in the future. There is some element of risk connected with investing in accounts owning stocks; they can go down as well as up. But the past record appears to confirm that the best hope of keeping up with and even doing better than inflation is with a portion of your money in stocks. The nice thing is that you can allocate as much or as little as you like to one or more of the accounts holding stock; you can change your mind as often as you like and you can move more money into those accounts or move some out, all without having to sell shares and pay taxes.*

# Diversification

## *Dealing with Risk: Using Diversification to Advantage*

A number of investors, especially first-time investors and older people, are concerned with keeping risk at a low level. For many people, low risk levels translate principally into guaranteed interest rates. While making use of the guaranteed interest account is a good tactic, it can be overdone, especially when people forget to consider the other way of dealing with risk—diversification. Diversification within and among the variable accounts allows the variable annuity buyer to address risk while still investing in accounts that can appreciate in value, thereby possibly hedging inflation.

*M/M Customer, some of the things you have said give me the sense that you are concerned about the risk of investing in variable accounts, which are the ones that have the potential for appreciating and keeping up with inflation. That is not unusual; I hear it frequently. Often, people are just more comfortable with guaranteed interest rate accounts even though they continue to worry about future inflation. What we have here is the risk of losing your principal pitted against the risk of losing some of the purchasing power of the money you are saving and investing.*

*Many financial experts point out that the risk of losing principal can best be addressed by diversifying your investments. When you diversify, you invest in many different types of investments – stocks of various types, corporate bonds and government securities, and so on – and many different investments within each of the types. When one investment goes down, another goes up; when one industry has a slowdown, another is doing pretty well; when one major product or service becomes less popular, another sells particularly well. Diversification, these experts say, is the way to deal with many of the risks of investing.*

*It is hard for an individual investor to diversify; he/she doesn't have the money to make enough investments fast enough. But an individual investor can diversify with the variable accounts in a variable annuity. Each of the variable accounts has investments in any number of different companies and organizations; one of the criteria that the investment managers use in selecting what to buy is maintaining diversification. Then, you can do your own diversifying; you can allocate your money among as many of the variable accounts as you like. And if you take a look, later on, at the accounts you own and decide you want to change to achieve more diversification, you can do that easily and quickly.*

## Using Guarantees

### *Cementing Your Successes: Strategic Use of the Guaranteed Interest (or Money Market) Account*

Sometimes we must remind customers that it is all well and good for the values in variable accounts or other investments they own to increase; they have nice gains on paper. But gains are not realized until the investments are sold and the money received. Until that happens, the paper gains can go away as the values or prices fall. As customers contemplate the gains, they must consider whether to stay invested as they are, awaiting further gains, or get at least a portion of the money out and realize the gains. When there are taxes to pay on the sales, the dilemma can get worse. Strategic use of the guaranteed account or the money market account offers ways, unique to the variable annuity, of dealing with the situation. (Note that there may be limitations on amounts which may be transferred in or out of the guaranteed account during any one year.)

*M/M Customer, when the account value of one of your variable annuity accounts or the price of another investment you own has increased substantially, you have a nice gain, a happy thought indeed. But some of my customers have said this otherwise happy situation can pose a bit of a dilemma for them. They know that they must sell the investments and take the money if they are to realize the gain. Otherwise, the investments' value may fall. On the other hand, the investments may continue to rise and they will wish they hadn't sold. Adding to this is the fact that, with most investments, the gains from the sales they will make are subject to current tax. If the investments go down, they don't feel so bad about the tax because they have made a smart move. But if the investments continue to rise, they feel doubly bad because they are not in the investments any more and they have had to pay taxes.*

*A variable annuity gives you the opportunity to cement your successes by moving money out of some accounts and into others without a current tax to pay. For example, you could move a portion of the money in a variable account that has risen in value into the guaranteed account (or money market account). Then, if the value of that variable account should fall, you have the money out, earning a guaranteed rate of interest (in the guaranteed account). If the value continues to rise, too bad, but at least you haven't had to add insult to injury by paying a tax on the gain. And another nice thing: when you perceive that the value of the variable account is on its way up again, you can move some of the money back into it. (I do need to call your attention to one more point: there is a limit on transfers involving the guaranteed account, etc.).*

### *Cementing Your Successes: Availability of the Death Benefit and Optional Death Benefits*

One of the unique features of a variable annuity is the death benefit. As discussed in more detail in Chapter 7, the traditional death benefit, which is paid to the designated beneficiary, is the amount of premiums paid (less any surrenders and applicable charges, including surrender charges in some cases) or the annuity's contract value, accumulated value, account value, etc. (all refer to the same figure) whichever is greater.

But there also are optional enhanced death benefits, generally funded by charges assessed against the various accounts. There might be a "stepped up" benefit based on a percentage of the premium paid in the last year, a "reset" on particular anniversaries, an annual "ratchet" up annually, a "roll up" feature adding the value of premium payments at a given rate of interest. Some of the optional death benefits have requirements in addition to the charges to the annuity accounts. For example, it might be required that the contract be in effect a minimum number of years. All death benefits are subject to different calculation procedures when the annuitant reaches some age such as 75 or 85. No annuity has all of the optional enhanced benefits but many annuities have one or more of them in addition to the traditional death benefit.

*M/M Customer, one of the reasons that many of my customers choose to invest in variable annuities is the fact that variable annuities have a death benefit. In fact, they also have an optional enhanced death benefit. Most other ways of investing don't have these benefits. Though my customers don't dwell on it much, they understand that should they die before completing their investment plans, it just might be at a time when the market is down. What a shame it would be if a temporary downturn were to impact what they leave to their families. They like the idea that with variable annuities, the least they can leave their families is the total amount of premiums they have paid, less any withdrawals they may have made; on the other hand, if the value of their accounts is more than that, the higher amount goes to their families.*

*What I have just described is the regular death benefit. As I said, an optional enhanced death benefit is available. With this enhanced benefit, some portion of the gains in account values (or some portion of the premiums paid) over the years can increase the minimum that is paid to your family in the event of your death. Let me show you how it works.* (Describe the principal provisions of the enhanced death benefit available.) *Before we leave this subject, let me point out that the enhanced death benefit is paid for with charges made to the accounts in your variable annuity.*

*Let me show you what I mean.* (Discuss charges for the optional enhanced death benefit as well as any conditions or requirements applicable.)

### *Cementing Your Successes: Availability of Guaranteed Living Benefits*

As discussed in Chapter 7, optional guaranteed living benefits, which go by various names, take some of the uncertainty out of the inevitable fluctuations in variable annuity account values. These benefits, which are funded by charges made to the various accounts, go a long way in providing comfort to potential customers who frequently are uneasy about not knowing what their accounts will be worth or the possibility of downturns occurring just at the wrong times, thereby affecting their financial and estate plans. Many optional guaranteed living benefits require that the annuity owner participate in the company's asset allocation program.

The Guaranteed Minimum Accumulation Benefit (GMAB) guarantees a specified account value, according to a formula, after a waiting period such as 10 years. There may be additional provisions which bring about further increases in guaranteed amounts. These guarantees provide more definite knowledge of how much will be accumulated in the accounts.

The Guaranteed Minimum Income Benefit (GMIB) guarantees a minimum, and often growing contract value amount, to be available for annuitization after a waiting period. It commonly requires that all applicable values be annuitized. There may be a provision permitting earlier annuitization than after the usual waiting period and there frequently are "resets or "ratchets" that serve to increase the amounts involved which usually are percentages of a certain amount, often referred to as the "protected amount."

The Guaranteed Minimum Withdrawal Benefit (GMWB) provides for income through withdrawals from the contract rather than as a result of annuitizing the contract values. Systematic withdrawals are permitted with amounts based on a percentage of a "protected amount." Unused withdrawals serve to extend the length of the income stream. In some cases, there are provisions for making larger withdrawals if no withdrawals are made for a certain number of years.

*M/M Customer, as we have been talking, it seems clear that you recognize that making investments in accounts that own stocks and bonds are definitely necessary if you are to accumulate the amount of money you believe you should have in the future, Yet, you have indicated that it would be awfully nice to have at least some conditional assurances with respect to what will be accumulated or the income that can be produced. There is an optional benefit (or there are some optional benefits) that can help give you some of those assurances.* (At this point, what you say depends on which of the guaranteed living benefits you discuss.)

*I am referring to the Guaranteed Minimum Accumulation Benefit. With the GMAB, a specific amount plus X% of the premiums you pay is assured at the end of 10 years, the first year that the benefit takes effect. Let me show you how it works.* (Explain the GMAB provision of the contract.)

*I am referring to the Guaranteed Minimum Income Benefit. With the GMIB, once the contract has been in effect for 10 years, when you take its values as an annuity, the minimum amount you will receive is assured, except that it can be more if it is more than 10 years before you begin your annuity payments. Let me show you how it works.* (Explain the GMIB provision of the contract.)

*I am referring to the Guaranteed Minimum Withdrawal Benefit. With the GMWB, when you take systematic withdrawals from your contract values, the amount of the withdrawals is assured, based on a stated percentage of the contract values. Let me show you how it works.* (Explain the GMWB provision of the contract.)

(In all three cases where applicable, the following should be added.) *This benefit is paid for by means of a charge against your account values. Obviously, these charges will reduce somewhat the amounts accumulated in those accounts. Also, in order to elect this option, it is necessary that you also use the company's asset allocation program free of charge. Let me show you what I mean.*

## Income Planning

### *Effective Income Planning: Defer, Withdraw, Annuitize*

When a person considers various sources of income from savings and investments, both during the working years and at retirement, it frequently is the case that planning the amounts to receive at various times and under various conditions is difficult. Apart from knowing the unknown, there is the fact that so many financial services products do not offer a range of choices that includes not taking income and deferring the tax, taking as much as you need, and maximizing income later through annuitizing. Of course, all of those choices are available with a variable annuity.

*M/M Customer, in our discussions, you have indicated that the income you will be able to receive, later on, from your savings and investments is of high importance. Most of my customers feel the same way. They also tell me that they very much like the idea of being able to control the income flow so that they can make the best use of it. What they mean by that is this: During your working years, what is most efficient is not to have to report income as taxable that you don't need and intend to leave accumulating in order to build up your future accounts. Around retirement time, what is most efficient is to be able to take just what income you need and pay taxes on it. What you don't need, you leave accumulating for the future and don't pay taxes on it. Then, later in your retirement years, in the event you have not been able to build up as much as you would have liked, what is most efficient is to have the option to get the absolute maximum income from that which you have accumulated.*

*That is what you have with a variable annuity. During your working years, values accumulate but you do not pay taxes on any of it unless you take some of it out. At retirement, you may withdraw as much or as little as you like, and the rest will remain accumulating without any tax on the gains. Then, if for some reason you would need more income than you would be able to realize from interest and earnings alone, you can elect an income option. Typically, the amount of income is equivalent to the amount you might receive from interest earnings as high as 10 or 12% or more. The income comes from a combination of principal and interest and lasts as long as you live. Under that arrangement, the principal is used up, but the income, which can be either fixed or variable at your option, is paid to you for as long as you live and will serve you well. Arrangements can be made so that payments are continued to someone else if something happened to you within just a few years.* (A comparison of one or two annuitization examples, with what can be withdrawn yearly while maintaining principal, can dramatize the value of annuitization, something not available with most other financial services products.)

## Penalty Tax Perspective

### *Keeping the Penalty Tax in Perspective: Don't Be Put Off by It*

Some people considering the purchase of variable annuities are put off, perhaps even frightened, by something that sounds pretty ominous – the penalty tax on premature distributions. Not surprisingly, the issue often is raised by those competing against the purchase of the variable annuity; for dramatic effect, they make the penalty tax sound nearly like the impugning of the character of the annuity owner. It is spoken of as something akin to the sword of Damocles hanging ready to seriously wound the unwary. Yet, the fact is, it is only a tax, one of 10%. It seems foolish to put off the benefits of tax deferral and the many other benefits of owning a variable annuity just for that.

*M/M Customer, several times now you have mentioned the 10% penalty tax that comes about when withdrawals are made from variable annuity accounts before the owner is age 59½. I think we should discuss it for a few moments. First, Congress put the extra tax in as a kind of balancing weight to compensate for the tremendous value of being able to defer income taxes on the interest and earnings in the variable annuity accounts during all the years leading up to the time when a person starts taking regular income at or near retirement. The deferral results in much more money built up than if the interest and earnings were subject to tax each year as they are with most savings and investments.* (Here, an example similar to "Maximizing Accumulation: Taking Advantage of Tax Deferral" discussed above might be used.)

*But let us suppose that you do have a need to withdraw money from your variable annuity before age 59½. The tax is assessed against the amount of money that is included in income. If you withdraw in the early years, not all of the money you withdraw may be interest or earnings; the amount that isn't is principal from payments made with money already taxed and not subject to regular or penalty tax. If you withdraw later, the entire amount withdrawn is likely to be interest and earnings and subject to tax. But the tax is assessed only on the amount you take out, not some larger amount, not the entire amount of interest and earnings. The amount not withdrawn remains with its tax deferral in place, still a better position than if you had had to pay taxes each year as they accrued* (See Note, just below).

*And why would you decide to make a withdrawal prior to a time near retirement? Isn't it either because you need the money due to a temporary loss of income or emergency, or because you have an unusual opportunity? If you have a loss of income, the 10% will be applied to a lesser amount of taxable income than your usual taxable income. If you have a good opportunity, the extra 10% will be worth it. The point is, the 10% tax is there but it should be kept in perspective. A great many annuity buyers will never have occasion to deal with it. Those who do are apt to find it more an annoyance than anything else. And all agree that it is not all that big a price to pay for tax deferral on accumulations.*

Note: As described in more detail in Chapter 10, certain dividends from stock, termed "qualified dividend income" are eligible for lower income tax rates currently. (These special provisions are scheduled to expire at the end of 2008, at which time the former, higher rates would apply.)

## Large, One-Time Amounts

### *Handling Large, One-Time Amounts: Take the Pressure Off but Put the Money to Work*

Surveys of nonqualified annuity buyers have shown that quite a large number of people buy with proceeds from one-time events: an inheritance; the sale of a home, farm, or business; an insurance benefit; a bonus; or a gift from a relative. They do so because they want to use the money to bolster retirement income. But they also do so because annuities offer a place to put the money to work without people needing to make many difficult financial decisions within a short period of time. Quite often, this type of event will not come along again. Perhaps more than anything else, people are fearful of making mistakes that will cost them money that never will be replaced. That motivation may be more powerful than any desire to "make a killing" by means of "brilliant" investments.

*M/M Customer, surveys have shown that many buyers of variable annuities are people who have (inherited money from their parents, sold their businesses, etc., whatever is the case) as you have. Most often, the reason is that they can relieve themselves of having to make a whole series of financial decisions all at one time; yet they can put the money to work right away, rather than leaving it in a checking or saving account while they fret over what to do with it. Nobody likes to be rushed into making these types of decisions; the more rushed you are, the more likely you are to make mistakes. After all, it's not as if these opportunities come along every day.*

*With a variable annuity, you can put some of the money into those accounts you know enough about to have some confidence. Then, you put the rest into the VA's money market account or the account that pays a stated rate of interest. When you have satisfied yourself that you want to move some of the money out of those accounts and into others that might produce higher earnings, you just do it, no muss, no fuss. You can take days to decide; you can take weeks; you can take months or years. It's up to you. And the thing that makes this even better is the fact that once you put the money into the variable annuity, whatever accounts you choose, the income earned from interest and earnings is not subject to current tax. The tax is deferred until you take the money out of the contract. This means that you don't even have to pay extra income taxes while you do your investigating and research about where to put your money.* (If the guaranteed interest account has limitations on internal transfers, that fact should be brought to the customer's attention.)

When people retire early, whether by their own choice or otherwise, they sometimes receive a cash settlement or, perhaps, their retirement plans are such that the proceeds need to be rolled over, probably into an IRA. These people have the same concerns as those just discussed, except that the rollover to the IRA must be done according to certain rules. See Chapter 11 for more on distributions from retirement plans and related subjects.

## Social Security Benefits Taxation

### *Annuity Buildup Not Counted for Social Security Benefits Taxation*

The buildup of funds inside an annuity is not counted for determining what is called "provisional income" with respect to the taxation of social security benefits at retirement. For most taxpayers, provisional income is the sum of adjusted gross income, tax-exempt interest, excludable U.S. savings bond income used for higher education, and one-half of social security benefits received at retirement. If the provisional income exceeds a threshold of $32,000 for couples filing jointly or $25,000 for single taxpayers, an income tax must be paid on up to 50% of the social security income. If this provisional income exceeds $44,000 for couples filing jointly or $34,000 for single taxpayers, income tax must be paid on up to 85% of the social security income. How much of a person's social security income is taxed depends on how much the benefits are and how much provisional income they have.[15]

For example, if a couple receives $20,000 of social security income during the year, 85% of it is taxed if they have provisional income of at least $56,941. There is a formula for determining how much is taxed. The fact that the buildup inside an annuity is not counted means that an annuity might be a better choice for someone to use for saving and investing than, say, tax-exempt securities, where interest is included in provisional income. The closer the couple's income is to $44,000 and below $56,941 the better. Before leaving this subject, we need to point out that the interest and earnings credited to the variable annuity are taxed when they are withdrawn from the contract. But in the meantime, they accumulate without having an adverse effect on social security earnings.

## Annuity Payouts and Life Insurance

### *Annuity Payout and Life Insurance Combination*

As discussed in Chapter 7, an owner-annuitant may elect to take an income for life. The amount of income depends on the person's age and sex and whether a guarantee is provided for another person. Couples frequently elect to take joint and survivor income payments so that the payments will last as long as either of them lives.

When joint and survivor income is elected, the amount of income is usually considerably less than if income were to last for the life of the annuitant alone. In some instances, it can be shown that the person might be better off to take the higher income and use a portion of it to buy a life insurance policy for the benefit of the person who otherwise would be the joint annuitant. This can be the result where, for example, the beneficiary is considerably younger. It is also true that if the second person predeceased the annuitant, the higher income would continue for the life of the annuitant and the life insurance could be used for another purpose. How much and what type of life insurance and when it is feasible to consider this approach depend on the amounts needed and ages of the people involved.

As discussed in Chapter 12, when someone elects a life income payout, only a portion of it is subject to income tax each year; the rest is a return of the investment in the contract.[16] Some annuity owners decide that they will take withdrawals at retirement, rather than a life income payout. They want to do this so that the principal they have accumulated in the annuity can be left to their families. These withdrawals will be subject to current income tax until they exceed the amount of income that the annuity has earned.[17] Therefore, these individuals might be better off to elect a life income option, with only part of the income subject to tax, and buy a life insurance policy for the benefit of their families. The premium for the life insurance would come from the savings resulting from lower taxes. For those who have an estate planning need, there would be no annuity value includable in the person's estate at death and the life insurance policy could be owned by someone other than the annuity owner or by an irrevocable life insurance trust, presumably keeping the proceeds out of the estate.

## Small Employer Retirement Planning

### *IRAs for Smaller Employers*

Smaller employers, who want to provide their employees with a retirement plan that is affordable and easy to administer yet has some of the attributes of larger plans, can make use of SIMPLE (Savings Incentive Match Plan for Employees) IRAs. These plans are salary reduction plans, which mean the employer already is paying the portion of the contribution made by the employee. The employer then makes a matching contribution on a dollar-for-dollar basis up to 3% of compensation, but the match is provided only for those who contribute. There is an alternative arrangement for making smaller contributions for all employees.[18] These plans may bridge the gap between employers who feel unable to have any plan and those who are able to do so. (Further SIMPLE IRA information as well as information on SIMPLE 401(k) plans is in Chapter 11.)

Employers who feel unable to provide even a SIMPLE IRA plan sometimes take steps to facilitate employees purchasing their own individual IRAs or Roth IRAs. Through their payroll systems, the employers arrange to withhold personal IRA contributions so that they can be put into the employees' individual plans. By doing so, they enable employees to save for the future by taking the money out of their paychecks before the employees receive them. The employers must be sure that they remain in a position of doing this as a convenience only and that they not acquire any fiduciary responsibility with respect to the money withheld as might be the case with a qualified retirement plan.

### *Providing for Supplemental Retirement Income*

Most businesses find it desirable to provide some sort of supplemental retirement income for their more highly compensated employees, quite often as an incentive for those employees to remain with the business and not look elsewhere. For a smaller business, a popular way of doing so is by means of an executive equity arrangement with the employee, who often also is one of the owners of the business. Under such an arrangement, the business increases the compensation of the employee (by bonus or otherwise) so that the employee can purchase a variable annuity or other financial services product. The extra compensation is tax deductible, provided that it is reasonable compensation,[19] and the employee includes it as additional income. The employee's cost is the tax on the added income. In some instances, additional compensation is given with which to pay the tax.

Another way of providing supplemental retirement income is through the use of deferred compensation arrangements or supplemental retirement plans. With these arrangements, there is no current deduction available to the business but the business builds in some restrictions on when the employee receives the compensation. When the contract between the business and the employee operates to remove the restrictions and the employee receives income, the business may take a deduction and the employee includes the income. The business usually owns the funding financial services product. Because of the "nonnatural person" rule that applies to annuities, variable annuities usually are not used with these arrangements. Life insurance often is used when the arrangement is started far enough in advance for the cash values to accumulate adequately.

The executive equity plan and supplemental retirement plans, as well as the "nonnatural person" rule, are discussed in Chapter 11. Also discussed in Chapter 11 are several estate planning aspects of annuities, including annuities that are not of the usual commercial variety.

## After the Sale

One final point relating to providing service to a customer, perhaps, long after the sale—those representatives who have many annuity customers frequently receive calls from their customers relating a financial emergency, need, or opportunity that the customers must address. These customers, under age 59½, are disappointed when they are reminded of the 10% penalty tax applicable to withdrawals. They begin considering other ways of getting the money they need.

It is important to remember the thoughts raised above under "Keeping the Penalty Tax in Perspective." Depending on the particular circumstances, the penalty tax may turn out to be a reasonable price to pay for the benefit of all the tax deferral on accumulations over the years. The admonition is, "Do the math." Get the facts before jumping to a conclusion that the values in the variable annuity are beyond reach until age 59½. In the long run, it seldom is a mistake to save and invest money regularly, especially in a product as versatile and dynamic as a variable annuity.

## Chapter Endnotes

1. IRC Sec. 219(b), 219(c).
2. IRC Sec. 219(g)(3)(B).
3. IRC Sec. 72(t).
4. IRC Sec. 408A.

5. IRC Sec. 72(t).
6. IRC Secs. 402(h)(2), 415(c)(1)(A).
7. IRC Sec. 414(v)(2).
8. IRC Sec. 457(b)(2).
9. IRC Sec. 25A.
10. IRC Sec. 221.
11. IRC Sec. 222.
12. IRC Sec. 530.
13. IRC Sec. 72(t)(2)(E).
14. Dohm, Arlene and Wyatt, Ian, "College at Work: Outlook and Earnings for College Graduates, 2000-2010, *Occupation Outlook Quarterly*, Fall 2002, Bureau of Labor Statistics, Washington, D.C.
15. Wilson, Stephen C., "Using Annuities to Reduce Taxes on Social Security Benefits, *National Underwriter*, Life and Health/Financial Services edition, November 14, 2003.
16. IRC Sec. 72(b).
17. IRC Sec. 72(e).
18. See generally IRC Sec. 408(p).
19. IRC Sec. 162(a)(1).

# Chapter 5

# Marketing and Sales Support

## Achieving Customer Satisfaction

When marketing and selling variable annuities, a major goal, perhaps *the* major goal, is to come as close as possible to achieving customer satisfaction. Customers are most likely to be satisfied when two things occur. The first is when they, in fact, do save and invest money as planned, rather than remaining on the sidelines gathering information and hesitating to take action. People worry about making mistakes and, as a result, put off acting. Often, they do not understand that when they do not act by saving and investing, they are acting not to do so.

The second occurrence leading to customer satisfaction is saving and investing in a satisfying way. By a satisfying way, we mean that customers understand the reasons they are selecting to purchase what they are purchasing and they understand how they will benefit from the performance of what they select. A satisfying way may also include the convenience of the purchasing method, as well as the services provided by the sales representative, his office, and the broker/dealer. Later on, customer satisfaction is retained and enhanced by good service after the sale, including timely and informative reports and other communications.

Products in which customers invest will have their ups and downs, as well as periods when there is very little movement up or down, often to customers' consternation. Some will perform at overall levels that are less than expected or less than average. At these points, if customers know and understand the reasons they selected the particular accounts, they are in a better position to make decisions either to "stay the course" with what they have, at least for the time being, or to make the shifts in allocation of accounts that are more likely to bring about results that are more satisfactory. What does harm to customer satisfaction is not being pleased with the results at hand, not understanding why those accounts were the ones they selected, and not knowing what to do about the situation. In fact, the people may feel worse off than they did before they made their purchases, even though they really may be better off from an objective standpoint.

## Expectations for the Future

There are many sides to customer satisfaction, including expectations for the future. Any number of studies over various periods of time has produced average returns for stocks (often measured by the S & P 500) that are quite agreeable. For the most part though, these studies include periods when returns have been low or negative; the low periods are usually offset by periods of high returns so that it becomes easy to forget that there are low periods, sometimes lasting for months or years. It is one thing to consider that there are times when returns will be pretty small; it is another to realize that there will be times when one actually can lose money, perhaps a good deal of money.

Similar developments have affected thinking on the volatility of equity markets. Market volatility is not readily apparent in studies of average returns. Yet, there can be extended periods when prices rise and fall frequently and significantly. This volatility is very unsettling to some investors and not at all in keeping with their expectations for the future.

All of this means that the work you do with customers to get them to commit to putting a certain amount, or continuing amounts, into variable annuities and the work you do in helping them select accounts among which to allocate their premiums is of great importance. You start out knowing that your customers may have at least somewhat unrealistic expectations about the performance of the accounts, based on mostly recent information. Customers also may have little patience for the inevitable ups and downs in account values. For these reasons, you need to call on support information, concepts, and tools designed to inform them and provide a basis of understanding for the financial events which will follow.

## Timing the Market

Many articles are written about the difficulty of attempting to "time the market"—that is buying when prices are at their low points and selling when they are at their high points. Those potential investors who are not frozen in place, and actually do act, often miss the lows and highs, sometimes by a substantial margin.

And, if money is held in liquid, but low-interest, accounts awaiting action, there can be a further loss. Occasional savers and investors often do poorly in the market because they react to a kind of herd mentality. Large numbers of purchases take place, following extensive publicity about the success of stocks or accounts, resulting in purchases made at or near the high for the current period. And many occasional investors sell near the low points due to a generalized fear of falling prices and further exercise of the herd mentality.

We should pause here in order to point out a similarity of terms used to describe very different things. As just discussed, timing the market has to do with making purchases and sales at what is hoped to be the best time to do so. A similar term is "market timing," which is the practice of moving assets from one subaccount to another with great frequency in order to profit from such exchanges. Market timing (discussed more in Chapter 6) is considered an abusive practice because the costs and fees generated by the many changes works to the detriment of the buyers of the variable annuity as a group. Many variable annuity prospectuses state that the practice of market timing will not be permitted.

## Dollar Cost Averaging

The opposite of trying to time the market is making regular and consistent premium payments. This approach allows the customer the opportunity to engage in dollar cost averaging, a most important concept. Dollar cost averaging is paying a fixed amount of premium at regular intervals—monthly, quarterly, semi-annually, annually—regardless of the unit values of the selected variable accounts (or the current interest rate on new premiums paid into the guaranteed account). The equal dollar amounts will result in relatively fewer variable account units purchased when unit values are higher and more units when unit values are lower. Figure 5.01 illustrates the mechanics of dollar cost averaging.

FIGURE 5.1

## DOLLAR COST AVERAGING*

| Time | Premium | Unit Value | Units Purchased |
|---|---|---|---|
| 1 | $200 | $10.00 | 20.00 |
| 2 | $200 | $12.00 | 16.67 |
| 3 | $200 | $ 9.00 | 22.22 |
| 4 | $200 | $ 7.00 | 28.57 |
| 5 | $200 | $10.00 | 20.00 |
| Totals | $1000 | $ 9.60 Average | 107.46 |

* Charges against premiums, if any, have been disregarded in this example.

In Figure 5.01, $200 of premium is paid into a variable account each period of time. The unit value of $10 at the time of the first premium payment results in 20 units purchased. As the unit value goes up, fewer units are purchased. When it goes down, more units are bought. For ease of calculation, we bring the unit value back to $10 at the end so that we can look at what has happened. Since 107.46 units have been purchased and each unit is worth $10 currently, the value in the account is $1,074.60 at that point.

There is an automatic benefit to dollar cost averaging due to the fact that more units are purchased when unit values are lower and fewer when unit values are higher. As we see from Figure 5.01, the average unit value at the time of purchase was $9.60. But the average cost of a unit purchased was $9.31 ($1,000 premium divided by 107.46 units), a $.29 per unit gain. This gain is always the case with dollar cost averaging and the more volatile the accounts, the more gain there will be. Of course, the unit value of the account must eventually at least regain the starting level for the gain in units to be of beneficial effect.

It can be argued that dollar cost averaging greatly reduces the stress involved in investing in accounts that can fall in value as well as rise. It is particularly useful when purchasing variable annuities because the customer can pay premiums in convenient, regular amounts and designate accounts in which the premiums are to go. The variable annuity owner can change the allocation amounts going to particular accounts or change the selection of accounts. Sometimes, the principle of dollar cost averaging can help give a prospective customer the confidence to begin making regular payments into the contract.

Dollar cost averaging can also be used to reallocate money already in the variable annuity contract. As explained in Chapter 7, some variable annuities provide that the owner may direct the regular movement of funds from one account, such as the money market account, into other variable accounts on a regular basis, e.g., monthly, quarterly. The reallocation continues until there is no longer money in the account from which the reallocation is made or until the contract owner directs that dollar cost averaging be discontinued.

## Asset Allocation

In the early chapters of this book, we discussed the need for a potential customer to diversify investments and savings primarily to achieve safety. With diversification, the downs of one investment might be offset by the ups of another. Some of the risk and uncertainty of investing could be reduced, a defensive strategy. But there is another side to diversification and it has to do with achieving the customer's objectives. In this context, selecting different kinds of investments is referred to as asset allocation. It involves identifying the mix of assets that will produce the desired results while maintaining a balance between risk and return.

With asset allocation, the customer is not seeking to maximize return in the usual sense, but to obtain the maximum return that can be had while keeping risk at an acceptable level. If we could predict which investments or class of investments would perform the best over a period of time, asset allocation would not be needed. But since we cannot predict with certainty, we select asset categories and determine what percentage of the total will be in those categories. We will not eliminate fluctuations, but we can reduce the fluctuations of assets in the aggregate while moving toward our objectives.

Asset allocation can be used both in a long-range way and in a manner that is more short-range. Viewed at long range, the customer can establish an asset allocation that will remain unchanged until some major changes occur. Along the way, he may need to rebalance accounts so that the allocation remains as has been decided. In the short range, from time to time, the customer may want or need to make modest changes in allocation to achieve better returns. There come times when long-range changes must be made. For example, when the person who has been accumulating for retirement reaches that age, he may need to change to an allocation with more emphasis on income and less on growth.

## Asset Allocation Model

A useful tool to help a potential customer decide on an asset allocation is an asset allocation model. There are a number available, many of them in computer programs that present allocations with charts and graphs. Most ask for answers to a series of questions from which a possible asset allocation is derived. The asset allocation models represent that what they are presenting is one possible strategy based on the responses to the questions. They should be viewed as broad guidelines, and any investment decisions should come after a careful examination of the person's own situation and circumstances and careful review of the prospectuses and other materials associated with the financial products being considered.

The questions asked in asset allocation models are those having to do with the

- person's investment objective;
- period of time available to reach the objective;
- person's age grouping;
- person's income tax bracket;
- importance of current investment income;
- amount of cash reserve the person has;
- importance of inflation to the person;
- future prospects with respect to current income and assets;
- person's tolerance for risk and volatility; and
- person's tolerance for asset loss.

The answers are scored and the possible asset allocation percentages are presented. In one allocation model program, three of the possible allocations are shown in Figure 5.02.

FIGURE 5.2

## ALLOCATIONS FROM MODEL ASSET ALLOCATION PROGRAM

| | Growth | Conservative Growth | Income |
|---|---|---|---|
| Capital Preservation (Guaranteed Acct., Money Mkt.) | 5% | 23% | 30% |
| Income (Corp. & Govt. Bonds) | 10% | 16% | 28% |
| High Yield Bonds | 8% | 5% | 10% |
| Growth & Income Portfolio | 24% | 20% | 12% |
| Growth Portfolio | 23% | 11% | 5% |
| Aggressive Growth Portfolio | 15% | 11% | 5% |
| International Portfolio | 15% | 14% | 10% |
| Total | 100% | 100% | 100% |

There are other allocations in the particular model program illustrated in Figure 5.02. As the explanation of the program indicates, the allocation is just one that is possible. The portfolio choices usually refer to broad classes and not to the particular accounts in any one variable annuity or to any particular mutual fund.

The potential customer's own likes and dislikes will overrule anything suggested by a computer model. For example, the potential customer may not care for high yield bonds or international stocks and, when all is said and done, he may particularly like several of the portfolios in the variable accounts for one reason or another. Nonetheless, a suggested allocation can do much to focus the person's thinking and help him decide which actual accounts to choose.

We have been referring to the asset allocation model as part of the process whereby the customer purchases the variable annuity. A model can be used earlier in the sales process as well. When approaching a potential customer, you can offer it as a service in helping to decide whether a variable annuity might be appropriate for consideration. Use of an asset allocation model also can be offered to those attending seminars. Or, a shortened version can be used as a part of the seminar.

A new use for asset allocation has come into play. It is in connection with many of the guaranteed living benefits now available with variable annuities. As discussed in Chapter 7, these benefits provide for guarantees such as certain specified account value accumulations, certain specified income on annuitization, or certain minimum withdrawal amounts. A requirement of many of these benefits is that the annuity owner must participate in the company's asset allocation program.

## Performance Histories

When deciding on the purchase of a variable annuity, a buyer is, or should be, interested in the provisions of the contract itself and in the various accounts that might be selected for the allocation of premiums. Performance histories and records of past performance can be quite useful in the selection of accounts. The broker/dealer distributing the variable annuity will provide past histories and performance data as well as information about the accounts' money managers and the company issuing the annuity contract. Detailed information on the contract is in the prospectus. We will take up prospectuses later in this chapter.

## Third Party Sources

In addition to the account information available from the broker/dealer, there are a number of third party sources that may be used to learn about the variable accounts. Because there are so many more mutual funds to report on than variable annuity accounts, most of the information available has to do with mutual funds. But there is considerable variable annuity account data that can be obtained. Following is a sampling of what is available. It is not a complete listing.

*Morningstar, Inc.*, www.morningstar.com – This company is a leading provider of investment information, research, and analysis of mutual funds, stocks, and variable annuities and has data available in both print and electronic media. Morningstar rates funds on the basis of total return, as well as risk. It concentrates its attention on selected funds and because there are fewer funds, the reports are more detailed, include more analyses, and take up more factors than would be possible if more funds were included.

*Lipper Analytical Services*, www.lipperweb.com – This service tracks the performance (total return) of a large number of funds worldwide and its data are often quoted in the general press, financial press, and on television. There are numerous performance rankings, but not as much analysis as the sources that report on fewer funds.

*Value Line*, www.valuline.com – This company publishes both print and electronic products and is best known for *The Value Line Investment Survey*, which provides information on stocks, the stock market, industries, and the economy.

Many regular publications, such as *Business Week* and *Consumer Reports*, contain articles of mutual fund performance. Many of the articles include ratings of the funds.

Stock and mutual fund information is nearly limitless on the Internet. A brief survey brought forth these sites: www.reuters.com; www.Bloomberg.com; CBS.marketwatch.com; finance.yahoo.com; and money.CNN.com. For a less traditional approach, there is www.fool.com, the site for The Motley Fool. No doubt, the use of *Google* would turn up many more.

Since these publications and websites are concerned primarily with mutual funds and the variable accounts in variable annuities, less information is provided on the annuity contract itself. Rather complete summaries of contract provisions, as well as information on fees and charges is available from Finetre/VARDS, www.vards.com, through their services *VARDS Online* and *VARDS Advisor*. The SEC and NASD offer some rather basic tools for analyzing information on charges and fees. The SEC fee analyzer is at www.sec.gov/investor/tools/mfcc/mfcc-int.htm. The NASD fee analyzer is at www.nasd.com/investor/tools/calculators/fundcalc/expense_analyzers.asp. Of course, the websites of individual companies issuing variable annuities contain analytical information, especially that information contained in the prospectuses of the products being offered for sale

## Insurance Company Rating Services

Since variable annuities are issued by insurance companies, on their own or in partnership with mutual fund or other financial services companies, the financial ratings of the companies, by independent rating agencies, is of importance. The ratings are not quite so important as they are when life insurance and fixed annuities are considered, chiefly because the variable accounts are separate from the general assets of the insurance company and free from the claims of its creditors. However, the ratings are important with respect to the guaranteed or fixed accounts that are supported by the company's general assets. And should a company have financial problems, some of the services and procedures provided might be curtailed. We will discuss five of the rating services here.

*A. M. Best Company*, www.ambest.com – The oldest is the A. M. Best Company, which has published *Best's Insurance Reports* since 1906. The objective of Best's rating system is to evaluate the factors affecting overall performance of an insurance company in order to provide an opinion as to the company's relative financial strength and ability to meet its contractual obligations. A large number of companies are rated by Best although some are not assigned ratings due to unique or unusual business features.

*Moody's Investors Service*, www.moodys.com – A credit research firm founded in the early 1900s, Moody's began rating debt securities of insurance companies in the mid-1970's. It introduced insurance financial strength ratings in 1986 to provide institutional and retail investors with objective and independent credit opinions. Life insurance company ratings are called financial strength ratings and are opinions of the company's ability to repay punctually its senior policyholder claims and obligations. Moody's rates fewer U. S. and Canadian companies, but they are the largest companies in terms of reserves.

*Standard & Poor's*, www2.standardandpoors.com – Standard & Poor's has been providing ratings of financial strength and credit quality for more than 75 years; it assigns ratings to debt issues of a wide variety of municipalities and corporations throughout the world, including insurance companies. In the early 1980s, S & P extended its rating business to include the claims-paying ability of insurance organizations. Several hundred companies are rated via a comprehensive process and many more are assigned a claims-paying rating using a quantitative process.

*Fitch Ratings*, www.fitchratings.com – Fitch Ratings, which took over the ratings being handled by *Duff and Phelps*, covers many kinds of financial analyses, including a large number of insurance companies. Founded in 1913, it began rating services in 1924. It has been a worldwide organization since its merger in 1997 and its acquisitions in 2000 and 2001.

*Weiss Ratings*, www.weissratings.com – Weiss Ratings is one of the newest rating services, but it has grown considerably in recent years. Each quarter it evaluates more than 15,000 institutions, including a large number of insurance companies. Weiss makes a point of indicating they do not accept compensation for ratings and do not allow the companies to preview their ratings.

The rating designations used by the services differ but the patterns are similar. Where one has high-end ratings of AAA, AA, and A, other services use Aaa, Aa, and A, or A++, A+, and A. The pattern is for all the services to have ratings that they describe as superior, excellent, and very good, or exceptional, excellent, and good, or highest, very high, and high.

These high-end ratings differ somewhat from each other but all are considered to denote financially secure companies. There may be lower ratings than those just mentioned that also are secure. But below those are ratings that the services describe as vulnerable, uncertain, possessing risk, or questionable.

Although some ratings are assigned from quantitative data, the methodology of determining ratings is similar for the most part. The companies usually, but not always, submit considerable data on many operational and marketing aspects of their operations as well as supplementing the financial data that may be obtained from public sources. As a rule, the services confer with management and financial representatives of the companies for further development of the information. The ratings themselves are arrived at independently and published. In most cases, the companies pay to have the ratings determined.

## The Prospectus

One important document in the variable annuity sales process is the prospectus, which is looked on either as very helpful or as something that must be endured. Though efforts continue to bring simplification, most prospectuses are highly detailed and quite lengthy. But the fact of the matter is that the prospectus must be presented at or in anticipation of the first contact with the potential customer when a variable annuity product is to be discussed.

The prospectus contains a complete description of the workings of the contract and the various accounts, albeit in language some consider to be more legalistic than necessary. When comparing one contract with another, the prospectuses are valuable sources of information. There should not be any significant information about the contract and accounts left out. Rather than treating the prospectus as a necessary evil, some registered representatives use highlighted portions of it to explain the contract and the accounts. They feel that by doing so, they portray themselves as capable of handling complex information and able to make it relatively easy to understand. They can reinforce the veracity of the briefer, more eye-catching sales materials they are using.

Most prospectuses begin with broad descriptions of the contract and the accounts in which premiums will be invested. These descriptions can include definitions of terms and a summary of

1. contract provisions, including workings of the contract, premiums, units of purchase, transfers, etc.;

2. the various accounts offered;

3. contract fees and charges;

4. account fees and expenses; and

5. performance data of the accounts.

Following the broad descriptions are elaborations and more detailed explanations. With respect to the variable annuity contract, there are explanations of

1. premiums, units of purchase, crediting, valuing of units;

2. transfers among accounts, limitations, rebalancing;

3. surrenders and withdrawals;

4. charges, including contract fees, mortality and expense charges, charges for riders or special features, investment advisory fees, surrender charges, waiver of charges, etc.;

5. death benefits; and

6. fixed and variable payout options.

If the contract is used in qualified retirement plans, there is some discussion of pertinent information. Disclosures, e.g., an IRA disclosure, sometimes also are included.

Each of the fixed and variable accounts is described; those sections include

1. investment objectives and policies of the account;

2. account expenses;

3. financial summaries, including investment activities, asset values and expense ratios;

4. risk factors applicable to the account;

5. other investment information, such as participation in futures contracts, options, repurchase agreements, etc.; and

6. information on the investment advisor and fees charged.

In addition to the proprietary funds of the annuity contract issuer, many variable annuities have variable accounts managed by outside investment advisors. These accounts also must be described in the same detail and usually are housed in the same prospectus, or attached to it. However, although the same types of information are included as those describing the proprietary funds, the formats often are somewhat different.

## Risk Disclosure Document

The complexity of prospectuses has been a subject of considerable discussion over the years. No one is very happy about the situation. The SEC has permitted the use of a so-called profile to accompany the prospectus; the profile has been used by a number of companies, but its success has been limited. Most recently, the NASD has proposed a rule that calls for the use of a separate, brief, and easy-to-read (written in "plain English") risk disclosure document that highlights the main features of the particular variable annuity transaction.[1] The document would accompany the prospectus and include

1. liquidity issues, such as potential surrender charges and the tax penalty for distributions before age 59½;

2. sales charges;

3. fees, such as mortality and expense charges, administrative fees, charges for riders or special features and investment advisory fees;

4. federal tax treatment of variable annuities;

5. any applicable state and local government premium taxes; and

6. market risk.

Most of these items have to do with charges and expenses. Market risk is rather less specific since it is common to all securities of the same class (i.e., the likelihood of the investment to rise or fall in value as general market conditions rise or fall).

Note that the use of the risk disclosure document is a proposed rule at the time of publication of this book. Considerable opposition has been brought forward, mostly on the grounds of the repetitiveness of the information in the document and the desirability of including any needed additional information in the prospectus, which already was required.

## Sales Illustrations

Sales illustrations are used with most insurance and annuity presentations. When explaining a fixed annuity or the fixed account of a variable annuity, projections into the future may be shown, using the current rate and the guaranteed rate. Projections of assumed interest rates also may be used so long as the current and guaranteed rates are illustrated as well. As a matter of practice, these illustrations are used extensively with fixed annuities, but much less so with variable annuities.

Illustrating the variable accounts is a much different process. No future projections involving the variable accounts may be shown. A portrayal of illustrative amounts of premium put into the variable accounts in the past, and remaining or continuing for ten years to today may be shown. With these portrayals, you are in a position to illustrate amounts of premium discussed with the potential customer in order to give your discussions more realism. But, of course, you never may imply that the situation will continue to be the same; in fact, you must make a point of saying it is very unlikely to be the same.

We should point out here that the rules applicable to variable annuities and those applicable to variable life insurance and variable universal life insurance are different. With the life insurance products, you may use hypothetical interest rates projecting into the future to illustrate the variable accounts. The rates you may use are limited to those prescribed by the National Association of Securities Dealers (NASD), but you may project into the future. Not so with variable annuities since future projections may not be used.

## Account and Balance Summaries

Contract owners receive a flow of written communication beyond the usual sale confirmations and delivery of the policy. A summary of account activity and balances is sent, usually several times each year. The account activity includes payments made since the last report, transfers in and out of the account, surrenders, and any fees charged to the account. The account balance section includes the number of units held, the value of each unit, and the accumulation value (or contract value) in the account. A sample account activity summary appears in Figure 5.03.

FIGURE 5.3

**ABC Life Insurance Company**
**100 Main Street**
**Washington, D.C. 20020**

STATEMENT FOR: John Taylor
200 Jefferson St.
Washington, DC 20020

REPRESENTATIVE: Melissa Morgan, CLU

**CONTRACT DATA**

Owner: Taylor, John
Annuitant: Taylor, John
Contract Number: 123456ABC
Plan: Nonqualified
Contract Date: 1-1-2000
Social Security Number: 123-45-6789

STATEMENT PERIOD: 12/31/2004 to 06/03/2005

**CONTRACT ACTIVITY**

| Sub-Account Name | No. of Units as of 12/31/2004 | Unit Value as of 12/31/2004 | Dollar Value as of 12/31/2004 |
|---|---|---|---|
| Growth | 455.529 | 33.167 | 15,108.88 |

| Sub-Account Name | No. of Units as of 6/30/2005 | Unit Value as of 6/30/2005 | Dollar Value as of 6/30/2005 |
|---|---|---|---|
| Growth | 455.529 | 36.756 | 16,743 |

**CONTRACT SUMMARY**

| | |
|---|---|
| Beginning Annuity Value: | $15,108.88 |
| Total Payments: | 0.00 |
| Total Withdrawals: | 0.00 |
| Total Charges: | 0.00 |
| Ending Cash Value: | $16,415.89 |
| Ending Annuity Value: | $16,743.61 |

## Periodic Reports

Once each year, and sometimes more often, a printed report is sent pertaining to the variable annuity in general, and the fixed and variable accounts in particular. This report contains comments and information from the issuing company management and from certain of the investment advisors, general economic and investment information that may have an impact on the accounts and investors in them, and some performance data pertaining to the accounts. The report also contains specific listings of the investments held in each of the variable accounts as of the close of the previous reporting period.

## Product Features

Many of the features of the variable annuity contract can be considered marketing and sales support aids. Product features are taken up in detail in Chapter 7. Consider the following list of product features that may be used in the sales process:

1. The ease of allocating premiums to the various accounts, and the ease of changing the allocation as desired. The allocation may be changed with a simple notification.

2. The ease of making transfers among accounts, including telephone transfers; some transfer limitations may apply. Generally, a number of transfers may be made each year without fee, and even more with a modest fee.

3. The ease of maintaining an asset allocation balance in the accounts, including the use of automatic rebalancing, if available. Even without automatic rebalancing, the ease of making transfers can maintain asset allocation balance.

4. The value of dollar cost averaging among accounts, when available, as discussed above.

5. The value of the ability to guarantee a minimum amount of accumulation, income, or withdrawal, when available.

6. The ease of making withdrawals from the contract, including the availability of periodic withdrawal plans which provide for systematic withdrawals as requested by the contract owner.

7. The waiver of any remaining surrender charges for withdrawals requested when the annuitant is in a nursing home or terminally ill.

8. The existence of a death benefit (i.e., a payment to a beneficiary that will never be less than a certain amount, no matter what the experience of the variable accounts).

9. The multitude of payout options available to the annuitant, or to the annuitant and spouse (or other individuals) on either a fixed or variable basis. Nearly any arrangement can be accommodated, along with guarantees of payments to others, when the annuitant does not live long enough.

We began this chapter with some statements about customer satisfaction, and achieving it when the customer feels comfortable in taking action and feels that he is saving and investing in ways that are comfortable. The methods of attaining comfort in taking action mentioned here, as well as the publications and tools discussed, should go a long way in accomplishing a desirable level of customer satisfaction.

## Chapter Endnotes

1. "Proposed Rule Governing the Purchase, Sale, or Exchange of Deferred Variable Annuities," NASD Notice to Members 04-45, June 2004.

# Chapter 6

# Licensing, Compliance and Ethics

## Federal and State Regulation

Both federal and state agencies are involved in the regulation of variable annuity products, their marketing, and the activities of registered representatives who market them. As we see in this chapter, this combination regulation sometimes leads to conflict, although it appears to be effective for the most part.

### *Registered Products*

Variable annuities are registered products. That is, they are registered with the Securities and Exchange Commission (SEC) and governed by provisions of the securities laws of the United States and the states where the issuing companies are domiciled and operate.

The most prominent federal laws are the Securities Act of 1933, which regulates variable annuities and securities, and the Investment Company Act of 1940, which regulates them as periodic payment plans. In 1996, the National Securities Market Improvement Act made changes affecting pricing as discussed in Chapter 8. Marketing and sales activities are regulated on the federal level by the National Association of Securities Dealers (NASD), a self-regulatory organization.

State laws also regulate securities and securities marketing activities within their borders. States have exclusive jurisdiction over the licensing of agents, the approval of insurance policies and contracts, and the marketing of insurance products (including annuities). In this context, a variable annuity is considered to be an insurance product with regulation by the state insurance department; although in some states, the state securities department also regulates some of the actions of sales representatives. Thus, a sales representative who intends to market and sell variable annuities must be a licensed agent or sales representative in the state, as well as a registered representative with the proper licenses and registrations as administered and supervised by securities authorities. The state requirements vary from state to state; generally, the requirements supervised on the federal level do not. A registered representative who wants to market and sell in more than one state must be mindful of the requirements of each of the states. The broker/dealer usually is in a position to make him aware of what is required.

### Broker/Dealer Products Only

A registered representative must be associated with a broker/dealer whose duty it is to see that the representative is qualified as a sales person and to supervise the representative's marketing and sales activities. The insurance company, with which the broker/dealer is affiliated, often takes responsibility for the licensing of the person as an agent; it often also assists the broker/dealer in administering its securities licensing activities. Since the representative often is licensed and contracted to sell other products of that company, this is a natural extension.

The registered representative may market only the products of the broker/dealer (in addition to the non-registered products of the company(s) with which he is associated). A broker/dealer may handle a great number of products, especially several families of mutual funds, but it may have only one or a few variable annuities available. Some of these may be products of other insurance companies with which the broker/dealer has selling arrangements. This means the sales representative may sell only that one or those few. This is a marked departure from the prevalent practice with respect to fixed annuities. Since fixed annuities are not registered products, it is common for many sales representatives to offer not only those products issued by their primary companies but those of other companies with which they have brokerage affiliations.

### Federal-State Regulatory Matters

The business of insurance has been regulated primarily by the states since regulation began. Over the years there have been many proposals, a number of them having been adopted, for more regulation and related matters to be performed at the federal level. The matter of market conduct is one such subject. The National

Association of Insurance Commissioners and the National Conference of Insurance Legislators have come up with a model law that will be the basis for state laws regulating market conduct. At the same time, Congress has proposed legislation that would mandate certain national uniform standards, perhaps even a national accreditation. Other federal agencies, such as the Government Accountability Office, also have made proposals. While there are some practical matters that could be handled on a uniform basis nationally (e.g., a uniform method of handling the approval of new products, and a uniform procedure for performing company inspections), the states will not give up overall regulation of the business of insurance easily. They believe the states are much better able to do it effectively.

Of course, the regulation of securities and securities marketing is different from the other regulation of the insurance business. Because these products necessarily must be subject to regulation by the Securities and Exchange Commission (SEC) and the NASD, and because the regulation of the marketing of the products necessarily must be a joint effort between federal and state agencies, it is likely that variable annuity regulation will remain pretty much as it is today. That does not mean there will not be some adjustments, however.

### *Fund-Level Disclosure and Certification*

The SEC requires disclosure on the part of portfolio or fund managers on registration forms and on supplements to prospectuses.[1] The registration statement must give the name, title, length of service, and experience of the members of the portfolio team. The Statement of Additional Information, accompanying the prospectus, must disclose the names of other portfolios the manager manages, the manager's ownership interest in the portfolio, and the manager's compensation structure. The back cover of the prospectus must either tell investors how to find additional information statements on the portfolio issuer's website, or explain why it does not offer the statements. On the front cover, a toll-free number must be shown where additional statements and documents may be obtained, and the Web address of the SEC must be listed.

Pursuant to the Sarbanes-Oxley Act of 2002,[2] the SEC adopted rules requiring chief executive officers and chief financial officers to certify to the accuracy of periodic reports filed under the Securities Exchange Act. Also, the SEC's rules establish minimum standards of professional conduct for attorneys appearing before the SEC. The rules require that the attorney report any evidence of a material violation of an applicable federal or state securities law to the company's legal counsel or chief executive officer.[3]

## Securities Licenses

A number of different securities licenses may be required in order to sell different types of securities. Since some of them are required at the state level, there are variations.

1. For variable annuities, mutual funds, and variable life insurance, NASD Series 6, Investment Company/Variable Contract Products. This is the shortest route to licensing for variable annuities.

2. For limited partnerships, NASD Series 22, Direct Participation Programs. This license is needed to sell oil and gas programs, real estate, and other limited partnerships.

3. For municipal bonds, etc., Municipal Securities Rulemaking Board (MSRB) Series 52, Municipal Securities. This license is needed to sell municipal and U.S. government and government agency securities.

4. For stocks and bonds, etc., NASD Series 62, Corporate Securities. In addition to stocks and bonds, this covers rights, warrants, closed-end funds, real estate investment trusts, and other asset-backed securities.

5. For comprehensive securities licensing, NASD Series 7, General Securities. This license takes the place of the four preceding licenses and permits the license holder to sell all of these products.

6. For futures, NFA Series 3, Commodity Futures. This license is needed to sell agriculture, financial, government securities, and precious metals futures.

7. For state-level registration, North American Securities Administrators Association (NASAA) Series 63, Uniform Securities State Law Exam. This exam, which may be required in addition to one or more of those above, is needed in states requiring state-level registration.

8. For state-level registration as a registered investment adviser (RIA), NASAA Series 65, Uniform Investment Adviser Exam. This exam, which may be required in addition to any of those above, is needed in states requiring state-level registration as an RIA.

9. For combination state-level registration, NASAA Series 66, Uniform Combined State Law Exam. This exam combines material from both Series 63 and 65, and may be taken in place of them.

All of these examinations are of the multiple-choice variety and are taken on computer terminals in exam locations. The time permitted for taking the exams varies, but most are in the range of two to three hours. There is one notable exception and that is Series 7, which permits six hours. In nearly all cases, a passing grade is 70%; in some cases, a passing score is needed in each of the major areas covered.

Frequently, it is debated as to whether one should "go the whole route" by taking Series 7 or take the other four exams one-at-a-time, preparing for each separately. There is no one answer. Some people are able to remember large amounts of information easier than others. Some are better off "biting off a little at a time." Some people will have an easier time "gearing up" for one big effort than exercising the necessary self-discipline to follow through with a series of examinations.

Sometimes, the point is made that a sales person should be knowledgeable on all of the types of product choices the customer may have. While this is a worthy goal, it may be somewhat unrealistic. There can be little doubt that much of the information learned for an exam is soon forgotten if it is not used on some regular basis. Learning about the great variety of financial services products is a formidable job, one that requires continuous attention and effort long after examinations have been passed.

## Supervisor Licensing

Those who supervise registered representatives, whether the representatives are engaged in sales or in administrative functions that require licensing, are required to also be licensed as principals (or sales supervisors in the case of General Securities registration). Following are the licenses available:

- NASD Series 4, Registered Options Principal
- NASD Series 9 and 10, General Securities Sales Supervisor
- NASD Series 24, General Securities Principal
- NASD Series 26, Investment Company/Variable Contracts Principal

- NASD Series 27, Financial and Operations Principal
- NASD Series 39, Direct Participation Program Principal
- MSRB Series 53, Municipal Securities Principal

These examinations, too, may be taken on computer terminals in exam centers. Similar time periods are permitted and a score of at least 70% is needed to pass.

State examinations for licensing as an insurance agent and additionally, if needed, to be able to sell variable annuities are administered in a variety of ways. Since a number of states now use examinations prepared by professional testing organizations, there is more standardization among the states than once was the case. Most examinations are multiple choice and a score of 70% or 75% is needed to pass. Besides examinations, there may be additional state filings and other requirements to qualify to sell securities in a particular state.

A sales representative's broker/dealer registration may terminate because of a change of companies, because he is not doing the required quantity of business, or because the representative has not paid applicable fees. The representative may remain unaffiliated with a broker/dealer for up to two years. After that, the representative must take the various tests anew in order to affiliate with a broker/dealer. For this reason, representatives are keen to make a new affiliation before the two-year period has expired.

## Registered Investment Advisor

Many registered representatives who concentrate on advising customers about their financial affairs and about selecting financial services products choose to register themselves as registered investment advisers (RIA). In some states, one must be an RIA (or RIA associate) to charge fees for such activities as financial planning. Even when it is not required, some registered representatives will want to be in a position to inform their customers that they have this additional registration, and the knowledge and supervision which go with it.

A registered investment adviser is registered with the Securities and Exchange Commission, which means his office is subject to inspection by the SEC. Additionally, an RIA is held to a higher standard of conduct. As we have seen, he must have passed the NASAA Series 65 or Series 66 exam and, in some states, must be registered with the state securities department, which also has the right to inspect his office. Some states also require that an RIA hold a Series 7 license. Obviously, RIA status is not to be taken lightly. Considerable responsibility, time, and some added expense are involved.

An alternative to individual RIA status is that of being an RIA associate. A broker/dealer who is registered as an RIA may appoint certain of its registered representatives as RIA associates. Those appointed must pass the same exams, and be trained by the broker/dealer that remains responsible for supervision. There may be additional state filings required. But the RIA associate is in compliance with state laws regarding charging fees and similar matters.

A registered investment adviser must adopt a code of ethics.[4] The code must set forth standards of conduct and require compliance with federal securities laws. Codes also must address personal trading: they must require advisers' personnel to report their personal securities holdings and to obtain pre-approval of certain investments. Advisers must describe their codes of ethics to their customers.

## Compliance Meetings

The NASD requires broker/dealers to have their registered representatives attend annual compliance meetings. These are meetings where a major portion of the time is devoted to compliance matters and issues. Those attending are reminded of the rules of conduct and potential pitfalls, and any new procedures are explained and implemented as needed.

Compliance meeting practices vary from one broker/dealer to the next. Some of the larger ones consider it up to the registered representative to take the opportunity to attend, and expect their representatives to present themselves at one of the announced times and locations. Other broker/dealers take a more active role by having compliance officers and others conduct meetings in some of the affiliated offices. Nearby representatives can also attend.

Annual attendance at these meetings is required by the NASD. The broker/dealer will be held responsible if a registered representative does not attend. For that reason, it is the broker/dealer who must impose any sanction on the registered representative. The most common sanction is suspension of the representative's ability to do business through the broker/dealer until the compliance meeting requirement is met. Since suspension interrupts the flow of commissions on broker/dealer products, this sanction usually is effective.

## Continuing Education

Since 1995, there have been two NASD requirements for continuing education. First, within 120 days following the second anniversary of their registrations, and every three years thereafter, registered representatives must participate in computer-based updating sessions. Those participating are given 3½ hours to answer questions on pertinent information and procedures. If they are not able to answer enough questions correctly in the allotted time, they must participate on subsequent occasions.

Second, each broker/dealer must provide an annual continuing education program for all of its registered representatives. The broker/dealer must formulate the content of this program based on an analysis of the needs of the broker/dealer and its representatives. A representative's registration is not at risk for failure to meet the continuing education requirements, but the broker/dealer may need to suspend activity involving the representative until the requirements are completed.

## Supervision and Designated Offices

The chief executive officer of a broker/dealer-NASD member firm must certify annually that executive management has in place processes reasonably designed to achieve compliance with applicable NASD rules.[5] Important among these rules are those related to supervision. A person who is senior or "otherwise independent" must perform day-to-day supervisory reviews. Supervisory procedures must be sufficient to assure verification of proper compliance, or they must be amended. Very small offices may be able to fall under a "limited size and resources" exception, but otherwise the SEC is requiring heightened supervision through the NASD.[6]

A broker/dealer may designate certain of its field offices as "branch offices." Generally, these are the larger offices that perform many of the sales functions the broker/dealer would otherwise handle. As branch offices, they are subject to inspection by the NASD and must conform to NASD rules. For example, the office files of investors must be kept apart from the files of those who purchase other products handled by the office.

Some very large broker/dealers will designate "offices of supervisory jurisdiction." These offices perform essentially all of the services of the broker/dealer and are subject to inspection by both the SEC and the NASD. Smaller broker/dealers generally will not have any offices of supervisory jurisdiction, but have all the broker/dealer services performed at the same central location.

There are a number of other sales practices governed by rules of conduct and broker/dealer and insurance company procedures. As discussed in Chapter 5, the variable annuity prospectus must be presented at, or mailed in advance of, the first contact with a potential customer when a variable annuity product will be discussed. The prospectus is the primary disclosure publication, and it must be available to the potential customer from the start.

Also, as mentioned in Chapter 5, the complexity of prospectuses has been a subject of considerable discussion over the years. No one is very happy about the fact that it can be very lengthy and complex. Some companies have been successful in redesigning their prospectuses so that they are easier to read and understand. The SEC has permitted the use of a so-called profile to accompany the prospectus; the profile has been used by a number of companies, but its success has been limited. Most recently, the NASD has proposed a rule that calls for the use of a separate, brief, and easy-to-read (written in "plain English") risk disclosure document that highlights the main features of the particular variable annuity transaction.[7] The document would accompany the prospectus and include

1. liquidity issues, such as potential surrender charges and tax penalties;

2. sales charges;

3. fees, such as mortality and expense charges, administrative fees, charges for riders or special features, and investment advisory fees;

4. federal tax treatment of variable annuities;

5. any applicable state and local government premium taxes; and

6. market risk.

Most of these items have to do with charges and expenses. Market risk is rather less specific since it is common to all securities of the same class (i.e., the likelihood of the investment to rise or fall in value as general market conditions rise or fall).

The use of the risk disclosure document is a proposed rule at the time of publication of this book. Considerable opposition has been brought forward, mostly on the grounds of the repetitiveness of the information in the document and the desirability of including any needed additional information in the prospectus that already was required.

Broker/dealers and their registered representatives are required to participate in the National Do-Not-Call Registry.[8] Telemarketers generally are prohibited from making telephone solicitations to people on this list. There are exceptions for established business relationships, as well as where there is prior written consent, and where the caller and customer have a personal relationship. The rule provides for a "safe harbor" from violation where the office has established effective procedures and an error has occurred. Obviously, registered representatives must comply with the rules that the broker/dealer office has established.

## Sales Presentations and Practices

### *Sales Literature*

The broker/dealer is responsible for assuring that proper procedures are followed in field sales offices and the use of sales literature and other procedures are in compliance. Many companies accomplish this by conducting inspections of field offices from time to time. The inspections usually are carried out by compliance personnel during visits for other compliance activities, or by company sales management personnel in their compliance capacities.

A registered representative may use only those sales materials approved by the broker/dealer. Most of the materials are either prepared by the issuing company or come from outside fund manager organizations and are approved by the broker/dealer.

Generally, sales materials are filed with the SEC for comment. For the most part, the SEC's comments pertain to adequacy of disclosure. They may require additional information or suggest that certain wording be changed to improve disclosure. Note that the SEC does not "approve" the sales material as such. For that reason, it is not proper to say or imply that the sales material has been "approved by the SEC." Rather, the SEC has reviewed the material and has become satisfied that the level of disclosure is adequate. NASD rules of conduct also prohibit the use of sales material that is misleading. The broker/dealer is charged with enforcing these rules as it understands them.

Registered representatives may originate their own sales materials. Business cards and stationery must be printed as approved by the broker/dealer. Any advertisements or pre-approach letters must be approved in advance. Most broker/dealers have sample advertisements and letters that have been approved and can be used as they are. About the only items that do not need to be approved in advance are individual communications with customers involving clerical and other matters not having to do with specific investment advice or the solicitation of business. Newspaper and magazine articles may be sent without approval, as long as there are no comments added that can be seen as providing specific investment advice or soliciting business.

The fact of the matter is that issuing companies produce a great deal of good information that has been approved for distribution to the public. As long as so much of it is available, it seems unnecessary for registered representatives to go to the work of originating their own to any significant extent. Some representatives do write newsletters to send to their customers, or to have published in customer publications. They also make articles produced by the issuing company available for publication. These newsletters and articles do not need approval so long as they contain only general investment information. Of course, the ones originated by issuing companies usually have been approved in any event.

### *Suitability Statement*

When a customer applies to purchase a variable annuity, the registered representative usually is required by the broker/dealer to complete a suitability statement. As discussed below, the NASD has proposed an extension of the rules with respect to suitability. The current NASD rule states that the registered representative "...shall make reasonable efforts to obtain information concerning: (1) the customer's financial status; (2) the customer's tax status; (3) the customer's investment objectives; and (4) such other information used or considered to be reasonable...in making recommendations to the customer."[9]

Questions for determining suitability usually are a part of the application, frequently found on the back or adjacent to it. Generally, the issuing company will not accept an application if the suitability portion has not been completed. Answers to the questions should lead to the conclusion that the variable annuity applied for is a suitable investment for that person.

Premiums paid by the potential customer must be credited to annuity accounts within five days following the day they were collected. For this reason, the application must specify what accounts the customer wants to use. When the allocation has not been made, the company may temporarily retain the money in an account, such as the money market account, but only with the express direction of the customer. Obviously, everyone is better off if the details of the allocation are settled by the time the application is sent to the issuing company for action. We should note here that the time requirement for funds settlement for variable annuities differs from that of stocks. Stock purchases must be made within three days following the collection of purchase funds.

As discussed in Chapter 5, there are limitations on the use of sales illustrations of variable annuities. With respect to the guaranteed or fixed account, although they are used only to a limited extent, projections of interest rates into the future may be made using the current rate and the guaranteed rate. An assumed interest rate also may be used provided that the current and guaranteed rates are also shown. This is the same rule that applies to fixed annuities.

On the contrary, no future projections involving the variable accounts may be shown. However, a portrayal of illustrative amounts of premium put into the variable accounts in the past, and remaining or continuing for ten years to today may be shown. These illustrations are instructive as to how the accounts operate, but it is improper to imply that the situation will continue to be the same in the future. In fact, one must make a point of saying it is very unlikely to be the same.

That no future projections of variable accounts may be shown is a different rule from the one that applies to variable life and variable universal life insurance. With life insurance products, hypothetical interest projections into the future may be made. The rates that may be used are the ones prescribed by the NASD.

### *Proposed Additional Suitability Rule*

Proposed rules by the SEC and NASD expand on what needs to be done to assure that a variable annuity purchase is suitable for the proposed customer. At the time of the publication of this book, the rule is still in proposed form. The principal provisions are:

1. A determination that (a) the customer has been informed of the unique features of the variable annuity, (b) the customer has a long-term investment objective, and (c) the variable annuity as a whole, and the underlying subaccounts, are suitable for the particular customer.

2. The customer must be presented with a current prospectus, and a separate risk disclosure document (see above under "Supervision and Designated Offices") and informed of any "free look" period in effect.

3. A registered principal is required to review and approve the transaction, taking into account (a) the customer's age, liquidity needs, and appropriateness of the investment, (b) the amount invested as a percentage of net worth or similar measurement, (c) whether there was a contract exchange involved, and (d) related matters.

4. NASD member firms are required to establish and maintain effective supervisory procedures.

5. NASD member firms must develop specific training policies and programs so that those who review transactions comply with the principles and issues involved.[10]

### *Contract Exchanges and Bonus Annuities*

The SEC and NASD are particularly concerned about the ever increasing number of contract exchanges involving variable annuities. Here we are referring to exchanges under IRC Section 1035, which are tax-free assuming they are done properly. The new annuity may contain some very desirable new features and provisions, such as the guaranteed living benefits described in Chapters 4 and 7. Regulators' concerns center on whether the customer has been fully informed, through adequate disclosure, of the potential drawbacks to the exchange.

The drawbacks may have to do with the fact that the new contract has higher fees and charges than the old contract. Another is that almost certainly the new contract will have longer-running and, perhaps, even higher surrender charges than the old contract. The different surrender charge patterns must be evaluated in light of the customer's liquidity needs in particular.

Bonus annuities, discussed in more detail in Chapter 7, have become popular candidates for exchanges in recent years. The bonus may be an extra amount of interest credited or an extra amount of contribution added to the premium. In some cases, there is increased producer compensation paid. The money with which to credit the bonus must come from somewhere. Sometimes there is a higher contract charge and, nearly always, there are higher or longer-running surrender charges.

Many exchanges are justified based on all of the circumstances surrounding the customer. The issue, as far as the SEC and NASD are concerned, is whether there has been full and adequate disclosure of the important facts involved. Without that, the customer is likely not well served. In the proposed suitability rule discussed just above, some of the factors to be considered in the review by the principal are whether the transaction is an exchange, how much exchange activity there has been in the customer's account, and whether there has been a high rate of exchange activity on the part of registered representative.[11]

### *Market Timing Disclosure*

Market timing is the term that has been applied to the practice of making frequent transfers from one variable annuity subaccount to another or several others. While making transfers from one account to another is one of the contract features that make variable annuities popular with the public, making excessive transfers has a detrimental effect on customers as a whole unless the contract has been designed for such transfer activity. The fact is, most variable annuity contracts are not designed for it. They have contract charge and fee structures that anticipate a relatively low level of transfer activity. This is in keeping with the long-term investment strategy employed by the vast majority of variable annuity buyers. Excessive transfers, designed to capture very small short-term gains, run up the costs for all buyers, thereby reducing the returns on their investments.

The SEC has ruled that there must be disclosure in the filings of the funds in a variable annuity contract, as well as in their prospectuses, of the risks of frequent purchases and redemptions of shares, and that there must be policies and procedures adopted stating

1. whether or not frequent purchases and redemptions are discouraged;

2. whether or not frequent purchases and redemptions are accommodated; and

3. any policies and procedures for deterring frequent purchases and redemptions.

The descriptions of these provisions must include any restrictions on the number of transfers within a stated period of time, any costs or fees applicable, any minimum holding period, any restrictions as to electronic transfers, and any right of the company to reject, limit, delay, or impose other conditions on transfers, as well as any right to limit based on the annuity owner's transfer history.[12] In their most recent prospectus revisions, many companies have made it clear that they intend to discourage market timing activities. Of course, the SEC ruling requires that they also have procedures in place to determine when they are taking place and to take action to curtail them.

Before leaving this subject, we should draw a distinction between "market timing" and "timing the market," which is the term applied to the idea of waiting until just the right time to put new money into an investment or to sell it, as discussed in Chapters 4 and 5. In various places in this book, we have stated that regular investing over a period of years almost always is more successful than trying to guess the best time to put substantial amounts into an investment or to sell it.

## Contract Delivery

A most important practice is for the registered representative to deliver the variable annuity contract promptly and obtain a delivery receipt. Generally, the contract provides that the owner will have a brief period of time, e.g., 10 days or 20 days, to examine it and, if he chooses, to return it for a full refund. This is the so-called "free look" provision. The free look period does not start to run until the contract is delivered; therefore, the delivery must be prompt.

The situation involving "free coverage" that arises when an insurance policy is not delivered promptly is serious enough. But when there are variable accounts involved, as is usually the case with a variable annuity, the situation is even more serious. After all, the value of the accounts may diminish significantly before the free look period has ended. Issuing companies sometimes place the premiums in less volatile accounts temporarily awaiting the return of the delivery receipt or the running of the free look period to end. Some companies also withhold the crediting of new business, and payment of sales compensation, until the delivery receipt is received.

## Ethical Practices

The SEC and NASD, on the national level, and state insurance and securities departments, on the state level, have devised various compliance practices, procedures and tests to serve the public. They are designed to assure, to the extent possible, that there will be proper disclosure of pertinent information pertaining to financial services products, that the products will be suitable for people in particular circumstances, and that those with whom the public consults will be competent, knowledgeable, and will follow good business practices. That is to say, the authorities are doing what they can to see that broker/dealers, and their registered representatives, engage in ethical conduct. Of course, there is more to good ethics than "crossing the T's and dotting the I's" with respect to licenses, sales literature, compliance meetings, and continuing education.

What people do publicly often is not as important as what they do in private. A person can attend all the classes, get all the licenses and registrations, and sign all of the suitability forms and statements of ethical conduct—the public things—but not do nearly so well in private. In other words, there are the attitudes the person has toward good ethics and the practices and habits the person actually maintains. It is said that though attitudes and values influence ethics, the clearest way to differentiate between highly ethical and unethical insurance professionals is to focus on their habits. Habits are the typical, conditioned approach people have for dealing with their professional conduct.

## Customer Focused

The sales process of the highly ethical professional is customer focused. The needs of the customer are the first concern. Though we indicated in preceding chapters that a significant volume of sales is needed for most sales people to be successful selling financial services products such as variable annuities, this does not mean shortcuts should be taken.

To be sure, shortcuts sometimes can be taken, but the ethical (and ultimately successful) sales representative will not take this route. One shortcut in particular that should be avoided is to assume, with little investigation, that customers know exactly what they need, and that the task of the sales representative is to merely proclaim the virtues of the product he is selling. As we also have said earlier, because of all the publicity and financial reporting that has appeared, the customer may very well have a good idea of what is needed. But it is a mistake not to verify this assumption with solid fact finding and detailed analysis.

When your sales process is customer focused, you will gather fact finding information, analyze it, present your conclusions, determine what the customer's interests are, and present a product or products that serve those interests and provide answers to the needs ascertained. You will also want to educate your potential customers so that they know what is proposed and, presumably, purchased. There are a number of steps to this process, but it does not necessarily need to extend over many meetings or consume a great deal of time. Potential customers may have come to some tentative conclusions that you will only need to verify.

A highly ethical professional will engage in continuing education that is considerably in excess of that required to maintain licenses and registrations. There is constant change in financial services products, in financial markets, in interest rate markets, in the tax law, and in other laws and regulations affecting the registered representative's marketplace. One would never want to discuss a product with which one is not familiar. On the other hand, neither would one want to overlook a product that might be useful and the answer to a customer's needs. One would never want to be unaware of a tax or other law change that can impact a customer. As it is said, you must "sharpen your tools" regularly. Besides that, changes present perfect opportunities to contact customers so that you can offer additional services or bring up financial needs that had been discussed previously. Many things could have happened in the customer's life since your last discussion.

## In-Office Documentation

Highly ethical professionals are careful to make sure paperwork is in order. They keep copies of fact finding and other forms, such as asset allocations and similar items used in the sales process. They are careful to complete and have the customer sign all disclosure forms, retaining copies. It is required that many disclosure forms be given to customers for their records, but it is not wise to depend on customers to retain them where they can be found.

Having good documentation can be of immense value if the customer claims, justified or not, that he has not been dealt with fairly; something more apt to happen when account values drop. Documentation not only offers legal protection to you, the registered representative, if that becomes necessary, but it can also be used to refresh the customer's recollection of what transpired during the sales process, in the event he remembers things differently. The value of good documentation in deterring a potential problem is often more valuable than its legal value because, after all, you want to retain good customers, not gather ammunition to fight them.

## Remember—Something Will Go Wrong

We must never fail to make it clear to customers that variable annuity values can be volatile, and at times very volatile. Great enthusiasm, sometimes rising to euphoria, takes place at the time of a sale. Sales representatives are enthusiastic because recommendations have been accepted, and a sale has resulted. Customers are enthusiastic because they have done a most difficult thing—they have made a decision.

This enthusiasm can lead to a feeling that "nothing can go wrong." Whereas, it is assured that something will go wrong. Even if the customer's accounts do very well indeed, they may not do as well as the customer's hopes had projected them to do. Some of the customer's accounts can actually lose money, an unthinkable outcome at the time of a sale. This is especially so in the short term. Again, remember that values will go down as well as up.

## Chapter Endnotes

1. "Disclosure Regarding Portfolio Managers of Registered Management Investment Companies," RIN 3235-AJ16, Effective Date: October 1, 2004.
2. P.L. 107-204.
3. DeGeorge, Michael, "Regulatory Initiatives," *NAVA Outlook*, September/October 2003.
4. "Investment Adviser Codes of Ethics," RIN 3235-AJ08, SEC Rule 204A-1, effective August 31, 2004.
5. "Supervisory Controls," NASD Notice to Members 04-71, October 2004.
6. *Ibid.*
7. "Proposed Rule Governing the Purchase, Sale, or Exchange of Deferred Variable Annuities," NASD Notice to Members 04-45, June 2004.
8. "Do-Not-Call Registry," NASD Notice to Members 04-15, March 2004.
9. NASD Conduct Rules, Rule 2310, "Recommendations to Customer (Suitability)." *National Association of Securities Dealers Manual.*
10. "Proposed Rule Governing the Purchase, Sale or Exchange of Deferred Variable Annuities," NASD Notice to Members 04-45, June 2004.
11. *Ibid.*
12. "Disclosure Regarding Market Timing and Selective Disclosure of Portfolio Holdings," RIN 3235-AI99, April 19, 2004.

# Chapter 7

# Product Features and Characteristics

## Annuity Classifications

Annuities are traditionally classified in several ways:

1. how premiums are paid;
2. when the annuities mature;
3. whether there is more than one annuitant;
4. whether the annuities are fixed or variable; and
5. whether the annuities are qualified or nonqualified.

There are other descriptive titles used in recent years, including what types of guarantees apply to the account values and to the amounts of income that may be paid out under the contract, as we will explore later in this chapter.

If classified according to premium, annuities are either single premium or periodic premium (which includes annual, semi-annual, quarterly, and monthly). As to the maturity date, annuities are either immediate or deferred. An immediate annuity begins payouts at the end of the first payout period; that is, the first monthly payment occurs at the end of the first month after the annuity is purchased. In contrast, a deferred annuity does not begin payouts until sometime later.

Regarding the annuitant, which is the person whose life is used to measure the annuity payout periods, annuities are either single or joint. A single annuity has a single annuitant while a joint annuity has more than one.

Finally, annuities are either fixed or variable, and either qualified or nonqualified. A qualified annuity is one used to fund a qualified retirement plan while a nonqualified annuity is not part of a qualified plan. Generally speaking, most variable annuities are periodic premium, deferred, single life, nonqualified annuities.

## Premiums

With a variable annuity contract, the issuing company must agree to accept the initial premium. This initial premium, when accepted with the application and any additional requirements, puts the contract in force. Subsequent premiums will be accepted automatically, provided that the contract's minimum and maximum premium requirements are met. Companies must be careful to see that compliance and suitability requirements have been met before accepting the first premium, which must be applied to the accounts specified by the contract owner within a few days, unless the owner has requested that it be held longer.

Typically, companies have minimum premium requirements for initial premiums and for subsequent premiums. Initial premiums may be relatively low, such as $50, $100, $1,000, or $2,000. Or, they may be relatively high, ranging from $5,000 to more than $25,000.

Subsequent premiums are often less than the initial premium. Companies frequently have maximum premiums as well, which sometimes can be waived in accordance with the provisions contained in the prospectus.

The usual methods of paying premiums are used with variable annuities-–annual, semi-annual, quarterly, and monthly, especially by preauthorized check. Since most variable annuities have flexible premiums, meaning that they may vary at the will of the contract owner within the minimums and maximums, the premium notices are more on the order of reminder notices. The contract owner will make additional premium payments when he decides to do so.

Generally, when new premiums have not been paid for some period of time and the account values are minimal, companies reserve the right to terminate the contract and return the values to the owner. Of course, contracts with high minimum initial premiums do not encounter this minimal account values situation unless there have been large withdrawals.

## Issue and Maturity Ages

Variable annuities are issued to young and middle-aged persons, as well as to individuals who are fairly well along in years, often up to the ages of 80, 85, or even 90. Immediate annuities, which begin paying out benefits right away, can be issued at nearly any age, providing that suitability requirements are met. The National Association of Securities Dealers (NASD) has taken note of the fact that variable annuities may not be suitable for most investors unless they have long-term investment objectives.[1]

Most variable annuities have a maturity date that is the contract anniversary date upon which the annuitant reaches a certain age. Annuities used in Tax Deferred Annuities (sometimes called Tax Sheltered Annuities), "eligible" 457 Plans, and qualified retirement plans must begin distributions near when the annuitant reaches age 70½ unless the annuitant-employee retires after that time. Annuities used in Individual Retirement Arrangements (other than Roth IRAs) must begin distribution by age 70½. These provisions are discussed in more detail in Chapter 11.

Nonqualified annuities have maturity dates at higher ages (e.g. 75, 85, or 90). The reason for this is traditional; the thinking is that in order for an annuity to be considered an insurance and annuity product, it must not too closely resemble a security such as a mutual fund. One of the ways of distinguishing an annuity is the prominence of payout features. Therefore, there must be a discernible time when payouts will begin—a maturity date. Because people are living to older and older ages, the need for higher maturity ages is recognized. For that reason, some annuities today are rather vague about their maturity dates.

## Accumulation Units

When premiums are received, any applicable charges are deducted, and the balance is credited to the guaranteed or fixed interest account, if available, and to the variable accounts selected by the owner in the form of "accumulation units." Accumulation units are determined by dividing the amount allocated to each variable account by the accumulation unit value for that account on the date of allocation. Thus, the premium allocated purchases a given number of units and fractions of a unit. The value of the accumulation units in the different accounts will vary in accordance with the investment experience of the account and the expenses charged to that account. The contract value (accumulation value or similar designation) of the variable annuity contract is the sum of the different variable accounts and the guaranteed interest account, if applicable.

The value of the accumulation units in the variable accounts is expected to change frequently, and will depend on the investment performance and expenses of the portfolio in which the variable account invests. The value of the units is determined every day that the stock markets are open. It is determined at the close of business one day and then is determined next at the close of business on the following day. As we see, the variable annuity contract owner's contract value is derived from the value of the accumulation units and guaranteed interest account, not directly from the prices of the securities held in the variable accounts. Naturally, it is true that the stocks and bonds provide the basis for calculating the accumulation units.

When the contract reaches the date at which annuity payments are to begin, the annuitant generally can have a fixed or a variable payout, or a combination of the two. The amount of variable payments is determined using a similar valuation method. These units are sometimes referred to as "annuity units." We will take up the various payout options later in this chapter.

## Variety of Variable Accounts

A prominent feature of today's variable annuities is the large number and variety of variable accounts available for investing. An examination, or even a perusal of variable annuity prospectuses (many of which are available on the Internet), shows that nearly all the contracts listed offered at least eight variable accounts, and a large number of the annuity contracts maintained at least twenty, thirty or even more variable accounts. This is a great deal of variety, perhaps more than some potential annuity owners wish to deal with. But no one can complain over a lack of choices.

Each variable account is characterized by type and has a stated objective and investment policy or strategy. For example, a bond portfolio might be listed as an income or bond type. The objective might be to seek as high a level of current income as is consistent with reasonable investment risk, investing primarily in long-term, fixed-income, investment-grade corporate bonds. The investment policy or strategy might mention that at least 75% of the value of the assets will be in publicly traded debt securities rated BBB or Baa or higher, or guaranteed by the government, etc.

In addition to a conventional bond portfolio, as well as other bond portfolios (such as one concentrating on short duration bonds or one specializing in high yield bonds), a variable annuity might offer other variable accounts similar to these:

1. *Growth or equity* – seeking long-term appreciation without incurring unduly high risk; investing in special opportunity securities that are selling at a discount from theoretical price/earnings ratios and seem capable of recovering.

2. *Growth with income* – seeking to provide reasonable current income and long-term growth of capital and income; investing at least 65% in common stock or convertibles that are believed to have long-term prospects for growth and income, including foreign securities.

3. *Aggressive growth* – seeking better-than-average capital growth; investing in common stocks and equity equivalents that meet certain fundamental and technical standards of selection and have better than average potential for appreciation.

4. *Balanced or asset allocation* – seeking high total returns by investing in equity securities, debt instruments, and money market instruments; proportion of types of securities determined by the advisor based on value analysis, analysis of historical long-term returns, and other market influencing factors.

5. *Mid-cap value* – seeking capital appreciation in equity securities of medium-sized U.S. companies believed to be undervalued.

6. *International* – seeking long-term growth of capital principally from a diversified portfolio of foreign equity securities; investing primarily in equity securities of established companies listed on foreign exchanges that the advisor believes have favorable characteristics.

7. *Equity income* – seeking current income (with capital growth of secondary importance) in equity securities of large U.S. companies with a focus on income-producing securities believed to be undervalued by the market.

8. *Real estate* – seeking current income and long-term capital appreciation in equity securities of companies in the U.S. real estate industry, including real estate investment trusts (REITs) and real estate operating companies (REOCs).

9. *Money market* – seeking stability and current income from a portfolio of market instruments with an average maturity of 90 days; investing in money market securities such as U.S. Treasury, finance company and corporate commercial paper, domestic and foreign certificates of deposit, and corporate obligations.

10. *Small company or small capitalization* – seeking high long-term growth primarily from younger, small-to-midsize capitalization companies; investing at least 80% in common stocks of small and medium-size companies that have just begun their life cycles but have the potential to become major enterprises.

11. *Specialty portfolios* – investing in particular portfolios of investments (such as those having to do with natural resources, utilities, precious metals, real estate, government securities, etc.).

12. *Equity-indexed accounts* – interest crediting based in part on increases in an external equity index (see the discussion of equity-indexed annuities in this chapter).

This list is not intended to be complete but just to present some examples. Further, the listings themselves have been abbreviated. Those actually found in prospectuses, and in sales materials are usually longer and provide more details. When variable annuity contracts have 15, 20, or more variable account choices, there usually is more than one of a particular category. Since accounts with similar objectives and investment policies or strategies own different investments, have experienced different performance results, and have employed different managers, there can be reasons for selecting one over another, even though the characteristics of the accounts appear similar.

The popularity of particular types of accounts changes from quarter to quarter and year to year as the investment market changes. According to *The VARDS Report*,[2] assets in the various types of variable accounts stood at the following percentages at the end of the second quarter of 2004:

| | | |
|---|---|---|
| 1. | Fixed Income/General Account | 26% |
| 2. | Growth and Income | 21% |
| 3. | Growth | 19% |
| 4. | All Other Equity Funds | 14% |
| 5. | Balanced/Asset Allocation | 8% |
| 6. | All Other General Fixed Income | 7% |
| 7. | Money Market | 3% |
| 8. | Corporate Bond High Quality | 2% |
| 9. | Balanced/Other | 1% |

## Choices Popular

The large number of choices available is appealing to potential customers. While they sometimes can find themselves confused by all of the choices, they usually can find at least a few that they like in particular; and since they can make changes virtually any time they like, they should not be put off by the array of choices. Among the many choices are some managed by outside money managers; that is, money managers who are not directly associated with the company issuing the annuity are managing some of the portfolios. Although companies prefer that their own proprietary funds be used as much as possible, since they make more money from those funds, they are happy to provide outside managed funds in order to increase the appeal of their variable annuities to potential customers.

Many of the outside funds are managed by companies with high levels of name recognition, most often because of performance records, news articles, and publicity surrounding their mutual funds. This is even more appealing to buyers.

In the course of this discussion, it must be noted that it is not possible to place an existing mutual fund in a variable annuity. In other words, if the ABC Mutual Fund has produced high returns and seems a desirable place to invest money, neither a variable annuity contract owner nor the issuing company, may make the ABC Mutual Fund a variable account of the variable annuity. However, a portfolio with many of the same characteristics as a mutual fund, like the ABC fund, often called a "clone", may be one of the variable annuity's variable accounts. Note, however, that for this tactic to be appropriate, the mutual fund must share the variable annuity's long-term objectives, including accumulation for the retirement years. Further, it is not proper to imply that a particular mutual fund and a variable account are similar unless, in truth, they are similar. The facts that they are from the same company, have the same objectives, and use some of the same money managers may not be enough.

## Guaranteed Interest Accounts

Most variable annuities have guaranteed interest accounts (also called guaranteed accounts, fixed interest, general, or deposit accounts); these are similar in most significant respects to fixed annuities, except that money in them can be allocated to variable accounts while remaining within the variable annuity.

Often, there is a limit on how much may be reallocated *from* the guaranteed interest account at any one time or during a year. For example, the limit may be 10% in any one year. There also may be a limit, such as 10%, on the amount that can be reallocated *to* the guaranteed interest account. In fact, some annuity contracts do not allow any reallocation to guaranteed interest accounts; only new premiums may be added. The reason for these limitations is that the issuing company has made investments, usually in corporate and government bonds and similar instruments, with maturity dates of several years or longer into the future, in order to be able to pay the promised rate of interest on the funds in the guaranteed interest account. Shorter maturities would have rates too low to earn enough to pay the promised rate. The issuing company has had to factor in the knowledge that, for example, as interest is paid on the bonds it is buying for the guaranteed interest account, the interest earned will need to be invested at going rates, rather than at the rates the bonds are earning. It cannot afford to also sell the bonds ahead of maturity at a probable discount. Therefore, most of the funds must remain in the guaranteed interest account.

Interest is credited using a variety of methods. A common practice is for the current interest rate on money placed in the guaranteed interest account to be guaranteed a given rate of interest for a certain period of time. One year is a common current interest guarantee; other common ones are six months, three years, five years, and seven years. But practices include nearly any period from 30 days to seven years or longer. Once the initial period has run, renewal rates apply. Renewal rates can be for multi-year periods as well, but it is also common for them to be renewed for one year at a time. Since the underlying investments for the initial period and for the successive renewal periods will vary as interest rate markets change, initial rates and renewal rates are apt to be different. In fact, an initial premium paid one month may have a different declared current rate than an initial premium paid in the next month.

Companies review current declared interest rates frequently, even if they change them rather infrequently. When changes are made, the new rates usually take effect rather quickly, within a few days or a week or so. There are times when market interest rates are quite volatile and other times when they are rather stable. To remain competitive in the guaranteed account, it is necessary that rates rise when market rates rise; it also is necessary for rates to fall when market rates fall. It does not take long to attract a good bit of money when the company's rate is out of line on the high side. Because of the current interest guarantee period, it may take a while to recover from such a situation.

When discussing the guaranteed interest account, one other application of the word "guarantee" is very important. It is the minimum interest guarantee. The variable annuity contract states that no less than a certain rate will be paid on funds in the account. In times of low interest rates, contracts issued usually have low interest guarantees, although those issued in prior years may have higher rates. Contract provisions limiting the amount that may be put in the guaranteed interest account serve to minimize the adverse effect of having a minimum interest rate guarantee that is out of line with current rates in the market. There is no other standard (non-optional) performance guarantee in the variable annuity contract and none whatsoever with many other types of investments. When the volatility of markets affecting the variable accounts makes variable annuity owners uncomfortable enough to want to "pull in their horns," the guaranteed interest account is available to the extent that transfers into it are permitted. When the guaranteed interest account is not otherwise as available as might be desired, variable annuity owners can turn to the money market subaccount as a place to "rest" their funds for a while.

Guaranteed interest accounts have always been popular with variable annuity buyers. During the high interest days of the early 1990s, assets in those accounts were at or near 50% of the total assets held in variable accounts. During the unprecedented stock market run-up of the late 1990s and into 2000, guaranteed account assets percentages plunged through the 40s, 30s and into the low 20s. As we just saw above, most recently fixed income/general account assets had the highest percentage of assets in them. Clearly, it is very important to have this guaranteed interest account available. When variable annuity owners then seek to increase their investments in variable accounts, transfers may be made to the extent permitted.

## Death Benefits

A unique feature of variable annuities, as compared with mutual funds or individual securities, is the variety of variable annuity death benefits generally applicable while the annuity is in the accumulation phase and has not matured. (The term "death benefit" should not be confused with its use as the major component of a life insurance policy.) The traditional variable annuity death benefit that is paid to the designated beneficiary is the amount of premiums paid (less any surrender or other applicable charges) or the annuity's contract value, accumulated value, account value, etc., (all refer to the same figure), whichever is greater. As a result, the beneficiary will receive whatever the annuity is worth, unless its value has dropped below the amount of net premiums paid, in which case the beneficiary receives the net premiums paid. There is no risk of receiving less than the amount invested in the annuity.

It has occurred to a number of people that once the contract value of an annuity has increased to a substantial level above the net amount of premiums paid, it would be unfortunate indeed if a rapid downturn took place just before the death benefit was paid. While the beneficiary still could have what is promised, it could have been so much more. This situation has led to a multitude of methods for enhancing or stepping up death benefits. In fact, these types of enhancements have been on the increase in recent years with a variety of different approaches used. Most increased death benefits are paid for by means of a charge applied to the variable annuity accounts, usually including the fixed account.

One approach, sometimes referred to as a "stepped-up" benefit provides for an addition equal to the premium payments since the last anniversary plus a percentage (e.g., 25%) of premiums, less any withdrawals and charges. Another calls for a "reset" of the death benefit on particular contract anniversaries (e.g., every three years). Another approach features an annual increase "ratchet" that includes the current contract value plus premiums paid, less any withdrawals and charges. Another enhancement, sometimes referred to as a "roll up" feature, adds the value of premium payments at some rate of interest (e.g., 5%) less any withdrawals and charges. A method, similar to some of the others, is sometimes referred to as "enhanced earnings" where a percentage (e.g., 40%) of earnings or premiums in the last year is added to the death benefit, calculated after deducting withdrawals and charges.

Some of these enhanced death benefits have requirements in addition to the charges assessed against the values in the accounts. For example, in some cases it is required that the contract be in effect for a minimum number of years before some of the features become operational. Many, if not nearly all, variable annuities provide that once an annuitant reaches an advanced age (e.g., 75 or 85) death benefits are calculated differently. With some of the options, the upper age limit is lower (such as age 65).

An important thing to keep in mind about these enhanced death benefits is the fact that most, if not all, require charges to be made against the values in the variable and usually fixed accounts. Obviously, these charges reduce the net earnings produced in the accounts. For that reason, variable annuity buyers must choose their optional benefits carefully. It would be nice to have all of the enhanced death benefit options available under the contract, but such an approach is probably impractical from a net earnings standpoint.

## Guaranteed Living Benefits

The area of variable annuity product development that has seen the most activity in recent years is that of guaranteed living benefits. For the most part, variable annuity buyers are expressing considerable preferences for options that minimize some of the uncertainty associated with contract values that can fluctuate considerably, sometimes at just the wrong times for buyers' financial and estate plans. It is one thing to want to participate in investments that can keep pace with inflation over the years. It is another to realize that the inevitable downturns just may occur at times when buyers' plans are affected more than they had counted on.

Guaranteed living benefits are called by various names by companies, and they operate somewhat differently from company to company. All of them require charges to be made against the contract values of the variable annuity. Here we will use the generally recognized, somewhat generic names common in industry literature.

The Guaranteed Minimum Accumulation Benefit (GMAB) guarantees a specified account value after a waiting period (e.g., 10 years). Sometimes, the guarantee extends to both the guaranteed amount and to some portion of subsequent premiums. It may be required that the annuity be annuitized for the guarantee to be effective. It also may be required that the annuity owner participate in the company's asset allocation program. There may be "step-up" provisions that bring about increases in the guaranteed amounts. Company provisions vary on details such as the length of the waiting period, whether or when annuitization is required, and when "step-ups" may be used. Charges made for this benefit also vary, usually depending on the nature of the definitions and requirements for participation. With the GMAB, buyers can reduce some of the uncertainty they may have concerning how much they will accumulate at certain points in the future.

The Guaranteed Minimum Income Benefit (GMIB) guarantees a minimum and often growing contract value amount to be available for annuitization. It is exercisable after a waiting period (e.g., 10 years). The most common provision requires that all of the applicable contract values be annuitized. In some cases, GMIBs allow for annuitization sooner than the usual waiting period and in some cases partial annuitization is permitted. All of the usual fixed payout options (as discussed later in this chapter) generally are available when the contract values are annuitized. The values available to be annuitized vary among companies. At least the current contract value or something often referred to as a "protected amount" (the initial amount at some rate of interest (e.g., 5%)), is always available, but "resets" or "ratchets" sometimes are used, as are premium "rollups." Sometimes, it is required that the annuity owner participate in an asset allocation program. Some plans use enhanced annuity purchase rates or actuarial tables for determining the payouts. Charges vary according to the definitions and percentages involved. With the GMIB, buyers can be reasonably certain of the income they will receive once the annuity payout begins and, with some provisions, how it is possible for that income to be more when it begins.

Some variable annuity buyers do not want to annuitize their account values in order to be assured of a guaranteed amount available for taking as regular income. It is for these buyers that the Guaranteed Minimum Withdrawal Benefit (GMWB) was developed. With the GMWB, systematic withdrawals are permitted from the "protected amount" (as described just above); the withdrawals are based on a percentage (e.g., 5% to 7%) of the protected amount on a non-cumulative basis. Annuitization is not necessary. Unused withdrawals serve to extend the length of the income stream. There is no waiting period, although some benefits provide for an increase in the percentage available for withdrawal if withdrawals are not first made for a period of years (e.g., 3 to 5 years). In some cases, larger withdrawals are permitted, but those in excess of the stated percentages reduce the amounts that are guaranteed. Some of these provisions do not allow the annuity owner to cancel the rider for some stated period of time, unless the whole contract is canceled. Some provisions require that the owner participate in the company's asset allocation program and some limit investment selections, not allowing riskier investment accounts to be used. An additional option is a "step-up" to the current value at some future anniversary. As with the other guaranteed living benefits, charges applied to the contract values depend on how many and which provisions are included. By choosing the GMWB, buyers can make systematic withdrawals of a relatively certain amount, yet retain their flexibility since annuitization is not required.

Any discussion of withdrawals from variable annuity accounts, whether occasional or more systematic, must include information about the taxation of the withdrawals. When the withdrawals are made after the age of 59½, income tax is usually payable on the amount withdrawn. When withdrawals are made prior to age 59½, there is also a 10% penalty tax applicable unless one of the exceptions to the penalty apply. Taxation of annuities is discussed in detail in Chapter 12.

This has been a brief discussion of the principal guaranteed living benefits available with variable annuities. It is easy to see from the descriptions that there are a great number of variables, and comparing all of one company's provisions with each other is quite complex. Comparing several companies' provisions with each other is even more complex. It goes without saying that most potential buyers will benefit from advice from a registered representative who is well informed and able to describe the benefits in understandable terms. Of course, approved literature and prospectuses should always be used during the discussions.

As mentioned above, product development of provisions calling for guaranteed living benefits has been most active in recent years. Companies issuing variable annuities have attempted to meet two needs of potential buyers: First, potential buyers want to benefit from purchasing financial products that are designed to keep up with inflation and that will enjoy the financial rewards of investing in successful and growing companies in our economy. Second, they are willing to apportion a certain percentage of their earnings to reduce the effects of market fluctuations and to introduce more certainty into their savings and investments. The popularity of these benefits has shown that those needs are being met to a significant degree.

We should repeat what was said just above about enhanced death benefits. An important thing to keep in mind about guaranteed living benefits is the fact that most, if not all, require charges to be made against the values in the variable and fixed accounts. Obviously, these charges reduce the net earnings produced in the accounts. For that reason, variable annuity buyers must choose their optional benefits carefully. It would be nice to have all of the guaranteed living benefits offered by a company under the contract, but such an approach would probably have too great an impact on net earnings to be practical.

## Allocation to Accounts

When someone purchases a variable annuity, he must select which of the available accounts to use and indicate how much of the premium is to go into each account. This allocation of premium will continue until the owner changes it, which may be done essentially at any time. The variable annuity buyer makes the selection on his own or with the advice of the registered representative, financial planner, or other financial advisor.

Since the issuing company must place the money in accounts right away, the initial selection must be made at the time the application is submitted, or immediately thereafter. In Chapter 5, we discussed asset allocation programs to use when considering whether or not to purchase a variable annuity and, if so, which accounts to select. Using information supplied by the buyer concerning personal circumstances, financial goals, and investment risk tolerance, these programs calculate an asset allocation model that they state should be viewed as broad guidelines on how to invest. The portfolios identified may be descriptive of variable accounts and the guaranteed account, but usually are not the accounts themselves. Thus, variable annuity buyers must do some translating into those accounts from which they are able to choose. Since the asset allocation model is intended as a guideline, buyers may accept as much or as little of it as they deem appropriate.

Asset allocation programs have taken on even more importance because many guaranteed living benefits require that the annuity owner participate in the company's program in order to be eligible for the benefits. Presumably, this is so the annuity owner's accounts do not become so lopsided that the company will have trouble making good on the living benefits. In addition, some accounts, particularly the more risky ones, may not be eligible for the asset allocation program and, thus, will not affect the company's ability to fulfill the promised guarantees.

## Transfers Among Accounts

As has been mentioned numerous times, a big advantage to variable annuities is the fact that the owner can transfer funds among the various accounts. The owner might want to make transfers in order to change the mix of investments or to maintain the mix of investments originally selected in light of the fact that each of the accounts has performed differently from the others. Transfers among accounts are handled in a variety of ways.[3] However, the current trend is for there to be a certain number of free transfers permitted (e.g., six or twelve per year) with a fee (e.g., $10 or $20) applicable to additional transfers. Companies also have minimum amounts (e.g., $100, $300, $500) that may be transferred in a transfer transaction. Most people agree that this limited number of free transfers gives enough latitude to satisfy most variable annuity buyers, and those who want to engage in more active transferring ought to pay extra for the additional record keeping and handling.

## Automatic Rebalancing

Some people believe that keeping the investment mix as the buyer intended is so important that there should be a mechanism for doing so without having to depend on the buyer to check his statement regularly and make transfers from some accounts to others. It is for that reason that automatic rebalancing was introduced.

With automatic rebalancing, the variable annuity owner directs that, until further notice, the company will maintain the present balance of assets by means of periodic transfers from one account to another. Practices vary on how frequently the rebalancing may take place (e.g., monthly, quarterly, yearly). Some minimum total balance (e.g., $5,000) in the variable annuity is usually required, and other distribution or payout plans may not be available while the automatic rebalancing is in effect. Only those accounts that the buyer is participating in are included, and it may be that only the variable accounts may be included in the program.

As with many other things having to do with investing, not everyone thinks rebalancing is a good idea. Those opposed argue that by having the automatic system in effect, the buyer "stunts the growth" of an account that otherwise would climb to a considerable height by taking away from it, periodically, and transferring to other accounts. This might happen, of course, but the variable annuity owner can prevent it from going on for very long simply by directing that automatic rebalancing be discontinued. It can always be resumed later.

## Dollar Cost Averaging Among Accounts

Dollar cost averaging was discussed in Chapter 5. The principle is that investing regularly, as the prices of investments fluctuate up and down, has proven to be a good long-term strategy. When prices are lower, more shares are purchased; when they are higher, fewer shares are bought. Assuming a reasonable performance over the period by the security, the overall value will be greater than most people can achieve by picking when to invest and when not to invest (timing the market).

Some variable annuities offer dollar cost averaging with money already inside the contract. The buyer may authorize that periodically (e.g., monthly) the company will take a predetermined dollar amount, usually with a minimum (e.g., $100) and transfer it from one account (e.g., the money market account or the guaranteed interest account) to the variable accounts in which the buyer is participating. This will take place until all of the money in the first account has been transferred. If the buyer continues to allocate ongoing premiums into the first account, the dollar cost averaging will continue, although the buyer can accomplish much the same thing by allocating to accounts on his own.

## Surrender Charges

Surrender charges are made against surrenders or withdrawals from the contract value of most variable annuities for a period of time. The surrender charge (sometimes referred to as a "backload") is used in pricing instead of an initial charge against the premium (referred to as a "frontload"). In nearly all products, it is applicable to values derived from each premium for a certain number of years (e.g., 5, 7, 9) but the rate declines each year. It might start at 5%, 7%, or 9% and reduce by 1% each year, for example. There is further discussion of charges and fees in Chapter 8. Withdrawals from the guaranteed account are sometimes subject to a market value adjustment, which is discussed briefly later in this chapter. A relatively recent development in product design is the availability of optional shorter or lower rate surrender periods. These optional surrender periods are financed with a charge made against variable and guaranteed interest accounts.

## Charge-Free Withdrawals

When the annuity owner makes a partial surrender or withdrawal, surrender charges apply until they have run their course except that most contracts provide for surrender-charge-free withdrawals of some sort. The most common withdrawal provisions are those that provide that 10%, or sometimes 15%, of the contract value may be withdrawn in a contract year. The number of transactions in the year is often limited too.

Another common provision is one that permits a percentage, such as 10%, or the interest and earnings in that year, whichever is greater, to be withdrawn without surrender charges. In a minority of cases, the withdrawal provision is cumulative. That is, the annual percentage amounts may be accumulated for a limited number of years and the sum of the percentages withdrawn without surrender charges. Cumulative withdrawal provisions can more easily be applied to variable accounts than to the guaranteed account for the same reasons as those limiting transfers from the guaranteed account to variable accounts as discussed above. An optional modification in the surrender percentage (e.g., 15% instead of the usual 10%) is available from some companies. Sometimes, the percentage can be cumulative rather than noncomulative. These optional provisions require a charge to be made against the values of the variable annuity.

The surrender charge provisions applicable to withdrawals from the contract values are apart from any tax penalties that may apply for premature distributions. Unless the annuitant is age 59½ or an exceptions applies,[4] 10% of the amount withdrawn subject to income tax is payable as a penalty along with the regular income tax.

## Periodic Withdrawal Program

Earlier in this chapter, we discussed the Guaranteed Minimum Withdrawal Benefit (GMWB). A number of companies offer a periodic withdrawal program which is not a GMWB requiring a charge against account values and not one of the payout options. Under this type of program, the variable annuity owner may preauthorize withdrawals of a level amount of money or a percentage of the contract value each month, quarter, half-year or year. The arrangement may be discontinued any time. The withdrawals that are made may or may not be subject to surrender charges, depending on whether they fall within the surrender-charge-free amount permitted. If surrender charges are no longer applicable, there is no limit to the amount that may be withdrawn, except for any minimums or maximums applicable to the withdrawal program itself. Since a payout provision is not employed, the income tax consequences, including any premature distribution penalties, of the withdrawal program are the same as those applicable to individual, non-programmed withdrawals. The program is especially useful for the individual over age 59½, who wants to take withdrawals on a systematic basis prior to the time of turning to a payout option.

## Waiving Surrender Charges

Many variable annuities have provisions that waive surrender charges on surrenders or withdrawals under extreme conditions. The two most common conditions are when the owner is confined to an institution such as a nursing home and when the owner contracts a terminal illness. Under the first, the owner must have been confined for a certain length of time (e.g., 30 consecutive days) in an institution providing daily medical treatment, including certain nursing home facilities. Under the second, the owner must have contracted a condition that a physician states should result in death within twelve months. These provisions allow access to the contract values of the annuity without concern for surrender charges. This access can be of considerable benefit to the owner in paying for the expenses involved with the confinement or terminal illness.

It must be noted here that the fact that the annuity owner qualifies for a waiver of surrender charges under the terms of the annuity contract does not necessarily mean that he qualifies for the "disability" exception[5] to the 10% premature distribution tax. The applicable disability definition is the one in the Internal Revenue Code. That is, the individual must be "…unable to engage in any substantial gainful activity by reason of any medically determinable physical or mental impairment which can be expected to result in death or to be of long-continued and indefinite duration."[6]

In this chapter, we have discussed a number of the provisions contained in annuity contracts. As we have seen, there are a number of variations with respect to them. While it might be natural to assume that the best annuity contract is the one that has the most features and choices, this is not necessarily the case. There is a cost connected with most of the choices as we have seen in this chapter and will discuss in more detail in Chapter 8. Some are more evident than others. Sometimes, it is possible only to determine that the costs of a particular contract are relatively high on an overall basis. In any event, it is usually necessary to weigh features and options against costs and then attempt to determine how useful some may be to potential customers in light of the costs connected with them.

## Payout Options

When an annuity contract reaches its maturity date, it is time to make use of one or more of the many payout provisions. Payout provisions also may be implemented, at the annuity owner's request, prior to the maturity date. Payouts may be fixed or variable. We will discuss the options here in terms of fixed payouts. Fixed options are usually placed in the contract using factors for determining amounts. Once applied, the factors are guaranteed when, taken together with the guarantees being provided in the annuity, are an advantage of annuities over some other financial services products. The owner may use the factors in the contract or alternate ones, based on current interest paid by the company. Though most options involve a life income, two do not. Those two are the fixed amount and the fixed period payout options. The other payout options involve payments for life, or life contingencies, although some elements of fixed amount and fixed period options are sometimes involved as well.

### *Fixed Amount Payout Option*

With this option, the amount of the benefit payment is decided upon and the period of time over which this set benefit amount will be paid is calculated using the contract value of the annuity, or a portion of it, and interest. The benefit amount may be paid on either a monthly, quarterly, semi-annual, or annual basis. When the designated amount has been paid for the period calculated, all of the contract value used in the calculation, together with interest, will have been paid out. With a given contract value, the larger the fixed amount payment, the shorter the period of time over which the payments will be made.

### *Fixed Period Payout Option*

This is similar to the fixed amount option except it is the period of time that is known and the monthly, quarterly, semi-annual, or annual amount that must be calculated using the contract value, or portion of it, and interest. When the calculated amount has been paid for the period designated, all of the contract value used in the calculation, together with interest, will have been paid out. With a given contract value, the longer the period of time selected, the less each payment will be over the period.

### *Life Annuity Payout Option*

With this option, also known as the life income without refund, a monthly, quarterly, semi-annual, or annual income for life is calculated using the contract value, or a portion of it, and interest. The calculation uses annuity tables that indicate the probabilities of living for years into the future. The annuitant's age is used in the calculation, as is the annuitant's sex unless a unisex table is used. The older the age of the annuitant, the higher the periodic payment will be. Because females live longer than males, payments to males of the same age are higher than those made to females.

The amount calculated will be paid as long as the annuitant lives. If the annuitant lives for three years, the amount paid out will be less than the contract value and interest from which payments were calculated. If the annuitant lives for 30 or 40 years, the amount paid out will likely be far more than the contract value, plus interest. If someone, in his mid to late 60's, wants to have the highest income possible for life, and dependents and children are otherwise provided for, this option is the one to use. It pays the most but when the annuitant dies, no payments are made to others.

### Life Income with Period Certain Payout Option

This option combines a life annuity with a fixed period option. An income is paid for the life of the annuitant, with the further provision that if the annuitant dies before a fixed period or period certain (e.g., 5, 10, or 20 years) has been completed, payments will continue to a beneficiary for the balance of the period certain. For example, if a 10 year period certain has been selected and the annuitant dies after three years, payments continue to a beneficiary for seven more years. However, if the same annuitant lives for 12 years, no payments are made to the beneficiary since the annuitant received payments for the 10 year certain period during his life. The amount of income for life is calculated in the same way, except that the factors used include not only the probabilities of living and interest, but the cost of providing the period certain. Thus, the life income to be paid will be higher if a 10 year period certain is selected than if a 20 year period certain is used.

### Life Income with Refund Payout Option

This is a variation on the life income with period certain option. In this case, an income is paid for the life of the annuitant, but if he dies after only a few years, payments will continue until all of the original contract value, usually not including the interest used in the calculation, is paid to a beneficiary. The refund is paid in the same installments as those being paid while the annuitant was alive, although the beneficiary may be permitted to take a discounted amount in a lump sum.

### Joint and Survivor Annuity Payout Option

Under this option, a monthly, quarterly, semi-annual, or annual income for the life of two (sometimes more) annuitants is calculated using the contract values, or a portion of them, and interest. Payments continue as long as either (or any) of the annuitants is living. The calculation takes into account the probabilities of both and either of the annuitants living for years into the future. The same age and sex considerations apply. This payout option is also known as a joint and survivor annuity without refund payout option.

Of note is the amount of the payment that continues following the death of the first annuitant. It may be the same amount, an arrangement referred to as joint and full or 100% survivor annuity. It may be half as much as when both annuitants were receiving the payout, called a joint and half or 50% survivor annuity. Or it may be two-thirds the amount being paid before, a joint and two-thirds survivor annuity. Naturally, the size of the payment while both annuitants are alive is affected by the percentage that will be paid to the survivor.

### *Joint and Survivor with Period Certain Payout Option*

Here again, a life annuity, this time a joint and survivor annuity, is combined with a fixed period option. The income paid to the annuitants will operate as before, with the further provision that should both annuitants die within a short period of time (e.g., three years) payments will continue to a beneficiary for the balance of the period certain.

### *Changing the Payout Option*

When a payout option has been selected, it may or may not be possible to make changes once the payments have begun. It is sometimes possible to end a fixed period or fixed amount option and take the remaining proceeds, after a discount for lost interest, in a lump sum. This is referred to as commuting the proceeds. This type of procedure is not so common with life income options. The reason is that the principles of pooled risks and averages operate so that some annuitants will live longer than expected and some will live shorter than expected. To allow annuitants to change their minds after the payout period has started defeats this principle. For that reason, life annuitants frequently must stick with the arrangements they have made. On the other hand, some annuities provide for a limited amount of "mind changing" so long as the changes are not adverse to the interests of the group of annuitants as a whole.

## Variable Payouts

The fact that circumstances change during an annuitant's payout years, especially the costs of the goods and services he must buy, is one of the reasons for the popularity of variable payouts. The beginning calculation of a variable payout option begins with an assumed rate of interest used much in the same way as with the fixed options discussed above. Then, subsequent amounts are calculated using the performance of the variable accounts into which the buyer has allocated premiums. Payout amounts are usually recalculated annually with the same amount paid each period during the next year. If variable accounts appreciate in value, the payments increase; if the accounts depreciate, the payments decrease. There is no floor to the variable payout, but most people think it unlikely that all of the variable accounts will falter at the same time.

## Immediate Variable Annuities

Some variable annuities are referred to as immediate variable annuities. For the most part, these operate the same as those described above, except that they are of the single premium variety, do not accept additional premiums, and begin paying out benefits right away. Immediate variable annuities are particularly useful when customers have received large amounts of money, as discussed in Chapter 2. When a variable annuity is designed for single premium, immediate payout applications only, it is possible to make some pricing adjustments, including those affected by the cost of features otherwise available during a period of accumulation. It also may be easier to provide for changes once the annuity payouts have begun.

A relatively new optional benefit is the Guaranteed Payout Annuity Floor (GPAF), which guarantees that future annuity payouts will never be less than a percentage (e.g., 85% to 100%) of the first. GPAFs are paid for by a charge against the variable annuity accounts.[7]

## Bonus Annuities

The term bonus annuities has been used in several ways over the past 5 to 10 years. The variations involve what type of "bonus" is referred to. For some years, the bonus has referred to an extra amount of interest credited, especially to fixed annuities, but sometimes to the guaranteed interest accounts of variable annuities. Sometimes, the extra interest is just for the first interest guarantee period; at other times, extra interest is credited at particular times (e.g., the first year, the fifth, the tenth, etc.). In some cases, the bonus referred to has to do with producer compensation; the sales representative receives a higher commission than would be the case if a similar product without a bonus were sold. In recent years, the bonus refers to an additional amount of contribution added to the premium paid by the customer. A percentage of the premium (e.g., 4% to 5% or more, depending on the amount of the premium) is added to the premium paid.

Obviously, the money with which to credit the bonus to the annuity has to come from somewhere. Sometimes, there is a larger or additional contract charge. Nearly always, there are higher surrender charges that run for longer periods of time. In some cases, producer compensation is less on bonus annuities. (Contract charges and fees are discussed in Chapter 8 and compensation is discussed in Chapter 9.)

## Payments to Impaired Risks

As discussed above, the payout rates for annuities are calculated using annuity tables. On the other hand, the cost of life insurance is calculated using a mortality table. A mortality table tracks the number of people who die each year, while an annuity table tracks the number of people who remain alive each year. The individuals whose lives are measured by annuity tables generally live longer than those measured by mortality tables because they are different groups of people. People buy annuities assuming they will live a long time. People buy life insurance assuming they will die someday.

People whose health is such that they do not expect to live a normal lifespan can still benefit from buying variable annuities. They can have tax deferral, professional money management, a wide range of choices, guaranteed accounts, and most of the features discussed in this chapter. However, they probably should not elect life income payouts. Instead, they can take systematic withdrawals of the contract values. There are some annuity contracts designed especially for impaired risks and there also are products for the structured settlement market. Those who are compensated for injuries over many years often have shortened lifespans. A payout option providing for an income for life would calculate periodic payments with variations from the standard life expectancy for persons of the same age.

## Market Value Adjustment

Earlier, we referred to the fact that the guaranteed interest account in a variable annuity may be subject to a market value adjustment, although this provision more often is used with group annuities that also have variable accounts or separate accounts. Individual annuities with market value adjustments more often are fixed annuities. In many cases, these types of contracts are referred to as MVA Annuities or Modified Guarantee Annuities. A market value adjustment annuity provides an interest guarantee for a year or several years. Once the period has elapsed, for a brief period of time (e.g., 30 days) withdrawals may be made without any reduction or charge. Then, when a renewal interest rate guarantee takes effect, the market value adjustment provision is applicable for the new period.

The market value adjustment is a charge against the withdrawal or a credit, if appropriate, based on a ratio of the current rates in interest rate markets and the rate guaranteed in the annuity. The adjustment is occasioned by the need for the company to sell securities backing the interest guarantee at a discount in order to have the cash for the withdrawal. Selling at a discount will be needed when the interest rate on the underlying securities is lower than current market rates. It is when market rates are higher than the rate in the annuity that annuity owners have incentive to make withdrawals in order to invest the money elsewhere. When the annuity provides for a market value adjustment, the company is in a position for the contract to rely less, if at all, on surrender charges on withdrawals in the early years following payment of the premiums.

## Equity-Indexed Annuity

A product that closely resembles a variable annuity but is usually considered to be a fixed annuity is the equity-indexed annuity, still a relatively recent development in annuity product design. The premium that an equity-indexed annuity buyer pays is credited with interest on the basis of participating in increases (but not necessarily decreases) in an external equity index (e.g., the S&P 500 Index).

Buyers may also have the option of directing a portion of their premium to what is otherwise a standard fixed annuity with an interest rate guarantee. The rate of participation of money placed in the equity-indexed annuity or portion will vary from time to time. To illustrate, let us use the example of $100,000 being placed in the equity-indexed portion.

| | |
|---|---|
| S&P 500 Index at start of index period | 500 |
| S&P 500 Index at end of index period | 570 |
| Index gain | 14% |
| Participation rate | 80% |
| Equity index gain | 11.2% |
| Interest to be credited (on $100,000) | $11,200 |

The increase in the S&P 500 index from the start of the period to the end of the period is 70 points, a gain of 14%. Since the equity-indexed annuity has a participation rate of 80%, the annuity will be credited with an interest rate of 11.2%, which is arrived at by taking 80% of 14%. Thus, the equity-indexed portion begins the next period with $111,200; as a result, if the S&P 500 Index showed a loss during the following period, the equity-indexed portion would still have $111,200, at least until the next adjustment date. This ratcheting of increases is in some contracts and not others, but in the latter cases, the original premium amount may be guaranteed.

Participation rates can range from 75% to over 100%; there are a number of contracts with exactly 100%. There are several ways of determining the index change. The simplest measures the growth from the first day of the index period (usually one year) to the last day. Another measures the growth from the first day to an average of the final three to six months.

Equity-indexed annuities often have surrender charges for early withdrawals, as well as allowing limited withdrawals without surrender charges. There are usually minimum cash value guarantees that apply to the equity-indexed portion as well as the guaranteed portion. Most have waiver of surrender charges in the event of terminal illness, confinement in a nursing home, or death. When the contract has a guaranteed portion and an equity-indexed portion, transfers of existing values from one to the other are permitted with some limitations on amounts or percentages and maybe the timing of transfers.

Most equity-indexed annuities are designed in the hope that their features will not cause them to be treated as securities and, therefore, subject to registration requirements. The reason is that, as non-registered products, they can be offered to many more distribution outlets. There are those who think that the index-linked interest crediting mechanism, which results in the annuity owner not knowing the return on the annuity until the end of the index period, makes the product similar to a mutual fund and not within the "safe harbor" of Securities and Exchange Commission (SEC) Rule 151.[8] Others disagree and say these products fall within the provisions of that rule.

SEC Rule 151 provides that a contract must meet three conditions to be within the "safe harbor":

1. The contract is issued by a corporation (an insurance company) subject to the supervision of a state insurance commissioner.

2. The insurer assumes a prescribed investment risk under the contract.

3. The contract is not marketed primarily as an investment.

Equity-indexed annuities offer some of the "up side" of investing without much of the "down side;" an arrangement that will be appealing to many annuity buyers. There continues to be considerable product development activity in equity-indexed annuities. As more and more of these products come onto the scene, with more and more features and approaches, they may eventually be viewed as securities.

Of course, those who market variable annuities will be able to take such a development in stride. They already have the necessary registrations and licenses. It should not take their broker/dealers long to acquire the ability to market one or more equity-based annuities. In fact, those marketing variable annuities may already be marketing the equity-indexed products their broker/dealers will make available because the insurance company and broker/dealer are associated.

## Group Annuities

Most of the product information discussed in this chapter describing individual variable annuities also applies to group variable annuities, more often called group annuities with separate accounts. The biggest use of group annuities is in qualified retirement plans where, generally, securities registration is not required because the annuities are not marketed to individuals and because the characteristics and restrictions of qualified plans offer much of the consumer protection that registration provides. The buyers of group annuities are the plan sponsors, employers, or associations. Individual participants deal with their plan sponsors and are issued certificates of participation.

The pricing of group annuities may include more variations in loads and charges, as well as in available compensation arrangements. A question that always arises is whether to use group annuities with separate accounts or individual variable annuities when either can be used, such as in qualified plans. A rule of thumb many use is that the breakpoint is at about 15 participants. With fewer people covered, individual products may be the correct approach; with more people, group annuities may be preferable. Of course, factors other than number of participants may need to be taken into consideration.

## Developing New Products

New annuity products and features are introduced regularly. There is always excitement and interest when something new comes along. Sometimes, there is also a period required for marketers to learn about the new offerings and to visualize how they will fit into the marketers' plans and operations. It is said that a product has an average "shelf life" of three to five years. During that time, built in changes, such as interest rate declarations, help maintain interest. Other relatively small changes, such as adding additional variable accounts or changing money managers of the accounts already included, and adding minor improvements, help maintain marketing momentum.

Eventually, so much will have transpired in the marketplace that a new product must be developed and introduced. However, issuers of annuities must always remember that they must continue to provide service for products marketed in the past and cannot announce that "parts are no longer available for this item," as it is possible to do with many non-financial products. Today, much of the service can be provided only when sophisticated and easily accessed data processing is at hand and available widely. In order to know when it is necessary to make substantial changes or to develop a new product and gain some idea of what needs to be developed, actuaries do a trend analysis. Generally, it takes about three years of data for an effective analysis.

## Chapter Endnotes

1. NASD Notice to Members 04-45, June 2004.
2. Rick Carey, "2Q Variable Annuity Sales Dip Slightly to $33 Billion," *National Underwriter*, Life and Health/Financial Services edition, September 6, 2004, p. 30.
3. Kosnett, Jeffrey R., "The Year In Annuities," *Life Association News*, December, 1996.
4. IRC Section 72(q)(2).
5. IRC Section 72(q)(2)(C).
6. IRC Section 72(m)(7).
7. Steve McDonnell, "Guaranteed Living Benefits Spur VA Sales, Grow in Complexity," NAVA *Outlook*, November/December, 2003.
8 SEC Rule 151 adopted by SEC Release No. 33-6645, May 29, 1986. Annuity contracts that meet the Rule 151 safe harbor provisions fall within Section 3(a)(8) of the Securities Act of 1933, which exempts the contracts from the provisions of the 1933 Act.

# Chapter 8

# Charges and Fees: Pricing

## Good Value, Adequate Return

A variable annuity product must provide good value to the customer while providing an adequate return to the issuing company. Leaving aside the performance of the variable accounts, customer value arises when the charges and fees are low enough that their effect on account values is slight; but they must be high enough that the company is able to provide the services that the customer needs.

The challenge in managing a profitable variable annuity is ensuring that fees collected exceed expenses and other obligations by a certain margin. Establishing the fees and charges for a product is a significant part of pricing. A profitable variable annuity also depends on critical mass; there must be adequate assets over which to spread the fixed costs. This means that there must be sufficient sales and, further, that those who purchase must remain contract owners to provide cash flow to the issuing company.

Naturally, in addition to being adequate, the charges and fees must be competitive with other variable annuity products and, to a lesser extent, with the charges and fees priced into mutual funds. However, in the case of mutual funds, an argument can be made that direct comparisons between variable annuities and mutual funds should be avoided because there are enough differences in the products and how they are used that comparisons "muddy the water" and lead to more confusion than anything else. This subject is discussed more in Chapter 10.

Variable annuity issuers, of necessity, must be mindful of how competitive their products are in comparison to other variable annuities. Registered representatives and buyers are interested as well. Looking at rankings of one kind or another can be helpful, but there is often more to the story. Since some of the charges and fees charged to the variable accounts are reflected in their performance figures, performance rankings might be used. But the fact is that the performance may have more to do with the selection of the investments, the buying and selling in the portfolio, and related matters than with the charges and fees.

The National Association for Variable Annuities (NAVA) does studies of company expenses for sales and marketing and for general expenses. Companies are able to use study findings as benchmarks to indicate relative expense levels and trends. However, NAVA does not suggest that the findings may be ranked for competitive purposes.

Similarly, while it is logical that companies with the most business on the books or that are selling the most would be able to spread their expenses over more units and, thus, be able to have products with the lowest charges and fees, this does not necessarily appear to be the case. Comparisons indicate that frequently there is no direct relationship between the size of the company and the expense level of its products. It may be that some larger companies have higher relative expenses that some smaller ones for reasons not having to do directly with the products that are marketed. If comparisons are needed, it is still necessary to research the various products individually. The most reliable way of doing so is to read the respective prospectuses, which include more and more examples of how the various fees are applied, thus making it at least somewhat easier to make comparisons.

## Securities Markets Improvement Act

As discussed in Chapter 6, variable contracts are regulated as securities under the Securities Act of 1933 and as periodic payment plans under the Investment Company Act of 1940. Periodic payment plans are subject to heightened regulation that focuses on the types of sales loads and related charges allowed and the manner in which they may be deducted. Consequently, variable contracts historically have been subject to regulation that goes far beyond that imposed on mutual funds or on most insurance and annuity products.

The National Securities Markets Improvement Act of 1996,[1] amended the Investment Company Act to provide for a considerably simpler charges and fees structure than had existed previously. It requires that aggregate fees and charges under a variable contract be "...reasonable in relation to the services rendered, the expenses expected to be incurred, and the risks assumed..." by the insurance company sponsoring the contract.[2]

There are two approaches to enforce the new reasonableness standard. First, an insurance company issuing a variable contract must affirmatively represent in the contract's registration statement that the fees and charges to be deducted meet the new reasonableness standard. Second, the SEC is authorized to make rules if variable contract charges become excessive.[3] The reasonableness representation does not have to be included in the product prospectus.

In determining whether the reasonableness standard applies, an insurer can take into account the nature and extent of services performed under the contract, the benefits conferred on the contract owner, and the nature and extent of the risks assumed by the insurer. Concerning sales loads, an insurer should consider the nature and quality of services necessary to ensure proper distribution of a particular contract. Thus, higher sales loads would be appropriate when relatively more selling effort is required. With respect to administrative charges, the nature and quality of the related administrative services should be considered.[4] All charges and fees must be considered in applying the reasonableness test, apparently including advisory fees charged to the various accounts.

Before the 1996 law, there was no numerical limit on administrative charges, but they were required to be "at cost." Today administrative charges are one component of an aggregate charge that must be reasonable. The same is true of mortality and expense risk charges, a change from the former SEC limit of 1.25%, plus additional charges for enhanced death benefits assessed on a case-by-case basis. Sales loads are no longer subject to a limitation under the Investment Company Act but to the aggregate charge that must be reasonable. However, National Association of Securities Dealers (NASD) Conduct Rule 2820 generally still limits variable annuity sales loads to 8.5% of premiums. The various fees may be combined and presented as one charge, although it appears the sales load must remain separate in order to demonstrate compliance with the NASD rule.[5]

Variable annuity issuers welcomed the changes since the pricing atmosphere became more open and they could do more fashioning of the pricing to fit the products they were marketing, as well as to fit their own operations. At the same time, the intense competition affecting these financial services products should keep charges and fees at levels in concert with reasonableness standards. It should not become necessary for the SEC to make new rules because charges have become excessive. However, there will always be changes in particular charges and fees that, in the aggregate, are reasonable and not much different from today. Yet, the changes might provide a competitive edge in the way the changed products perform under certain scenarios.

## Contract Fees

Some charges and fees are assessed to the contract as a whole and others are assessed to the various accounts. Many contracts have administration or contract fees, flat amounts (e.g., $30 or $40) to pay for maintenance of the contract, preparation of statements, premium notices, mailings, and other customer services. The flat fees are deducted pro rata from the various accounts in proportion to the assets in the accounts. They are sometimes described as "disappearing," since they may be waived once the contract value or accumulation value of the variable annuity has reached a certain amount (e.g., $25,000 or $50,000). As mentioned below, a percentage of the assets (e.g., .25%) is subtracted to pay for similar expenses.

## Guaranteed Interest Account: Interest Margin

A charge is assessed against the guaranteed interest or fixed account that is indirect. It is an interest margin, the same system used with fixed annuities. For example, the issuing company's investments in corporate bonds and government securities produce a certain rate of interest; then, a lesser rate is credited to the money in the guaranteed account. The difference between the two rates of interest (e.g., 2.25% or 225 basis points) is the interest margin.

The size of the margin (or "haircut") depends on how large the expenses are that need to be covered, with the most immediate impact coming from sales expenses. Companies attempt to manage the margins so that the interest rates they guarantee do not need to fluctuate as frequently as the bond markets, and so that the companies can hold some cash reserve against rising and falling market interest rates to remain competitive both with rates on new premiums and rates on renewing premiums.

Interest rate competitiveness is all the more important since the bonds and other securities that are purchased often have maturity dates five or more years in the future and early liquidation, necessary to provide for customer cash withdrawals, will be at a discount. As a result, the company may find it difficult to pay the interest rate(s) it has promised. Surrender charges (discussed later in this chapter) may also help restrain customer withdrawals.

In recent years, some direct charges against guaranteed interest accounts have been assessed to pay for certain optional enhanced death benefits and for optional guaranteed living benefits, such as the Guaranteed Minimum Accumulation Benefit (GMAB), the Guaranteed Minimum Income Benefit (GMIB), and the Guaranteed Minimum Withdrawal Benefit (GMWB). In addition, direct charges against guaranteed interest accounts may be made for optional reduced surrender charge periods or for optional charge-free withdrawals from the account values of the contract. These benefits are discussed in Chapter 7.

## Mortality and Expense Charge

In addition to the administrative charge to assets and to any charges for optional benefits, there is a mortality and expense (M & E) risk charge, a percentage subtracted from the variable accounts. M & E pays for three guarantees:

1. The guaranteed death benefit (but not optional enhanced death benefits) payable to the designated beneficiary;

2. The fixed payout options that guarantee a certain amount will be paid for the life of the annuitant or annuitants; and

3. The guarantee that contract expenses will increase no more than the maximums stated in the prospectus.

The administrative expense charge and the M & E fee are often combined in a single charge, ranging from just over 1% to a little over 1.5%.

The mortality risk portion is affected by the type of guaranteed death benefit, and by the payout amounts guaranteed in the contract. As discussed in Chapter 7, the higher the probable death benefit, due to enhanced or stepped-up provisions (but not optional enhanced death benefit provisions), the more is needed to pay for the benefit. Life income payout provisions are determined according to annuity tables that are used to estimate how long a person of a particular age and sex will live; guaranteed payout factors are often printed in the contract. When there are two or more annuitants, all lives must be considered. While the contract owner may elect instead to use annuity payout provisions currently in effect at the time income is to begin, the more favorable the provisions guaranteed in the contract are, the higher the mortality risk portion of the M & E fee needs to be.

When the M & E charge for one contract is higher than for another, there may be a variety of reasons. One reason may be that the issuing company has decided to make that fee higher and another fee in the contract lower. Another reason is that the contract may provide more customer benefits. For example, if the guaranteed death benefit (but not any optional enhanced death benefit) is one that provides for generous enhancing or stepping up, there may be a need for a higher fee. Or, there may be such a need if the contract provides for many other services (such as automatic rebalancing, internal dollar cost averaging, a large number of free transfers among accounts, etc.).

## Investment Management Fees

Investment management fees are charged directly to each variable account and impact the performance figures of the account. They consist of both the investment advisory fee and a component covering other operating expenses. (Frequently, only the term investment advisory fee is used.) The operating expense portion is relatively small since services are provided to only the insurance company variable account and not to a number of other shareholders. If expenses are such that it would otherwise be necessary to charge more than the maximum amount stated in the prospectus, typically a monthly percentage of assets in the account, the extra amount is usually absorbed and not charged to the account.

The investment advisory fee, also usually a monthly percentage of the assets in the account, is for the professional management of the investments in the account—a feature that many variable annuity buyers seek when they consider the advantages of variable annuities. The percentage amount of this fee depends on the type of account. The fee for accounts with only stocks or only corporate bonds and government securities might be lower than for accounts requiring more discretionary management such as balanced or asset allocation accounts that have a variety of types of investments and anticipate changes in the mix of investments on a regular basis. On the other hand, indexed accounts, which seek to emulate investments followed in external market indexes (such as the S&P 500), might have lower fees than the stock or bond accounts. International funds and special purpose accounts might have fees that are among the highest since they are apt to require specialized expertise and additional procedures.

The total investment management fee, which combines the advisory fee and an operating expense component, averages somewhere in the .80% to .90% range. Of course, an average cannot completely take into account the fact that different kinds of accounts require different kinds of investment management. Investment management fees are listed in the prospectus portions pertaining to the accounts, but the fees themselves are not shown on the contract owner's summary of account activity. The account values shown on the account balance section will be net of the fees that have been charged and deducted from the accounts.

## Charges for Optional Benefits

As discussed in Chapter 7, charges are assessed against the values in the variable accounts (as well as the guaranteed interest accounts in some cases) for optional enhanced death benefits and for optional guaranteed living benefits, such as the Guaranteed Minimum Accumulation Benefit (GMAB), the Guaranteed Minimum Income Benefit (GMIB), and the Guaranteed Minimum Withdrawal Benefit (GMWB). The charges vary since the terms of the various benefits, as well as the terms of each type of benefit, are different from each other among companies.

In addition, charges are assessed against the values in the variable accounts (as well as the guaranteed interest accounts in some cases) for optional reduced surrender charge periods and for optional charge-free withdrawal provisions when they are elected. Again, these provisions vary from company to company, so the charges will also differ among companies.

## Proprietary Accounts

When a variable annuity buyer allocates premiums to proprietary accounts, the variable accounts managed by investment advisors working for the company issuing the contract, the investment management fees are paid to the issuing company. When the buyer allocates to accounts managed by outside investment advisors, the outside advisors are paid the fees. Ordinarily, it is possible for the issuing company to provide the investment management and services at a lower cost because many of the services can be provided with systems and personnel already in place to serve other needs or with relatively small incremental increases in systems and personnel. For that reason, the issuing company greatly prefers that buyers take advantage of their proprietary accounts.

On the other hand, outside managed accounts, especially those managed by organizations with well-known names, are very popular with the public and have been given credit for much of the popularity of variable annuities. Issuing companies know this trend is good for them and seek out opportunities to include outside managed accounts not withstanding the fact that doing so may cause less to be allocated to their proprietary accounts. In the long run, the greater sales are expected to carry the day.

## Transfer Fees

Transfers of values in one variable annuity account to other accounts may be made without the necessity of buying and selling and paying the resulting income taxes. As discussed in Chapter 7, there are some limitations but, generally, transfers are easily accomplished. While there are a variety of practices applicable to contracts, the current trend is for a certain number of transfers each year to be free of charge, with a fee, e.g., $10 or $20 applicable to additional transfers. The number of free transfers is enough to satisfy most variable annuity owners' needs, and additional transfers are charged only for a higher than usual number of transactions. The expense of free transfers is accounted for by the administrative charges and fees discussed above. Similarly, the expense of transfers, which are the result of internal dollar cost averaging or automatic rebalancing, are handled by those administrative charges and fees as well.

## Surrender Charges

Some of the most important charges associated with annuities, including variable annuities, are surrender charges. Surrender charges are applicable to surrenders or withdrawals from the contract value or accumulation value for a period of time. In nearly all products, surrender charges are applied when surrenders or withdrawals are made within a stated number of years following the payment of the premium. Typically, the charge is one that reduces each year following the premium payment until it has reduced to zero. For example, the charge may apply for eight years, but the percentage used reduces through the years:

| Year | Percentage |
|---|---|
| 1 | 7 |
| 2 | 7 |
| 3 | 6 |
| 4 | 5 |
| 5 | 4 |
| 6 | 3 |
| 7 | 2 |
| 8 | 1 |
| 9 | 0 |

In this example, if premiums are not paid for eight years, no surrender charges are made when the contract owner makes a surrender or withdrawal. Typically, there is a maximum surrender charge percentage applicable to the contract as a whole. As discussed in Chapter 7, most contracts have surrender-charge-free withdrawals of some sort. The most common provisions are those that provide that 10%, or sometimes 15%, of the contract value may be withdrawn in a contract year. As also discussed in Chapter 7, and earlier in this chapter, optional benefits are available that provide for shorter surrender charge periods or larger withdrawal amounts. These optional benefits are usually purchased by means of additional charges assessed against account values of the contract. In addition, we should note here that the surrender charge provisions applicable to withdrawals are apart from any tax penalties that may apply for premature distributions. Those provisions are discussed in Chapter 12.

Surrender charges are needed for several reasons. The most obvious one is the need for recovery of sales expenses when surrenders or large withdrawals occur early after the contract takes effect or premiums are paid. Few, if any, variable annuities have sales loads subtracted from premiums when they are paid into the various accounts. That is, essentially the full amount of premium is paid in. (A small, annual contract charge may be deducted, but this deduction is frequently made at the end of the year rather than at the beginning.) Sales expenses, including sales representative and manager compensation, are recovered over a number of years as part of the interest margin on guaranteed interest accounts and by means of the contract fee and administrative fees charged to the contract.

If a contract owner surrenders or makes sizable withdrawals soon after making premium payments, there will be no time to recover the sales expenses. A surrender charge, assessed against a surrender or withdrawal, will help with the sales expense recovery. The charge also serves the purpose of discouraging early surrenders and withdrawals for less than compelling reasons. The surrender-charge-free withdrawals that are available make it possible to obtain more limited amounts of cash on a regular basis.

A couple of other points should be made about surrender charges. As discussed in other contexts, the bonds and other securities, purchased by the issuing company to produce guaranteed rates of interest for premiums allocated to the guaranteed or fixed interest account, usually have maturities of five or more years into the future. Early surrenders or withdrawals of account values will necessitate the selling of some of the securities held prior to maturity, usually at less than face value. Surrender charges help compensate for the losses incurred as a result of the early sale of the securities. They will also discourage withdrawals and surrenders unless there has been a marked increase in market interest rates, an increase sufficient to overcome the effect of the surrender charges.

There are similar considerations with respect to the variable accounts. Most contract fees are asset-based, yet many of the expenses involved are less dependent on the amount of assets in the accounts. Most contract provisions and customer services must be provided without regard to the size of the accounts. Surrender charges will help recover some of the expenses incurred when asset-based charges and fees have been depressed because of early surrenders and withdrawals. The assumption that is made when the various charges and fees are determined is that there will be a more-or-less consistent flow of premiums into and out of the contract. Surrender charges can serve to provide a reverse incentive for not interrupting this flow unnecessarily.

Finally, some states impose a premium tax on variable annuity purchases. These taxes are payable by the purchaser and reduce contract or accumulation values, although they are collected at different times by different states. They can range up to 4% of the purchase, but generally do not exceed 2%.

## Group Annuity Pricing

To this point, the discussion of pricing has been concerned primarily with individual variable annuities. Group annuities, which usually include separate variable accounts, are generally used to fund qualified retirement plans. The great popularity of 401(k) plans has extended the use of group annuities to smaller and smaller plans. A rule of thumb is that plans involving 15 or more participants probably will be better served with group annuities than with a collection of individual variable annuities. Group annuities, used in many qualified retirement plans, are not registered products because they are marketed to plans, not to individual participants. The requirements of these plans include many of the same disclosure and procedural safeguards as registered products.

Group annuity pricing includes the same sorts of asset-based fees as individual pricing. There are also contract charges and participant level charges. There is more latitude with respect to the handling of sales expense loads than with individual variable annuities. Some of these group cases are very large, and fees and charges have become very competitive. Existing cases that are taken over from another issuer might have different loads, charges, and fees applicable to existing assets or existing participants than those applicable to new participants or additions to existing accounts. In some cases, the sales compensation agreed to may consist only of asset-based fees with no compensation otherwise for new premiums. In other cases, combinations of sales commissions and asset-based compensation may be used. Thus, the pricing of group annuities and individual variable annuities is somewhat different, although composed of many of the same factors and considerations.

## Operational Differences

There are some operational differences between group annuities and individual variable annuities. The group annuity customer is the employer or other plan sponsor; the individuals are plan participants who have their business relationship with the plan sponsor, rather than the issuing company. Although many customer services are provided by the issuing company to plan participants, they are provided in the name of the plan sponsor.

Such items as changes of investments and reallocations are made by participant request to the plan sponsor. There may be limitations on the timing and frequency of such changes. Withdrawals may be more limited with respect to timing and frequency. With individual variable annuities, the annuity buyer is the customer and the business relationship is between the customer and the issuing company directly. We already have referred to the owner's right to make changes virtually at will, the fact that investment and other options are many, and that there is a great variety of withdrawal and payout provisions.

On the other hand, a group annuity and an individual variable annuity, from the individual's point of view, may look quite similar. The same sorts of premium allocations are often available, as are the same sorts of variable account choices and the same methods of paying premiums into the accounts. However, when the group annuities are used inside qualified retirement plans, there are differences having to do with taxation of premiums (plan contributions) and some payout options, among others. Qualified retirement plans are discussed in Chapter 11.

## Comparisons and Customer Value

This chapter began with the need to design a product that is a good customer value, as well as one that will be profitable for the issuing company. As discussed in Chapter 5, good customer value also includes satisfaction with having taken concrete steps to save and invest, rather than remaining on the sideline, and satisfaction with the way the product purchases were made. Additionally, good customer value encompasses a good experience with the sales representative: good advice and helpfulness, someone who listens, a good person to do business with; an expectation of a quality issuing company: good, efficient procedures, helpful and complete sales literature, the likelihood that future communications and transactions will flow smoothly; and quality product performance as a result of good investment management. The product is very important but all of these factors go into the complete package that is embodied in the relationship among the customer, sales representative, and company.

Purchasing registered products is done in an atmosphere of relatively high disclosure. There is considerably more easily obtained information available about the charges, fees, and operation of variable annuity contracts than about most things we purchase. Not infrequently, such detailed information about many consumer products can be had but only by going to considerable effort involving extra time. With registered products, most of it is right there in the prospectus, often also available on the Internet, albeit sometimes requiring effort to "wade through" the language. Some people are detail oriented and enjoy making their own discoveries by reading the prospectus and sales literature. Others are put off by the detail and depend on sales representatives to point out pertinent information to them. But, at least the information is at hand and can be referred to in concrete terms.

When comparing one financial services product with another, it is important to remember the relationship between those features that the potential customer believes are needed and the stated charges and fees that relate to them. Put another way, a small difference in a charge or fee between one product and another is important only to the extent that the charge or fee is important to the potential customer. For example, we see in Chapter 7 the variety of death benefits, enhanced death benefits, optional guaranteed living benefits, optional surrender charge options, regular withdrawal arrangements, transfers and transfer fees, and other product features; differences usually result in some variations in charges and fees. But how important are they to the customer? How "big a deal" should be made of the differences? Is this "much ado about nothing"? One of the most consistently made comparisons is between variable annuities and mutual funds. The issues involved in those comparisons are similar, and are taken up in more detail in Chapter 10.

## Chapter Endnotes

1. National Securities Markets Improvement Act of 1996, P.L. 104-290.
2. *Ibid.* Section 205(a), adding 15 USC 80a-26(e)(2).
3. Conner, W. Thomas and Mackey, Mark J., "Variable Contract Charges Simplified," NAVA *Outlook*, November, Special Edition, 1996. Blazzard, Norse N. and Hasenauer, Judith A. "Law May Change Structure of Variable Products," *National Underwriter*, Life and Health/Financial Services edition, November 11, 1996.
4. *Ibid.*
5. *Ibid;* NASD Rules, Rule 2820, "Variable Contracts of an Insurance Company—(c) Sales Charges." *National Association of Securities Dealers Manual.*

# Chapter 9

# Distribution of Products

## Variety of Distribution Outlets

Variable annuity products are developed by insurance companies alone or in conjunction or joint venture with other organizations such as mutual fund companies. The insurance companies' know-how in product development, dealing with life contingencies, annuitization, and death benefits and the investment management personnel they already have in place are put to use as products are developed. Additional investment management and development costs can be supplied by the joint venture partners. On the other hand, variable annuities are distributed by a large number of different organizations and there have been significant changes in recent years in distribution.

According to The VARDS Report for year end 2003,[1] 34% of the sales in the survey in 2003 were sold by agents directly associated with insurance companies, 26% were sold by independent NASD firms, 14% by banks and credit unions, 13% by New York brokerage houses, 12% by regional investment firms, and 1% through direct response marketing. When comparing the results with those of about five years ago, we see that the shares of sales made by independent NASD firms and by banks and credit unions have increased, while the shares of sales sold by agents directly associated with insurance companies and by regional investment firms have decreased.

One of the reasons for the changes we see is the financial services reform legislation that became law in 1999.[2] It made it possible for banks and other financial institutions to take on more and more of the functions that only insurance companies were able to do. These other financial institutions are able to profit, in some ways, from the manufacturing of products as well as the distribution of them. Even before those changes, insurance companies were constantly looking for sales distribution outlets, and many of them turned more and more to banks and independent brokerage firms. More and more partnerships have developed among insurance companies and large mutual fund companies to develop and market variable annuities.

## Producer Compensation

Annuity producers are compensated in at least two ways, though both methods are not used with all products. The first is a percentage of the premium paid by the annuity buyer. The second is a percentage of the assets managed in the various accounts, sometimes referred to as "trailer commissions." There is a relatively wide range of compensation patterns although, in the end, variable annuity sales loads are limited by NASD Rule 2820 to 8.5% of premiums.[3]

The wide range comes about because of the variety of products (especially involving minimum initial and continuing premiums), any specialized markets where the products are used, and how the products are distributed. For example, products with high initial premiums are sometimes marketed for special uses. Perhaps, they are marketed exclusively to a particular group of buyers. In these instances, the compensation on premiums may be on the low side, with asset-based compensation somewhat higher than usual. Products used primarily for rollovers from qualified plans, or as substitutes in existing plans, may rely almost exclusively on asset-based compensation.

Products distributed by agents and other registered representatives who are responsible for developing their own customers usually pay compensation based more on premiums and less on assets. How high these commissions are depends, in part, on the level of services provided by the broker/dealer and insurance company. Generally, if relatively few services are provided, the compensation is higher than when a greater number of services is provided. The services we are referring to here include sales consultation, sales training and compliance assistance, breadth of product line, access to certain fringe benefits, applicability of sales credits to sales conference qualification, and the like. Compensation of both types is also paid to local office or agency management.

When products are distributed through sources where the individual producers do not need to develop individual customers, such as banks or credit unions, producer compensation usually is lower. Of course, the total compensation paid to the bank or credit union also includes amounts for developing customers and administrative costs.

## Paid to Other Distributors

Compensation otherwise paid to agents or sales representatives and to managers is paid to the bank, credit union, or other financial institution that makes the sale; it is up to that institution to decide how much of this amount is paid to the individual producers. This is similar to the arrangement a broker/dealer makes to distribute a group of mutual funds. The mutual fund group pays what is called a "dealer concession" to the broker/dealer, which then decides how much of it must be retained for expenses and how much will be paid to producers and agency or local office management personnel. The arrangement the broker/dealer makes with producers often varies according to the producers' level of production.

It is likely that an insurance company will pay more in these situations than it will pay to agents and managers. That is because the financial institution will perform many of the services, and undergo many of the costs, that the insurance company or broker/dealer would otherwise have been responsible for assuming. It is not unusual for an insurance company and broker/dealer to determine that, although they are paying more in compensation for business produced by other financial institutions, the total direct and indirect costs of producing the business are lower than for business produced by agents with whom they have a direct relationship. However, the associated question of whether or not that business will enjoy as favorable premium persistency as business produced by associated agents needs to be taken into consideration. A continuing flow of premiums into contracts helps attain the critical mass needed in accounts to make them profitable. The number of withdrawals from accounts may also be different for customers of the various distribution sources.

## Percentages Paid

The percentage of premiums paid to producers can range from zero, as indicated above, to 5% and higher. The percentage of premiums paid to managers usually is lower, ranging from less than 1% to 2% or more. In the past, compensation arrangements sometimes had somewhat higher percentages paid during the first year or several years and lower percentages paid thereafter. Most of today's arrangements use constant percentages on all premiums intended to be continuing. Single premium products often have different percentages from their continuing premium counterparts. Sometimes, percentages vary by size of the premium being paid.

The percentage of assets or trailer commission rate also varies, although not over so great a range. Most asset percentages are less than 1%, perhaps ⅛, ¼, or ½ of 1%. Of course, over time, this fraction of a percent is applied to a larger and larger number until the compensation involved is substantial indeed. In some cases, there is a floor level of assets that must be reached before the percentage of assets compensation is paid. This is so that elaborate administrative systems do not need to be implemented for producers who only occasionally produce business.

Compensation arrangements that use both a percentage of premiums and a percentage of assets usually make use of a see-saw principle. A higher asset percentage means there is a lower premium percentage, and vice versa. As we have seen in Chapter 8, there is only so much that can be paid for the production of business, whether it is because of the need for the product to be profitable and competitive, or because of limitations imposed by NASD or SEC rules. Notwithstanding these considerations, some products are designed to attract business by paying commissions based on a higher than usual percentage of the premium. The design of these products is such that the higher costs can be absorbed by having larger or longer surrender charges or surrender periods or by having restrictions such as the requirement that the values be annuitized.

It is not unusual for the compensation on fixed annuities to be higher, especially with respect to the percentage of premiums, than on variable annuities. Fixed annuities are not subject to NASD or SEC rules. But more than that, some fixed annuities are designed with features that allow for higher sales costs to be built into the price. For example, some interest rates declared are also conditioned on the annuity being annuitized later. If the annuity holder surrenders instead of annuitizes, a deduction is made from contract values, thus providing a source to make up for the additional compensation that has been paid. Other features also relate to the length of interest rate guarantees and the like.

## Increasing Compensation

As seems clear, a producer of variable annuities earns more compensation by selling more premiums, by keeping premiums continuing on contracts sold earlier, and where applicable, by constantly building a book of business so that the percentage of assets compensation is applied to an ever increasing figure.

Selling more premiums each year than the year before obviously increases percentage of premium commissions from new sales. Not quite so obvious is the beneficial effect of customers continuing to pay premiums as planned and of assets continuing to grow so that percentage of assets commissions increase.

Registered representatives usually put most of their effort into finding, approaching, and selling new customers. As we see here, considerable effort also needs to be directed at keeping in consistent contact with existing customers so that they will remain happy enough to continue paying the premiums they have planned to pay. Consistent contact with customers will also uncover any disappointments serious enough to motivate customers to withdraw funds from their contracts and put them elsewhere.

## Variable Annuity Replacements

When a customer exchanges a variable annuity for a newly available annuity, compensation is paid on the new one and no longer paid on the exchanged one. Sometimes, there are good reasons for such an exchange, such as important and desirable new features that cannot be added to the old contract, desirable investment options that are not available under the old contract, and the like. Of course, from the producer's standpoint, it may be that he will now receive the compensation formerly going to a different producer. If the amount of compensation is comparable, the customer may be no worse off and, for that reason, not be concerned about the change from that standpoint. If it is substantially more, there may be reason for the customer to object.

We know from the information in Chapter 8 that there are costs connected with a new contract. For starters, we know that the customer almost surely is in a less favorable position with respect to surrender charge percentages and surrender charge periods. Also, it is not easy for a customer to fully comprehend the impact that additional charges and fees will have on the accounts. In fact, the new contract may have so many differences in charges and fees, compared with the replaced contract, that the customer is mystified and apt to consider that he has been mislead. The point of all of this is that when replacing one variable annuity contract with another, it is critical that there be complete disclosure. Dwelling on the benefits of a new contract while giving scant attention to the drawbacks is a formula for customer problems.

In a joint SEC/NASD report[4] on sales practices, it was found that there was unsuitable switching or replacement of products. The report said

- registered representatives gave unfounded, false, or misleading justifications for switches or replacements;
- registered representatives misrepresented or failed to inform clients of sales charges associated with switches or replacements; and
- excessive switching of variable annuities took place in customer accounts, often on a periodic basis, once every two or three years.

## Making a Profit

To conclude this discussion, we should look at how the insurance company and joint venture partner make money from developing and marketing variable annuities. Simply stated, it is from having income exceed expenses. As discussed in Chapter 8, sources of income are contract fees, interest margins, mortality and expense charges, optional benefit charges, transfer fees, surrender charges, and on accounts that are managed, investment management fees. Investment management fees vary according to the types of accounts involved. Not all of these charges and fees will be received on every contract. For example, if little or no money is in the guaranteed account, there will be little or no interest margin. If few transfers are made, few transfer fees, if any, will be charged. If there are no early surrenders, there will be no surrender charges levied. If the customer does not elect any optional benefits, no optional benefit charges will be assessed. The pricing actuary must use realistic assumptions as to how much revenue can be obtained from the various revenue sources. When actuaries set charges and fees, they must consider competition. In order to be competitive, the charges and fees must be set at levels without much "wiggle" room.

We have also discussed the need for critical mass—enough assets in the various accounts to spread the costs of managing and administering the accounts so that the cost can be covered by the investment management fee charged to each contract. In this context, the persistency of premiums coming into the accounts and the assets remaining there for a period of time are important. In earlier discussions, we mentioned the fact that companies prefer that their proprietary accounts be used extensively because some of the administrative costs are absorbed elsewhere in the company, and the investment management fees charged can go further. In other words, proprietary accounts are usually more profitable.

Distribution expenses must be kept in line if the products are to be profitable. Often, the best thing that can happen is for there to be more sales so that critical mass is achieved earlier in the product's life. For this to happen, there is often a need to acquire more distribution sources. This means more production from registered representatives from the ranks of existing offices and sources, as well as increasing the number of representatives in those offices. It also means contracting with sources not previously used for distribution, a tactic that must be carried out carefully. Not infrequently, disappointment arises due to misunderstandings and a mismatch between the new producers contracted and the existing products available for sale.

While increased production will help, controlling expenses is also essential. Reaching potential new customers has become more and more difficult, and sometimes more costly. Additional time and money is needed to find new customers. People's service expectations can only be met through the use of more and more technology. While the costs of hardware and off-the-shelf software are constantly falling, the costs of needed proprietary software is not. Local offices are faced with cost increases for office space, services, and administrative personnel. It is helpful that technology, including the Internet, has made it possible for many local offices to get by with a smaller administrative staff and less office space. Yet, in a competitive atmosphere that is apt only to intensify, commission compensation can increase only by selling more, keeping premiums coming in on contracts in force, and building the overall book of business. At the same time, expense increases must be kept within reasonable limits. When all is said and done, these are the factors faced by nearly all business people today.

## Chapter Endnotes

1. Carey, Rick, "Variable Annuity Sales Climbed 11% in 2003," *National Underwriter*, Life and Health/Financial Services edition, March 5, 2004.
2. Gramm-Leach-Bliley Act, PL 106-102.
3. NASD Conduct Rules, Rule 2820, "Variable Contracts of an Insurance Company - (c) Sales Charges." *National Association of Securities Dealers Manual.*
4. Joint SEC/NASD Report on Examination Findings Regarding Broker-Dealer Sales of Variable Insurance Products, June 2004.

# Chapter 10

## Other Financial Services Products

As we have seen throughout this book, variable annuities are excellent financial services product choices for a great number of people. However, even the most ardent variable annuity advocate would not insist that they are the only choice. Rather, they should play a prominent role in many people's overall financial plans, which should also include other products. In this chapter, we consider some of the more prominent other products and, to an extent where appropriate, compare and contrast them with variable annuities. This chapter is intended to touch many of the high points but is not an exhaustive discussion.

### Stocks and Bonds

Stocks and bonds traded on national and regional exchanges receive the most publicity in the general press. A share of stock represents ownership of a corporation and constitutes a claim on the corporation's earnings and assets. Common stock usually entitles the shareholder to vote in the election of directors and other matters taken up at shareholders' meetings or by proxy. Preferred stock generally does not confer voting rights but it has prior claim on assets and earnings. That is, dividends must be paid on preferred stock before any can be paid on common stock. A corporation can authorize additional classes of stock, each with its own set of contractual rights.

Common stock prices are the ones quoted most often in news accounts of the stock market, and the ones that usually rise and fall most substantially. When people talk about stocks keeping pace with inflation, it is common stocks they are describing. On the other hand, many investors like to hedge against some risk by investing a portion of their money in preferred stock. Though the preferred stock will probably not appreciate as much as the common, it will stand ahead of the common shares in the dividend paying line.

A bond is an interest-bearing or discounted government or corporate security that obligates the issuer to pay the bondholder a specified return, usually at specific intervals, and to repay the principal amount of the loan at maturity. Bondholders are creditors of the government agency or corporation, but they have no corporate ownership privileges. A secured bond is one backed by specific collateral that the bondholder may sell if the issuer fails to pay interest or principal when due. More common are unsecured bonds, referred to as debentures that are backed by the full faith and credit of the issuer but not by any specific collateral. A convertible bond is one that the bondholder may exchange for some other security, usually stock of the issuing company, at some future date under certain conditions. A callable bond is one that may be redeemed by the issuer before the scheduled maturity. The issuer must pay the holders a premium price if the bond is retired early. Bonds are usually called when interest rates fall so significantly that the issuer can save money by floating new bonds at lower rates.

Most stocks and bonds are traded on national securities exchanges, such as the New York Stock Exchange or the American Stock Exchange, or over the counter where they are tracked, in large part, on the NASDAQ (National Association of Securities Dealers Automated Quotation system). NASDAQ is a computerized system that provides brokers and dealers with price quotations for over the counter, as well as many New York Stock Exchange listed securities. NASDAQ quotes are published on the financial pages of most newspapers. Stocks and bonds are also listed on regional exchanges; some are available for sale only in particular states.

People may purchase treasury securities directly or through a broker or registered representative, although they are also purchased for certain mutual funds and variable accounts of variable annuities. Treasury securities are negotiable obligations of the U.S. government, secured by its full faith and credit, and issued at various schedules with various maturities. The income from treasury securities is exempt from state and local income taxes, but not from federal income taxes. Treasury bills have maturities of one-year or less and are issued at a discount from the face value. Treasury notes are intermediate securities with maturities ranging from one to ten years. Denominations range from $1,000 to $1 million or more.

Treasury bonds are long-term instruments with maturities of 10 years or longer and are issued in minimum denominations of $1,000.

We have referred many times to the usual methods of purchasing variable annuities; they are purchased through a registered representative who is associated with a broker/dealer that has an agreement to market one or more products of an insurance company. The insurance company sends regular premium notices that give the purchaser the opportunity to make additional purchases. The purchaser also has the right to make a number of adjustments in the variable accounts, thereby performing the functions of buying and selling among the accounts. We have also referred to the diversification and the professional investment management available when variable annuities are purchased.

Most of what has just been mentioned is different when the investor buys stocks and bonds directly. (Remember that the variable annuity purchaser buys shares of the variable accounts, not shares of the stocks and bonds bought for the variable accounts.) An investor may buy stocks and bonds in a number of ways; the most common is through a stock broker after consultation, and perhaps a recommendation by that broker. Today, there is great variety in the level of services provided by various brokerage firms, from what is called complete service, including consultation, research, recommendations, and the like, to a number of different kinds of discount brokerage services. As should be expected, the size of the sales charge has much to do with the level of service. People who want to do their own investigating and decision making often opt for a low level of service with a commensurate level of sales charge. Much of their work, including the purchases themselves, can be done over the telephone or on the Internet.

### Selecting Investments

People who feel competent to do so may enjoy selecting their own investments, whether they do so largely independently or after consultation with a broker. For example, when they select the stock of a company that does better than similar companies in the same industry, or better than others they might have selected, they are rewarded monetarily and psychologically.

But as we saw earlier, many people do not feel competent to make their own selections. Even more people do not feel competent, nor have the time to continue, making stock and bond selections on an ongoing basis. That is the reason for "hiring" professional investment managers through a variable annuity.

Stock brokers can help individual investors on a continuing basis, but they are not really paid to be professional investment managers in the usual sense. Investors with relatively large holdings often retain professional investment advisors to look after their accounts for a fee. Stock brokers can serve the purpose of encouraging the investor to continue making new purchases, investing more money in order to achieve the investor's future goals. This may or may not be as effective as regular premium notices and other contacts by the variable annuity issuer and registered representative.

People who select their own stocks and bonds need to have a reasonable level of diversification in order to spread risk. Obviously, it is easier to attain proper diversification when the investor has the funds to purchase a substantial number of stocks and bonds. It is not easy to diversify for the person starting out or the person who has limited funds available for investing. In order to achieve proper diversification, an investor must select the right stocks and bonds. Diversification is easier to achieve by purchasing shares of variable annuity accounts that are already diversified; and that is even more the case when the investor has limited funds to invest. Another option for investors in this situation is the purchase of mutual fund shares, as discussed below.

### *Income Tax*

The income tax aspects connected with buying individual stocks and bonds are also different from those applicable to variable annuities. Generally, earnings and gains from stocks and bonds are taxed currently; there is no deferral of earnings as is the case with variable annuities. However, certain dividends from stock, termed "qualified dividend income," are eligible for lower income tax rates. (These special provisions are scheduled to expire at the end of 2008, at which time the former, higher rates would apply.) Capital gains arising when stocks are sold are taxed at rates that are generally lower than ordinary income rates. Interest from bonds (other than tax-exempt bonds) is taxed at regular ordinary income tax rates. No capital gains treatment is available with variable annuities.

Since there is no deferral of income with stocks and bonds, there is no concern with penalties arising when premature distributions are made, as is the case with variable annuities. An important exception to the current taxation of earnings and interest is municipal bonds, which are debt obligations of state or local governmental entities. The interest from many of these is exempt from federal income tax and some also are exempt from state income tax. The interest income is completely exempt, not merely deferred to another time. (Note that income from certain municipal bonds, called "private activity bonds," may cause a taxpayer to be subject to the alternative minimum tax.)

## Derivative Investments

Before leaving the subject of stock market investing, we should mention derivative investments, which include options and futures. Options are rights to buy or sell property that are granted in exchange for agreed-upon sums. If a right is not exercised after a specified period, the option expires and the option buyer forfeits the sum paid. Options are associated with transactions tied to stocks, commodities, and stock indexes. They are traded on many exchanges. A call option gives its buyer the right to buy shares (usually 100 shares) of the underlying security at a fixed price before a specified date in the future, usually three, six, or nine months into the future. A put option gives its buyer the right to sell a specified number of shares of a stock at a particular price within a specified period of time. The call option buyer speculates that the price of the stock will rise during the period and he will be able to buy at a bargain. The put option buyer speculates in the opposite direction—that the price will fall and he will be able to sell at the option price instead.

A futures contract is an agreement to buy or sell a specific amount of a commodity or a financial instrument at a particular price on a stipulated future date. The price is established between buyer and seller on the floor of a commodity exchange, using what is referred to as the open outcry system. A futures contract obligates the buyer to purchase the underlying commodity and the seller to sell it, unless the contract is sold to another before the settlement date. The obligation passes to the buyer of the contract. This contrasts with options where the person chooses whether or not to exercise the option by the exercise date.

## Mutual Funds

The financial services product that is most similar to a variable annuity is a mutual fund. In fact, variable annuities are often described as mutual funds with a tax shelter, referring to the deferral of current income tax on the interest and earnings in the variable annuity accounts while the funds remain inside the contract. We should note that the special tax treatment afforded certain dividends from stock, discussed above, may also apply to mutual funds. If the income passed from the fund to investors is "qualified dividend income" in the hands of the fund, and not short-term capital gain or interest from bonds, the special rates are applicable.

Describing variable annuities as mutual funds with a tax shelter is an oversimplification, of course. There are some significant differences. More than that, the two are often competitors for the same investors' savings and investments. In part, this is because of the great number of similarities. Both variable annuities and mutual funds can be purchased in convenient amounts on a regular basis. There is professional investment management and diversification. The variable accounts in variable annuities are managed by people who also manage mutual funds. There is a ready market for the sale of shares; they will be repurchased by the fund when the investor wants them redeemed.

Numerous articles attempt to point out how mutual funds are better for certain people than variable annuities. The usual arguments point out the greater variety of mutual funds and assert that mutual funds have lower charges because they do not have the mortality and expense (M & E) charges that variable annuities do. There is no question that there are more mutual funds available to buy than variable annuities, although there is a question as to just how many choices are enough to suit the needs of the overwhelming majority of persons who would like to save and invest in this way. The product charges are another matter. The question is whether the additional charges in the variable annuity are worth paying, given the additional provisions and features available.

At times, the competition between mutual funds and variable annuities seems a bit strange. Most registered representatives who market variable annuities also market mutual funds. They are in a position to provide whichever product is the right one for the customer. What sometimes happens is that one registered representative recommends a mutual fund and a different one recommends a variable annuity, even though both representatives could have provided either. In such a case, arguments should center on which product is better for the customer, rather than which product seems to be better when compared with the other standing apart from the customer.

There is another aspect to this. While a registered representative may be able to provide both products, the organization preparing the sales arguments may not be so situated. It must prepare materials designed to sell its products without regard for any knowledge of a particular customer. The fact is that many people feel that head-on comparisons between mutual funds and variable annuities should be avoided. If made forcefully enough, the comparisons may confuse customers enough for them to avoid or put off buying either. However, there are differences we should look at.

Both mutual funds and variable annuities have investment expense charges. The charges for mutual funds tend to be higher than those for variable annuities. But variable annuities also have M & E charges that, when added to the investment expense charges, total more than the mutual fund investment expense charges.[1] One reason the investment expense charges can be less for variable annuities is that some of the administration charges are handled by the insurance company that issues the variable annuity. Presumably, the associated costs are handled through a portion of the M & E charge.

## Variable Annuity Features

As mentioned above, variable annuities have features and provisions that mutual funds do not have. The first is the deferral of recognition of current income due to interest and earnings while funds remain inside the contract and are not withdrawn. We need to point out that mutual funds inside IRAs and other plans do have this type of deferral. As mentioned above, if the income passed from the fund to investors is "qualified dividend income" in the hands of the fund, and not short-term capital gain or interest from bonds, a special tax treatment is given to this income (until the special provisions expire at the end of 2008). It should be repeated here that some of the annual mutual fund income is capital gains that is generally taxed more favorably than at ordinary income rates. Variable annuity earnings do not produce capital gains. Obviously, since mutual funds have no income deferral, no penalty taxes apply to premature distributions.

A related provision is the fact that money inside a variable annuity can be transferred from one account to another without any sales or new purchases resulting in recognition of gains (or losses). With mutual funds, changes can be made within mutual fund families with a minimum of expense, but there is recognition of gain (or loss) when one fund is sold and another purchased, even within the same family of funds. Annuities may also be exchanged for each other on a tax-free basis under Internal Revenue Code Section 1035, as discussed further in Chapter 12. Following such an exchange, the deferral of recognition of income on interest and earnings continues with the new annuity contract.

Variable annuities have death benefits, which can amount to considerably more than what a mutual fund will pass to a family member when the mutual fund owner dies. Additionally, variable annuities offer fixed and variable life income options. This means a person can receive an income for life, no matter how long. It also means that since principal and earnings are combined in the income payment, it is possible for a person at retirement age to receive more income than would be the case if only interest and earnings from a mutual fund or other financial product were the source of income. For those of more modest means, this is a very important feature. With mutual funds, a person may withdraw both principal and earnings, but there is no guarantee that the money will last for the person's lifetime. Variable annuities also have guaranteed living benefits that provide minimum accumulations of account values, minimum income guarantees, or minimum withdrawal amounts.

There is a point of comparison related to the performance of mutual funds and variable annuities. When one of the customer's primary objectives is to provide for retirement, it may be that variable annuities are a better choice due to product performance. This is due to the fact that the investment manager can consider a longer horizon for selecting investments. The buyer will not be looking for such immediate results as would be the case if the horizon were shorter. Also, the manager needs less invested in liquid assets that can be redeemed quickly. The tax deferral, possible penalties, and surrender charges in the early years of the variable annuity strongly discourage taking withdrawals from the contract.

Earlier in this part of the discussion, we stated that many people argue that variable annuity/mutual fund comparisons should be avoided. Though we have pointed out some of the differences here, the argument to avoid comparisons is a good one. The comparisons that are published use averages whether they pertain to expense charges, performance, or other criteria. Though data on the particular products a customer is considering are available from prospectuses and other published materials, how the products work in actual usage can only be determined retrospectively. Customers probably have enough to think about when they consider goals and objectives, the selection of fixed and variable accounts, and how much money to put in each one, without additionally considering the inside charges and fees; unless those charges and fees are out of line with other, similar products. As indicated previously, nothing good comes if the customer does not put anything into any decent product.

## Wrap Accounts

We should mention mutual fund wrap accounts here, which are more a service than a financial services product, although they do produce revenue. Wrap accounts charge a fee for analyzing a customer's investment needs, developing an appropriate asset allocation strategy, and selecting a portfolio of mutual funds. The basic services include a point of sale program, which is either paper-based or software-based, that assesses investors' risk profiles, investment objectives, time horizon, and suitability. The fee is based in part on percentages of assets and in part on certain flat charges. Generally, a relatively large amount of assets is needed for the fee to be justified and, as a result, wrap accounts frequently have minimum asset requirements for participation.

## Limited Partnerships, Unit Investment Trusts and Hedge Funds

Limited partnerships have at least one general partner in addition to the many limited partners. General partners manage a project and limited partners invest in it. (Limited here refers to the fact that the limited partner's financial liability in the enterprise is limited to what has been invested. Creditors cannot go beyond the investment to the partner's personal assets, as is the case with general partners.) Typically, limited partnerships invest in real estate, oil and gas, and equipment leasing; but they may also finance movies, research and development, and other projects. Public limited partnerships usually are sold through brokerage firms and broker/dealers.[2] Also, there are private limited partnerships that usually call for far fewer limited partners who invest larger amounts.

A unit investment trust purchases a fixed portfolio of income-producing securities, such as corporate, municipal, or government bonds, mortgage-backed securities, or preferred stock. Units in the trust are sold by brokers to investors for a load charge (e.g., 4%). Unit holders receive an undivided interest in both the principal and the income portion of the portfolio in proportion to the amount of money they invest. The portfolio remains fixed until all the securities mature and unit holders have recovered their principal. Most brokerage firms maintain a secondary market in the trusts they sell, so that units can be resold if necessary.[3]

Limited partnerships and unit investment trusts are invested in by a number of people, especially when they suit an investor's needs better than more common investments such as stocks, bonds, mutual funds, and variable annuities. In the recent past, some income tax provisions pertaining to limited partnerships made them particularly attractive. Eventually, Congress decided the provisions were too favorable and changed them. As a result, choosing to invest in limited partnerships is influenced more by their investment potential in accomplishing the investor's goals than by their income tax aspects.

Hedge funds are similar to mutual funds in that they are both pooled investment vehicles that accept investors' money and generally invest it on a collective basis. Hedge funds differ significantly from mutual funds, however. Because hedge funds are not currently required to register under the federal securities laws (though funds of $25 million or more are going to be required to register beginning in February, 2006), they may be limited to a small number of investors who invest large sums, and they currently are not subject to most securities regulations that apply to mutual funds for the protection of investors. Thus, hedge funds are permitted to engage in leverage and other sophisticated investment techniques to a much greater extent than mutual funds. Domestic hedge funds are generally set up as limited partnerships.

## Real Estate

Nearly all people invest in real estate; they do so when they buy their homes. One of the usual considerations is how easily and for what price a home may be sold later. There is always the hope that the real estate will increase in value so that it can be sold for more than was paid and the proceeds used to purchase a more expensive home. As a result, nearly everyone knows something about investing in real estate. People know that there are up markets and down markets. They have seen people "make a killing" in an up market by selling for far more than comparable homes in the recent past. They have also seen people not be able to sell their homes in a down market, and later "take a beating" by having to sell at considerably less than they paid not long ago.

Beyond buying homes, a number of people invest in other real estate by buying homes or buildings that are for sale. Sometimes, the people plan to rent the property and make a gain from rental income over the mortgage payments and maintenance expenses. Other times, they plan to improve the property and sell it for a higher price, usually within a relatively short period of time. With either of these approaches, those who know how to do maintenance and make improvements at a reasonable cost are usually better off.

People are generally pretty realistic about real estate investing because they have first-hand experience. There was a time when the prevailing view was that all real estate appreciates. Today, there is a more balanced view. Sometimes you win and sometimes you do not, but timing is extremely important and the investor must be in a position to "ride out" any temporary depression in the market. To be successful at real estate investing, you have to know what you are doing. Rarely are there reports and studies available to review. While there is much more disclosure required today on real estate sales contracts, there is still ample opportunity to miss important factors and make costly mistakes. There is no ready market when the investor wants to sell, such as with variable annuity variable accounts, mutual funds, and the stock exchanges and over-the-counter market. Real estate cannot be purchased in convenient quantities that may be changed frequently. There is no SEC or NASD to require adequate disclosure. Still, for those who are adept, there are good opportunities in real estate investing.

There are at least two ways of investing in real estate without actually purchasing particular pieces of property. One is through limited partnerships, as mentioned above. The other is through Real Estate Investment Trusts (REITs). REITs, usually traded publicly, manage a portfolio of real estate to earn profits for shareholders. They make diverse investments in real estate from shopping centers and office buildings to apartment complexes and hotels. Equity REITs take equity positions in real estate; shareholders receive income from the rents received from the properties and receive capital gains as buildings are sold at a profit. Mortgage REITs specialize in lending money to building developers; they pass interest income on to shareholders. Some REITs have a mixture of equity and debt investments. In order to avoid a corporate income tax, REITs must receive 75% or more of their income from real estate and 90% of their taxable income must be distributed to shareholders.[4]

## Savings Accounts and Certificates of Deposit

Of course, one of the most frequently used methods of accumulating savings is through savings accounts and certificates of deposit. Savings accounts are highly liquid in that withdrawals may be made from them at any time, an important point in some situations. The chief disadvantage to savings accounts is that their interest rates are low. That is because of the need for such a high degree of liquidity.

Certificates of deposit, generally referred to as CDs, pay higher rates of interest but they are purchased for a certain period of time (e.g., 3 months, 6 months, 24 months, 36 months, etc.). Generally, the longer the period of the CD the higher the rate of interest that is paid, although sometimes there is not much difference. If there is a need to redeem the certificates before the period has run, a penalty applies, thereby having the effect of reducing the interest rate paid. Most people have at least some of their savings in savings accounts, CDs, or interest-bearing checking accounts.

## In Conclusion

This has been a brief survey of a great number, but not all, of the many outlets for people's savings and investment dollars. We have not touched on some outlets such as precious metals, collectibles, and the like. As we have seen, some outlets require more knowledge, care, and attention than others. Some are easier to learn about than others because of the amount of information that is published and otherwise made available to the public. Some provide the opportunity to invest in equities, in order to attempt to keep pace with inflation, and some do not. Some have guaranteed minimum interest rates and some do not. Some are easier to purchase in convenient amounts and at convenient times than others. Some have tax advantages over others at certain times. Some are easier to take income from, whether on a regular basis or from time to time, than others. Some are better than others at maximizing income at retirement time. Some are easier to redeem or resell than others when the time comes for that action. Most importantly, some will have more attributes needed and desired by a particular customer than others.

## Chapter Endnotes

1. "The Real Cost of a Variable Annuity," *NAVA Outlook*, May/June, 2004, Source data: Morningstar, Inc.
2. *Dictionary of Finance and Investment Terms*, Barron's Educational Series, Inc.
3. *Ibid.*
4. *Dictionary of Finance and Investment Terms*, Barron's Educational Series, Inc.; IRC Secs. 856, 857.

# Chapter 11

# Variable Annuities in Business and Estate Planning

## Qualified Retirement Plans

As mentioned in earlier chapters, variable annuities have uses in business, particularly in retirement plans, and to some extent in estate planning. The discussions in this chapter are intended to be of an overview nature so that the places where variable annuities may be used can be identified. Treating the subjects fully requires much more development and is beyond the scope of this book. We begin with qualified retirement plans.

Qualified retirement plans, which include pension, annuity, profit sharing, and stock bonus plans, are particularly attractive because of their tax advantages:

1. The employer can take a current business expense deduction for its contributions to the plan even though its employees are not currently taxed on them;[1]

2. Generally, an employee pays no tax until the benefits are distributed;[2]

3. A lump sum distribution meeting certain requirements may be eligible for special tax treatment;[3]

4. Annuity and installment payments are taxable only as received;[4] and

5. The fund within the plan earns and compounds income on a tax free basis.[5]

A pension is defined as a plan established and maintained by an employer primarily to provide systematically for the payment of definitely determinable benefits to employees over a period of years, usually for life, after retirement. Definitely determinable benefits are provided by having either fixed benefits (also called defined benefits) or fixed contributions. Under a defined benefit plan, the size of the pension, or a formula to determine size, is set in advance, and by actuarial methods the annual contributions are determined that will gradually accumulate a fund sufficient to provide each employee's pension at retirement. The amount of the pension benefit usually is related to the employee's compensation, years of service, or both.

With a defined contribution pension plan (also called a money purchase plan), the annual contribution to the employee's account is fixed or definitely determinable, and the employee receives whatever size retirement benefit can be purchased with the funds accumulated in the account. Usually, the annual contribution (which usually is paid throughout the year) is a fixed percentage of the employee's compensation. There are limits on the amount of contributions that can be made to a pension plan, whether the plan is a defined benefit or a defined contribution plan.

### *Contribution Limitations*

The contribution limitation rules are complex but there are general rules that apply. With respect to defined benefit plans, the highest annual benefit payable must not exceed the lesser of (a) 100% of the participant's average compensation in his/her high three consecutive years of employment while a plan participant, or (b) $170,000, in 2005, as adjusted for inflation. (The maximum is indexed annually for inflation and changes only in increments of $5,000.)[6] The annual contribution limitation for defined contribution plans must not exceed the lesser of (a) 100% of the participant's compensation, or (b) $42,000 in 2005, as indexed for inflation. (This annual limit also is indexed for inflation and changes in increments of $1,000.)[7] Special rules may apply in the event the employer sponsors more than one plan.

As its name denotes, a profit sharing plan is one for sharing employer profits with employees. A profit sharing plan need not provide a definite, predetermined formula for determining amounts of profits to be shared. But in the absence of a formula, there must be recurring and substantial contributions made on behalf of employees. However, there must be a definite, predetermined formula for allocating the contributions among the participants, and for distributing funds to the employees after the lapse of a fixed number of years, at retirement, at death, etc. The allocation formula generally is related to compensation, although service and other factors may be given consideration. Since the contributions are related to compensation, the defined contribution limitations above apply.

A stock bonus plan provides benefits similar to those of a profit sharing plan but the benefits are distributable in stock of the employer, and employer contributions are not necessarily dependent on profits. For the purpose of allocating contributions and distributing benefits, the plan is subject to the same requirements as a profit sharing plan.

### *Plan Requirements*

In order to enjoy the tax advantages mentioned above, qualified plans must meet a set of requirements:

1. A plan must be established in the United States by an employer for the benefit of employees or their beneficiaries. Plan assets may not be used for any purpose other than for the exclusive benefit of employees or beneficiaries until all liabilities to those two groups have been satisfied.[8]

2. A plan must meet minimum age and service standards and minimum coverage requirements. The general minimum age and service standard is age 21, with one year of service; two years of service may be required if there is immediate 100% vesting.[9] The minimum coverage requirement will be met if the plan passes a ratio percentage test. Under this test, the percentage of nonhighly compensated employees who benefit under the plan must be at least 70% of the highly compensated employees who benefit under the plan.[10] There is also a minimum participation rule that applies only to defined benefit plans.[11]

3. A plan must provide for contributions or benefits that are not discriminatory. There are three basic requirements: (a) contributions and benefits must not discriminate in favor of highly compensated employees; (b) benefits, rights and features must be made available to employees in a nondiscriminatory manner; and (c) the effect of plan amendments and plan terminations must be nondiscriminatory.[12]

4. Benefits and contribution amounts must not exceed the limitations mentioned above.[13]

5. A plan must provide for minimum vesting standards. Generally, an employee must be given nonforfeitable rights to accrued benefits derived from employer contributions in accordance with one of two vesting schedules: (a) five-year cliff vesting; an employee who has five years must have 100% vesting of accrued benefits; (b) 3/7 vesting; an employee who has at least three years of service must have vesting in 20% of accrued benefits, with the percentage graduating each year until there is 100% vesting after seven years.[14]

6. A plan must provide for distributions to satisfy both the commencement rules and the minimum distribution rules. Unless the participant directs otherwise, distributions must commence within 60 days following the later of: (a) the close of the plan year of the earlier of normal retirement age under the plan or age 65; (b) the close of the plan year when the participant has 10 years of plan participation; or (c) the close of the plan year when the participant ceases employment.[15] The minimum distribution requirements are an interrelated set of rules which require that distributions from a plan must begin by a specific date and also that a participant's entire interest must be distributed within certain specified periods.[16]

7. Certain plans must provide that unless waived by the participant, with the consent of the spouse, the automatic survivor benefit is a qualified joint and survivor annuity.[17]

8. There must be provisions for actions to be taken should the plan become "top-heavy." A top-heavy plan is one where the benefits are disproportionately in favor of highly compensated and other key employees.[18]

9. A plan must provide that benefits generally may not be assigned or alienated (transfer the ownership), or subject to garnishment or execution (a court order). One notable exception is the collection of federal taxes from benefits. Another is what is referred to as a "qualified domestic relations order."[19]

### *Required Minimum Distributions*

With respect to individual account retirement plans (defined contribution plans, 401(k) plans, and most IRA plans), the entire interest of each employee must either be distributed to the employee in its entirety not later than the "required beginning date" or over the life (or life expectancy) of the employee (or the employee and a beneficiary).[20] The required beginning date generally is April 1 of the calendar year following the later of the year the employee reaches age 70½ or the year the employee retires.[21] (With respect to traditional IRAs, the distributions must begin whether or not the IRA owner has retired.) The amount of the required minimum distribution is calculated by dividing the employee's account by the applicable distribution period determined from the following table:

**Uniform Lifetime Table**

| Age of Employee | Distribution Period | Age of Employee | Distribution Period | Age of Employee | Distribution Period |
|---|---|---|---|---|---|
| 70 | 27.4 | 86 | 14.1 | 101 | 5.9 |
| 71 | 26.5 | 87 | 13.4 | 102 | 5.5 |
| 72 | 25.6 | 88 | 12.7 | 103 | 5.2 |
| 73 | 24.7 | 89 | 12.0 | 104 | 4.9 |
| 74 | 23.8 | 90 | 11.4 | 105 | 4.5 |
| 75 | 22.9 | 91 | 10.8 | 106 | 4.2 |
| 76 | 22.0 | 92 | 10.2 | 107 | 3.9 |
| 77 | 21.2 | 93 | 9.6 | 108 | 3.7 |
| 78 | 20.3 | 94 | 9.1 | 109 | 3.4 |
| 79 | 19.5 | 95 | 8.6 | 110 | 3.1 |
| 80 | 18.7 | 96 | 8.1 | 111 | 2.9 |
| 81 | 17.9 | 97 | 7.6 | 112 | 2.6 |
| 82 | 17.1 | 98 | 7.1 | 113 | 2.4 |
| 83 | 16.3 | 99 | 6.7 | 114 | 2.1 |
| 84 | 15.5 | 100 | 6.3 | 115 | 1.9 |
| 85 | 14.8 | | | | |

If an employee dies before the required beginning date, distributions must be made under one of two methods:

1. The entire interest must be distributed within five years,[22] or

2. If any portion of the interest is payable to, or for the benefit of, a designated beneficiary, that portion must be distributed over the life (or life expectancy) of the beneficiary, beginning within one-year of the employee's death. If the sole beneficiary is the employee's surviving spouse, distributions must begin by the later of (i) the end of the calendar year immediately following the calendar year in which the employee died, or (ii) the end of the calendar year in which the employee would have reached age 70½.[23]

### *401(k) Plan*

A 401(k) plan generally is a profit sharing or stock bonus plan (see above) that provides for contributions to be made pursuant to a "cash or deferred" arrangement (CODA) under which individual participants elect to take amounts in cash or to have the amounts deferred.[24] Amounts that are deferred are excluded from the participant's gross income in the year of deferral and treated as employer contributions. Thus, the deferrals are contributions made with before-tax dollars. Some plans call for all of the contributions to be from participant deferrals and others for some of the contributions to be ordinary employer contributions. The latter plans usually are referred to as matching since the scheme often involves the employer making contributions in amounts that are the same or a percentage of what the participant contributes.

The amount of elective deferrals an individual can exclude from income in a year is subject to a ceiling, which also applies collectively to other elective deferral plans such as tax deferred (or tax sheltered) annuities, in which the individual participates. The limit for conventional and so-called safe-harbor 401(k) plans for 2005 is $14,000, increasing to $15,000 in 2006, after which there are adjustments for inflation. In addition, there are catch up provisions, available to those age 50 and over, of $4,000 (in 2005) increasing to $5,000 in 2006.[25]

In order to meet nondiscrimination requirements, 401(k) plans must either satisfy one of two actual deferral percentage (ADP) tests or be SIMPLE (Savings Incentive Match Plan for Employees) 401(k) plans or safe-harbor design plans (plans that meet special notice and funding requirements).[26] The two ADP tests are not so complex in themselves but they require relatively elaborate records and data and they compare the current year with the previous year. Then, if a violation is found, remedial action must be taken such as refunding contributions and correcting accounts and records. Many small employers do not have elaborate enough data processing systems or are not in a position to pay outside administrators the fees necessary to administer 401(k) plans, notwithstanding the great popularity of the plans among the public.

### *SIMPLE 401(k) Plans*

That is the reason that SIMPLE 401(k) plans were created. These plans are for employers with no more than 100 employees earning $5,000 or more in the preceding year. Employees must be permitted to elect to have the employer make elective contributions on behalf of employees; the amount is a percentage of compensation up to $10,000 in 2005. These plans also have catch-up provisions for those age 50 and over of $2,000 in 2005, increasing to $2,500 in 2006. The employer must match dollar-for-dollar up to 3% of compensation. Alternatively, the employer may elect to make non-elective contributions of 2%. All contributions are immediately vested in full.[27] By using this type of plan, the employer is not required to deal with the ADP testing of conventional 401(k) plans. The SIMPLE 401(k) is a relatively new creation. It remains to be seen how popular it will become.

To this point, we have looked broadly at plans for relatively large employers, with the possible exception of the SIMPLE 401(k). Before we turn to other tax-advantaged retirement plans, we should again state the rule of thumb that qualified retirement plans usually are better served by group annuities, with separate variable accounts, than by individual variable annuities. Many of the reasons were discussed in Chapter 7. Nonetheless, there are opportunities to use individual contracts even in connection with these larger plans.

### *Using Variable Annuities in Qualified Plans*

In a number of cases, plan administrators are perfectly well equipped to provide complete service to participants of qualified plans while they are actively employed. However, when retirement time comes, different arrangements must be made. That is because these administrators are not in a position to administer all of the options the participant has under the law. They might be able easily to administer a life income of some kind but, perhaps, cannot administer periodic withdrawals at the participant's direction. They may not be well equipped to administer required minimum distributions, generally beginning at age 70½, should the participant want to leave a large portion of his account intact.

These and other needs may necessitate the rolling over of the plan proceeds, on a tax free basis, to an individual variable annuity capable of handling all of the options available. Rollover distributions from qualified retirement plans may be made to either another qualified retirement plan or to an individual retirement plan. In the examples discussed just above, which pertain to plan proceeds at retirement, the usual choice is an individual retirement plan. The rules pertaining to rollovers are simpler than they were some time back; a most important one to note is that the rollover must be completed within 60 days after receipt of the distribution.[28]

The distribution can be placed in a variable annuity that is an individual retirement annuity (IRA). Then, the many options and procedures that are part of the variable annuity can be available. Of course, the IRA participant will need to keep in mind that his actions will be treated in accordance with the rules pertaining to IRAs. While this discussion has been concerned with actions at retirement time, there are reasons for rollovers to IRAs prior to retirement, the most common being a termination of employment with an employer that had a qualified retirement plan and new employment or self-employment without a plan to roll over a distribution to. The IRA rollover distribution needs to be allocated to accounts and new contributions can be made in accordance with IRA rules.

A variable annuity also is a good place for a lump sum distribution from a qualified retirement plan. Certain people will determine it is best for them to pay the taxes on a lump sum distribution and save and invest the money on their own. Certain people, born before 1936, are eligible for potentially more favorable tax treatment with some of the distribution treated with a ten-year averaging and other of the distribution given long-term capital gains treatment. Obviously, there will be considerable competition among financial services providers to accommodate people who want to take distributions and put the money to work. A variable annuity is a good choice for many people who elect to take distributions.

## Individual Retirement Annuities

Many people use variable annuities in their individual retirement accounts or annuities (IRAs). IRAs are personal retirement plans, not dependent on an employer. An IRA also may be funded with mutual funds and other investments provided the arrangement is one that qualifies with IRA procedures. A disclosure statement, and a copy of the governing IRA instrument, must be furnished to the buyer at least seven days before the plan is established or purchased. That is why disclosure statements and related documents often are included in the prospectuses of variable annuities that may be used in IRAs. Earnings on the variable annuity inside the IRA accumulate with a deferral of income tax generally until the values are taken out. Of course, values in variable annuities, which are not in IRAs, also accumulate on a tax deferred basis.

### *Contributions*

What makes the traditional IRA (but not the Roth IRA) different from nonqualified annuities is the fact that the individual may be able to take an income tax deduction on the contributions. An individual, under age 70½ who has compensation of at least the amount contributed, may be able to deduct up to $4,000 per year for 2005 through 2007, and $5,000 for 2008 (after 2008 this amount is indexed for inflation). The same contribution also may be made for a non-working spouse; thus the total for both spouses can be as much as $8,000 in 2005 through 2007. When both spouses are working and earning at least $4,000 each (in 2005), the total for the two remains $8,000 (in 2005). A catch-up provision also applies to those age 50 and over. For 2005, the catch-up amount is an additional $500, which increases to an additional $1,000 in 2006 through 2010.[29]

The deduction for contributions made to individual and spousal plans may be reduced or eliminated if the contributing individual or the spouse is an "active participant" in a qualified retirement plan. A phase out of the deduction begins at $50,000 of adjusted gross income (AGI) for an individual in 2005 and after and the deduction is eliminated at $60,000. For a married couple filing jointly, where both spouse participate in retirement plans, the 2005 phase out begins at $70,000 and the deduction is eliminated at $80,000. These amounts increase by $5,000 per year until 2007 when the phase out begins at $80,000 and the deduction is eliminated at $90,000. In the case of married taxpayers who file a joint return where only one is an "active participant," the phase out begins at $150,000.[30] Thus, many persons who participate in qualified plans do not have IRAs available on a deductible basis. Roth IRAs, to which they may contribute on a non-deductible basis, are discussed below. Of course, financial services products may be purchased to fund traditional IRAs on a nondeductible basis. However, when annuities, including variable annuities, are used, there appear to be few advantages to nondeductible IRAs (other than Roth IRAs) that annuities do not already have. Further, some of the formalities and limitations of nondeductible IRAs do not apply to annuities when they are not in plans.

### Distributions

One of the limitations does apply to annuities as discussed in Chapter 12. Amounts distributed from a regular or spousal IRA, to the individual for whom the plan is maintained, before the person reaches age 59½ are premature distributions and subject to an additional tax of 10% of the amount includable in gross income. The penalty does not apply to distributions:

1. made to a beneficiary, or the individual's estate, on or after the death of the individual;

2. attributable to the individual's disability;

3. that are part of a series of substantially equal periodic payments made (at least annually) for the life or life expectancy of the individual, or

the joint lives or joint life expectancy of the individual and his/her designated beneficiary;

4. made for medical care but only to the extent allowable as a medical expense deduction during the year.

5. made to alternate payees pursuant to qualified domestic relations orders.[31]

Of more importance to most IRA participants are the required minimum distribution rules discussed above. Distributions from a traditional IRA must begin by April 1 of the year after the year in which the owner reaches 70½, whether or not the owner has retired. In addition, the rules above pertaining to distributions before or after the death of an employee also apply to IRAs.

Whether the owner dies before or after distributions have begun, the surviving spouse, if the sole beneficiary, may elect to treat the entire account or annuity as the surviving spouse's own plan. The surviving spouse may make contributions to it and make rollovers from it.[32]

The reason it is so important to comply with the minimum distribution rules is the tax assessed in the event of a shortfall. If the amount distributed from an IRA is less than the minimum required distribution for the year, there is an excise tax equal to 50% of the amount by which the distribution made in the calendar year falls short of the required amount. That is a stiff penalty which should be avoided. Variable annuity issuers who provide annuities for IRAs usually are equipped to handle minimum distributions adequately enough to avoid running afoul of the minimum distribution rules.

### SIMPLE IRA

A small employer (one with no more than 100 employees who received at least $5,000 of compensation for the preceding year) may set up a SIMPLE (Savings Incentive Match Plan for Employees) IRA plan. These plans resemble the SIMPLE 401(k) plans mentioned above in many ways. SIMPLE IRAs are salary reduction arrangements where employees may elect to receive payments in cash or contribute them to the plan. Contributions are expressed as a percentage of compensation and may not exceed $10,000 per year in 2005 and after. There also are catch-up provisions for those 50 or over of $2,000 in 2005, increasing to $2,500 in 2006. The employer must match or make nonelective contributions. The match formula is dollar-for-dollar up to 3% of compensation; however a special rule permits the employer to elect a lower percentage (not less than 1%). The employer may not use the lower percentage if the election would result in the percentage being lower than 3% in more than two out of five years. The nonelective employer contribution alternative is 2% of compensation for each employee who earned at least $5,000 in any two preceding years and is reasonably expected to receive at least $5,000 during the year. All contributions to a SIMPLE IRA must be fully vested and may not be subject to any prohibition on withdrawals, nor conditioned on their retention in the account. However, the premature distribution penalty for withdrawals is increased from 10% to 25% during the first two years of participation. Contributions are excludable from the employee's income.[33]

### *Simplified Employee Pension*

A simplified employee pension (SEP) is an individual retirement account or annuity that may accept an expanded rate of contributions from employers. The employer must contribute for every employee who is 21 years of age, has performed services for the employer during the year and for at least three of the past five years and who has received at least $450 (in 2005 indexed) in compensation from the employer for the year. Employer contributions must be determined under a definite written allocation formula, must not discriminate in favor of the highly compensated and must bear a uniform relationship to compensation. Contributions cannot be conditioned on keeping them in the plan and the employer may not prohibit withdrawals. IRA withdrawal rules apply. Contributions may not exceed the lesser of 25% of compensation (after reduction by the contribution itself) or $42,000 (in 2005 indexed).[34] Thus, a SEP is a good way for a very small employer, even one self-employed person, to set up a plan and make deductible contributions at the higher limits. Variable annuities can be used effectively to fund a SEP.

A SAR-SEP is a simplified employee pension offered on a salary reduction basis. No new SAR-SEPs may be established after 1996. However, plans established prior to 1997 may continue to operate, receive contributions, and add new employees.[35] Small employers interested in salary reduction arrangements may turn to SIMPLE IRAs or possibly to SIMPLE 401(k) plans. Small employers also may facilitate their employees setting up their own IRAs by providing for payroll deduction. The potential availability of deductible contributions of up to $8,000 total (in 2005) for a husband and wife makes IRAs more worthwhile than ever. In addition, employers can facilitate saving and investing on a nonqualified basis by providing for payroll deduction for purchases of variable and fixed annuities and life, disability income and other types of insurance and savings products.

### *Roth IRA*

With a Roth IRA, individuals make contributions to IRAs that are not deductible but do have some significant tax advantages. Values in the IRAs accumulate tax-deferred and, provided they are held for at least five years, are not subject to income tax on distribution if:

- the owner is at least age 59½;
- the distribution is made after the owner's death;
- the distribution is attributable to the owner becoming disabled; or
- the distribution is for qualified first-time home buyer expenses, limited to $10,000 for the owner and family members.

A 10% penalty tax applies to distributions not meeting one of the above exceptions. However, it applies only to the taxable portion of the IRA (essentially the earnings since the contributions were made with after-tax dollars). There are no required minimum distributions with Roth IRAs.

The annual contribution limit is 100% of compensation, up to $4,000 in 2005 through 2007, available to both spouses, The limit is scheduled to rise to $5,000 in 2008, after which it is indexed. There is a catch-up provision for those age 50 and over. It is $500 in 2005 and increases to $1,000 in years 2006 through 2010.[36] Unlike traditional IRAs, contributions may be continued beyond age 70½. The annual contribution limit is reduced dollar-for-dollar for contributions to traditional IRAs. The phaseout provisions of Roth IRAs are somewhat more generous than for traditional IRAs. The amount that may be contributed by a single person begins to phase out at $95,000 and is eliminated at $110,000. For married couples filing jointly, the phase out begins at $150,000 and the amount eliminated at $160,000.[37]

## Tax Sheltered Annuities (403(b) Plans)

Tax sheltered annuities (also referred to as tax deferred annuities, although the latter term also is used to describe nonqualified annuities) are available to employees of organizations that are either tax exempt as described in IRC Section 501(c)(3) or public school systems.[38] Many variable annuities are purchased by these employees, especially school teachers and hospital employees, including a number of highly paid professional medical staff members. Many registered representatives concentrate on marketing these annuities almost exclusively. Products other than annuities also can be used.

TSAs usually are purchased by employees through their employer on a salary reduction basis by payroll deduction. The employer collects the contributions and remits them to the insurance company or other product issuer. The amount of salary reduction eligible in 2005 is $14,000, increasing to $15,000 in 2006, with indexing after that.[39] A special additional limit may be available to employees of most 501(c)(3) organizations who have completed 15 years of service. The catch-up provision for those age 50 and over also is available in the amounts of $4,000 in 2005, increasing to $5,000 in 2006 and indexed after that.[40] The overall limits (lesser of 100% of compensation or $42,000, indexed in 2005) of qualified plans apply.[41]

Most of the provisions of other plans discussed above also apply to TSAs. There are provisions for employer contributions and matching but matching contributions are not common among plans involving teachers and hospital employees. Nondiscrimination rules apply when there are employer contributions, of course, and, to a lesser extent, to salary reduction contributions. The 10% penalty for distributions made before age 59½ applies with most of the same exceptions. There is an additional exception for an employee who separates from service after attaining age 55.[42] It is more common for employees to borrow from their plans than for them to take premature distributions. On the other hand, the loan is treated as a premature distribution if it is not repaid within five years. However, a loan used to acquire a dwelling that within a reasonable time is to be used as the participant's principal residence is not subject to the five-year repayment provision.[43] Minimum distributions are required to begin by April 1 of the year following the year in which the taxpayer turns age 70½ or retires, whichever is later.[44]

## 457 Plans

IRC Section 457 plans are available to employees of state and local governments and to some employees of tax-exempt organizations. So-called "eligible" plans usually have participants who are rank-and-file employees and these plans resemble the plans discussed just above. "Ineligible" plans are limited to a select group of management or highly compensated employees (a "top hat" group). They resemble the nonqualified retirement plans discussed next in this chapter.

Salary deferral contributions to eligible plans are limited to 100% of compensation, up to $14,000 in 2005, increasing to $15,000 in 2006, and indexed after that.[45] There are two catch-up provisions. Employees age 50 and over may defer an additional $4,000 in 2005, increasing to $5,000 in 2006 and beyond. During the employees' final three years before retirement, they may generally defer twice the amount they could normally defer.[46]

Eligible IRC Section 457 plans have required minimum distribution provisions. They are similar to other plans discussed earlier in this chapter, beginning in the later of the calendar year following the year the employee reaches age 70½ or the year he retires.[47] These plans have one additional provision for distributions; they may be made if there is an unforeseeable emergency, which is defined as extraordinary and unforeseeable circumstances arising out of events beyond the control of the employees.[48]

## Nonqualified Retirement Plans

Some employees, especially the more highly compensated, will need more retirement income than can be provided through qualified retirement plans. These plans, plus social security benefits, total a smaller percentage of higher paid employees' working years' income, because of the caps on social security retirement contributions and resulting benefits. To add to the retirement incomes of these employees, employers turn to nonqualified retirement plans such as supplemental retirement, deferred compensation, and employee bonus arrangements.

Supplemental retirement plans and deferred compensation plans (these terms sometimes are used interchangeably) operate in much the same way. An employer (for this discussion a regular C corporation) sets up a plan whereby either the employer makes contributions in addition to usual compensation (a supplemental retirement plan) or the employee forgoes or reduces compensation and has the employer make contributions (a deferred compensation plan). Since the arrangement is not a qualified retirement plan, contributions are not deductible when set aside but they are not included in the employee's current income because under the terms of the plan, these rights are both nontransferable and subject to a substantial risk of forfeiture.[49] This usually means that the employer owns the financial services product into which contributions are made.

At a later time—at retirement or other time in the future, or at the employee's death prior to retirement—supplemental or deferred compensation is paid out. At that time, the employer is entitled to take a deduction for amounts attributable to prior contributions that are paid to the employee. The employee includes those amounts as income.[50] Thus, the employee has postponed tax on the amounts until retirement when, presumably, he is in a lower income tax bracket. The employer did not get deductions over the years as contributions were made but does get deductions as amounts are paid out—better late than never. And besides, since this has been a plan for the more highly compensated, a group that may include the principals of the business, it is an incentive for those most valuable to the success of the business.

Note that new rules regarding nonqualified deferred compensation plans have been enacted. Among the new rules is a requirement that distributions generally can be made only on the occurrence of one of the following: separation from service; upon the disability of the participant; death; a fixed time (or pursuant to a fixed scheduled) specified in the plan at the date of the deferral; a change in the ownership or effective control of the corporation or assets of the corporation; or the occurrence of an unforeseeable emergency. In addition, certain key employees of publicly traded corporations may not take distributions until six months after separation from service.[51]

If the employer will make contributions over the years, and in that way informally fund the plan so that the needed money is most likely to be in place, the contributions will go to purchase a financial product or products. If the contributions are used to purchase variable or fixed annuities, the "nonnatural person" rule comes into play. When an annuity contract is owned by a corporation, partnership, or trust, "the income on the contract," (essentially the gain each year over the premiums paid) is taxable. (See Chapter 12 for further discussion of this rule.)

Though the rule with respect to annuities was different some years back, the nonnatural person rule puts annuities in a position similar to most other products. Life insurance stands pretty much alone as a product where the earnings are deferred into the future; where life insurance is appropriate to provide the informal funding, it should be considered. But if life insurance is not appropriate, for whatever reason, one should do the calculations, compare annuities with other products, especially giving weight to the income options, and choose the best product for informal funding.

## Executive Equity Plans

So-called executive equity plans for providing supplemental retirement benefits operate differently. Here, the employer (a C corporation) arranges to provide increased compensation to the employee so that a product may be purchased to fund supplemental benefits. The additional compensation is a currently deductible business expense for the employer, provided that the employee's total compensation is a reasonable amount,[52] and the employee includes it as additional income. Sometimes, the employer advances an additional amount that is sufficient for the employee to pay the income tax on the increased compensation thereby maintaining the employee's take home pay. This arrangement is sometimes referred to as a "double bonus" plan.

The employee owns the annuity or other financial product and, as a result, there are no restrictions on what can be done with it. For that reason, executive equity plans are offered to only the most valuable of employees, including the principals of the business who are employees. The "nonnatural person" rule does not apply to a variable or fixed annuity purchased by the employee because a natural person owns it. And a variable annuity is a most effective way of providing supplemental retirement income.

The supplemental retirement, deferred compensation, and executive equity plans we have discussed here are in their most straight-forward form. There are a great many variations of them, including the use of several kinds of trusts, to effect some measure of security from the creditors of the corporation and to impose at least some restrictions on the rights of either the employer or employee, depending on the type of plan. These variations are beyond the scope of this book.

## Education Funding

The education of children is one of the major reasons listed for accumulating money. The cost of education continues to rise faster than the overall rate of inflation so that today's college costs, high as they are, will be exceeded by costs in the future. And people's ability to pay continues to decline. At the same time, the gulf in earnings between those with college educations and those without is widening. Clearly, saving and investing in advance is called for.

### *From Personal Resources*

Funds for education that have been saved in advance are the best, of course. Money that is saved in savings accounts, certificates of deposit, stocks, bonds, mutual funds, life insurance cash values, and the values in annuity contracts have the fewest strings attached and can be used at will for the most part. (See further discussion in this chapter and in Chapter 12 on gifts and withdrawals.) When personal resources fall short, some students will be able to qualify for financial aid and many more may resort to student loans.

Since qualifying for financial aid is not easy, it would seem shortsighted to rely on its availability. It should be considered a fall-back position when other education financing is not available and family financial resources are limited. Student loans are much easier to get but they are loans that the student will need to pay back, usually for many years, following completion of college or professional school.

### *Tax Credits and Deductions*

A number of income tax credits and income tax deductions are available with respect to education funding. It is a rather intricate system with different credits and deductions applying to different expenses and different phase-out income amounts applying to different provisions, plus the fact that, in some cases, if you use one, you cannot use another. This discussion will hit the high points with no attempt to be completely thorough as to the particulars of the provisions.

The Hope Scholarship Credit[53] provides an income tax credit against taxes of up to $1,500 (as indexed) for qualifying expenses during each of the first two years of college. There are phase-out provisions. The Lifetime Learning Credit[54] against taxes is 20% of the first $10,000 for qualifying education expenses (up to $2,000 per year) during any year of post-secondary education. The two credits cannot both be used for the same expenses. There also are income-based phase-out provisions for these credits.

Interest paid on student loans is deductible from income.[55] The deduction is available from gross income so that the taxpayer need not itemize (and thus need not have deductions in excess of the standard deduction to benefit) to use it. It is for up to $2,500 of interest paid for qualified higher education expenses. Income phase-out provisions apply. Another education expense deduction of up to $4,000 applies but is set to expire at the end of 2005.[56]

### *Tax-Favored Education Savings*

Contributions to Coverdell Education Savings Accounts[57] are not tax deductible but earnings in the accounts are tax-free. Contributions of up to $2,000 may be placed in the accounts and may be distributed to pay qualified education expenses, which include elementary and secondary school expenses as well as post-secondary. Any balance remaining when the beneficiary reaches age 30 generally must be distributed. There are income-based phase-out provisions applicable to the amount of the contribution permitted.

IRC Section 529 Plans, or Qualified Tuition Programs, are state-sponsored or privately-sponsored arrangements that allow a taxpayer to purchase prepaid tuition credits or certificates, or to make contributions to educational savings accounts. There are significant differences among the plans available. Contributions or credit purchases are limited in some way, e.g., five years of education expenses or a dollar amount. Contributions are not tax deductible but earnings are deferred and payments for qualified higher education expenses are not taxable. Distributions of earnings that are not used for such expenses are subject to a 10% penalty.

Distributions from regular IRAs made prior to age 59½, used for qualified higher education expenses for the taxpayer, the taxpayer's spouse, or the child or grandchild of either spouse, are not subject to the 10% penalty for premature distributions.[58] Of course, the regular income tax applies to such distribution since the contributions had been income tax deductible. In general, the same treatment is given to distributions for education expenses from SIMPLE IRAs, SEPs, SIMPLE 401(k) plans, tax sheltered annuities, and 457 plans. Roth IRAs are different in that earnings distributed for educational expenses are not subject to the 10% penalty and any contributions themselves included in any such distribution have already been taxed. (These plans are discussed earlier in this chapter.)

United States Savings Bonds also may be used for accumulating money for education expenses.[59] In addition, when the taxpayer-student is employed, certain tuition reimbursement arrangements may be available from the employer and personal education expenses may be deductible, although this deduction is an itemized deduction and may or may not be useful, depending on total deductions compared with the standard deduction.

### *Role of Annuities*

Variable annuities can play a significant role in accumulating money for college. But as we have seen, things are not as simple as merely saving money and then using it, as with a savings account. A parent who purchases a variable annuity when a son or daughter is young can pay continuing premiums into a variable account, engage in dollar cost averaging, and accumulate a substantial sum by the time the child is ready for college. During the accumulation years, earnings on the savings and investments have been deferred so that the parent was not required to reduce payments somewhat in order to also pay income tax on the earnings each year.

If the parent has reached the age of 59½ by the time withdrawals are needed, income tax will be limited to the parent's rate on the amount withdrawn (until all of the earnings have been withdrawn, after which the remaining amounts may be withdrawn without tax). If the parent makes withdraws prior to age 59½, the 10% penalty on premature distributions applies.[60] This very well may be a disadvantage but someone in that position should do the tax calculation to be sure how disadvantageous it is. We always like to assume our customers will have high incomes when their children are ready for college, but some will not. Someone who has bought a variable annuity primarily for retirement, and then is confronted with higher college costs than anticipated, may have to turn to his variable annuity. The tax cost, including the penalty, may be worth incurring in such a situation.

A parent who is several years away from age 59½ at the time of college expenses may make delayed use of a variable annuity. The parent may be willing to borrow, using a second mortgage credit line for example, to pay the major costs of college knowing full well that he can take withdrawals without a penalty in a few years and pay off the second mortgage balance. Interest on the second mortgage credit line loan usually will be deductible. The calculation of the cost of the whole process takes several steps, taking into account deferral of tax on the variable annuity earnings, deductibility of the mortgage interest, and tax on the withdrawals (but no penalty tax).

It often is grandparents who fund a major portion of their grandchildren's college expenses. When a grandparent purchases a variable annuity, the same deferral of taxes on the earnings occurs. When the grandchild reaches college age, the grandparent is over age 59½ and can make withdrawals without penalty. Presumably, the grandparent is in a lower tax bracket than when the earnings deferrals were taking place while the grandparent was working. The grandparent pays the tax on the withdrawals and gives them to the parents or grandchildren for college expenses. In this case, the grandparent is in control of whom is to receive the money; should the grandchild not be a good college candidate or one or both of the parents not be as dependable as the grandparent would like to see, the grandparent can act accordingly.

Note that when the grandparent gives money for college to the parent or grandchild, the gift is subject to the federal gift tax. However, a gift equal to the annual exclusion amount ($11,000 as indexed) may be given each year to any number of recipients without incurring a gift tax. And if both grandparent-spouses join in the gift an amount equal to twice the annual exclusion amount may be given to each recipient without gift tax.[61] When there are several grandchildren and two parents, there are quite a few recipients. Obviously, a variable annuity can work very well in that situation.

## Gifts of Annuities

From time to time a family member will want to give a financial asset to another family member. He may want to do so either to help the other family member financially or so that the asset is removed from the estate of the owner for Federal estate tax purposes, or for both reasons. When the gift is to be of an annuity issued after April 22, 1987, things can be a little more complicated. The annuity owner has two choices: surrender the annuity and make a gift of the cash or make a gift of the annuity itself.

If the owner surrenders the annuity contract, the income tax on the gain in the contract must be paid. Further, if the owner is under age 59½, a 10% penalty applies to the amount subject to tax. Gifts of the cash are subject to gift tax, as just above, with the availability of the annual gift tax exclusion of $11,000 per recipient (as indexed).

The second choice is to make a gift of the annuity. However, in such a case, the person making the gift is treated as having received an amount equal to the gain in the contract for income tax purposes.[62] The donee of the gift of the annuity receives a contract where the investment in the contract now includes all of the previous gain. Therefore, future gain will be calculated from this higher starting point and income tax deferral of earnings goes on. The gift of the annuity is subject to the gift tax. The value above the annual exclusion amount ($11,000 or $22,000 if the owner-donor and spouse join in the gift, as indexed) will require a gift tax to be paid unless a portion of the donor's unified estate and gift tax credit is used. Again, careful consideration and a series of calculations are necessary in deciding which way, if either, to go.

## Gifts to Charity

Considerable use is made of annuities in estate planning, especially planning involving gifts to charity in one form or another. For the most part, however, these are not commercial annuities, the subject of this book. Here, the dictionary definition of annuity is applicable: a payment of a fixed sum of money at regular intervals of time, especially yearly (annual and annuity are from the same root). We will briefly review some of these charitable gift planning techniques.

There are several overriding considerations in charitable gift planning. One is to reduce the size of a person's estate, for federal estate tax purposes, and at the same time make a gift to a charity the donor is interested in supporting. Another is to reduce current income taxes somewhat by making the gift. A third is to not necessarily give up all of the benefit of the property given during the lifetime of the donor or one or more of his beneficiaries. Quite frequently, the property to be given has appreciated significantly in value and would be subject to a substantial capital gains tax if sold by the donor instead of given away. Assuming the charity to which the property is given is an exempt organization under IRC Section 170(c) it will not be subject to income tax if the property is sold by the charity for cash.

An individual may enter into a charitable gift annuity arrangement. This is an agreement between a charity and the person whereby the person donates property in exchange for an annuity to be paid by the charity for the person's life. A commercial annuity could be used but usually is not because the charity wants to make immediate use of the property or sell it and put the sale proceeds to use. The annuity payments are made directly from the charity and backed by the charity's assets and good name. Obviously, one would want to enter into such an arrangement only with a charity in a position to make good on the lifetime income commitment.

## Charitable Trusts

An often used charitable gift planning arrangement is the charitable remainder trust (CRT). A CRT involves an irrevocable gift in trust to a charity with payments continuing to a noncharitable beneficiary for life or for a term of years. At the death of the individual or at the end of the term of years, the property remaining in the trust, the remainder interest, becomes the property of the charity. There is a minimum (5%) that must be paid out of the trust each year, as well as a maximum permitted payout of 50% (beginning with transfers after June 18, 1997). Furthermore, the value of the remainder interest must be at least 10% of the initial net fair market value of the property placed in the trust (for transfers made after July 28, 1997). The requirements for setting up a CRT are complex[63] but charities that attract a number of these gifts (e.g., colleges and community and arts organizations) have put together standardized procedures for implementing them. If certain requirements are met, the gift of the property can result in an immediate income tax charitable deduction for the donor.[64]

There are two types of CRTs: the charitable remainder annuity trust and the charitable remainder unitrust. The annuity trust provides for a fixed payment of at least 5% and not more than 50% of the trust's fair market value at inception. Additional gifts to the trust may not be made. The unitrust provides for a variable amount to be paid to the noncharitable beneficiary. The percentage (at least 5% and not more than 50%) to be paid is fixed but the assets in the trust are valued annually resulting in possible variable payments. A unitrust may be designed to pay out only the net income of the trust.

In recent years, CRTs have been combined with what is referred to as a "wealth replacement trust," actually an irrevocable trust funded with life insurance. Typically, an individual gives appreciated property in trust to a charity with the individual retaining a life income from the property value. The wealth replacement trust purchases a life insurance policy on the donor, payable to the donor's beneficiaries, usually family members. Because of income tax savings resulting from the charitable gift deduction, dollars presumably are available with which to pay life insurance premiums. When the donor dies, the remainder interest goes to the charity and the beneficiaries receive life insurance proceeds. These are happy results when the arrangements have been designed properly.

With a charitable lead trust, the income and remainder roles are reversed. Under the trust, the charity receives the income (lead) interest and the remainder interest comes back to the donor or the beneficiaries at death or after a term of years. The lead trust must pay income in the form of either a guaranteed interest or a unitrust interest. The guaranteed interest is of a fixed amount; the unitrust interest is of a fixed percentage of the value of the property in the trust.[65]

Finally, there is the "pooled income fund." Donors make gifts of property that are placed in a pool. Each donor names a beneficiary to receive income from the fund, often for the life of the beneficiary. The amount of income generally is determined by the earnings of the fund. The charity receives the remainder interest in the property.

# Chapter Endnotes

1. IRC Secs. 402(a), 403(a), 404.
2. IRC Secs. 402(a), 403(a).
3. IRC Sec. 402.
4. IRC Secs. 72, 402(a), 403(a).
5. IRC Sec. 501.
6. IRC Sec. 415(b).
7. IRC Sec. 415(c).
8. IRC Sec. 401(a).
9. IRC Secs. 401(a)(3), 410(a)(1).
10. Treas. Reg. §§1.410(b)-2(b)(2)(i).
11. IRC Sec. 401(a)(26).
12. IRC Sec. 401(a)(4).
13. IRC Sec. 415.
14. IRC Secs. 401(a)(7), 411(a)(2).
15. IRC Sec. 401(a)(14).
16. IRC Sec. 401(a)(9).
17. IRC Sec. 401(a)(11).
18. IRC Sec. 416.
19. IRC Sec. 401(a)(13).
20. IRC Sec. 401(a)(9)(A).
21. IRC Sec. 401(a)(9)(C).
22. IRC Sec. 401(a)(9)(B)(ii), Treas. Reg. §1.401(a)(9)-3, A-1(a).
23. IRC Sec. 401(a)(9)(B)(iv), Treas. Reg. §1.401(a)(9)-5, A-5(c)(2).
24. IRC Sec. 401(k)
25. IRC Sec. 402(g).
26. IRC Secs. 401(k)(3), 401(k)(11), 40l(k)(12).
27. IRC Sec. 401(k)(11).
28. IRC Sec. 402(c)(3).
29. IRC Secs. 219(b), 219(c).
30. IRC Sec. 219(g)(3)(B).
31. IRC Sec. 72(t).
32. Treas. Reg. §1.408-8, A-5(a).
33. IRC Secs. 408(p), 414(v), 72(t).
34. IRC Secs. 402(h)(2), 415(c)(1)(A).
35. IRC Sec. 408(k)(6).
36. IRC Sec. 219(b)(5)(A).
37. IRC Sec. 408A(c)(3)(A).
38. IRC Sec. 403(b).
39. IRC Sec. 402(g)(1).
40. IRC Sec. 414(v)(2).

41. IRC Sec. 415(c), News Release IR 2004-127.
42. IRC Sec. 72(t)(2)(A)(v).
43. IRC Sec. 72(p).
44. IRC Sec. 401(a)(9).
45. IRC Sec. 457(b)(2).
46. IRC Secs. 457(b)(3), 414(v)(5); Treas. Reg. §1.457-4(c)(3).
47. IRC Sec. 457(d)(2).
48. Treas. Reg. §1.457-6(c)(2).
49. IRC Secs. 402(b)(1), 403(c), 83(a).
50. IRC Sec. 404(a)(5).
51. IRC Sec. 409A.
52. IRC Sec. 162(a)..
53. IRC Sec. 25A.
54. IRC Sec. 25A.
55. IRC Sec. 221.
56. IRC Sec. 222.
57. IRC Sec. 530.
58. IRC Sec. 72(t)(2)(E),
59. IRC Sec. 135.
60. IRC Sec. 72(q).
61. IRC Sec. 2503(b).
62. IRC Sec. 72(e)(4)(C).
63. See generally IRC Secs. 170, 664.
64. IRC Secs. 170(f)(2)(B), 664(d).
65. IRC Sec. 170(f)(2)(B).

# Chapter 12

# Taxation of Variable Annuities

## Federal Income Tax

Because annuities, including variable annuities, accumulate substantial amounts of money that are withdrawn and/or distributed in the future, their income tax aspects are of importance. So, too, are their estate tax and gift tax aspects. In this discussion, we will look at the principal provisions of the federal tax laws affecting annuities. Annuities also may be subject to applicable state income, gift, and estate or inheritance tax laws. In most instances, federal taxes are considerably more substantial and, therefore more important, but state taxes should be taken into account.

In Chapter 11, we consider annuities that are part of qualified retirement plans. These annuity premiums, which are plan contributions, usually are tax deductible. That is not the case with respect to annuities purchased outside of these plans. The general rule is that these premiums, whether paid on a single premium basis or on a periodic premium basis, are non-deductible. As we shall see, these non-deductible premiums are the basis for determining what is referred to as the investment in the contract, the amount that the owner may receive without any further income tax.

The interest or earnings credited to an annuity, which meet conditions of the Internal Revenue Code,[1] are not taxed at the time they are credited provided that they remain inside the contract and are not withdrawn or distributed. This statement is generally true only so long as the owner of the annuity contract is a natural person. If premiums are paid after February 28, 1986 into a deferred annuity contract owned by a corporation or other entity not considered to be a natural person under the law, the interest or earnings credited each year are taxable currently.[2] To be more precise, the amount to be taxed is calculated by taking the sum of the net surrender value at the end of the taxable year and any amounts distributed during the taxable year and prior taxable years. From this amount is subtracted the sum of the net premiums for the current and prior taxable years and any amounts included in gross income for prior taxable years (presumably amounts withdrawn).[3]

The nonnatural person rule does not apply to annuities held by qualified retirement plans, IRAs, tax sheltered annuities, "eligible" 457 plans, single premium immediate annuities, and damage award payouts. When an annuity contract is held by a trust, corporation, or other nonnatural person acting as an agent for a natural person, interest and earnings credited are income tax-deferred.[4] The place where this latter provision applies most frequently is trusts. Generally, the IRS has indicated that it views most types of trusts that have natural persons as beneficiaries to be acting as agents for the natural persons.

Note that the nonnatural person rule is directed at annuities where premiums have been paid after February 28, 1986. Thus, if all premiums were paid after that date, the rule clearly applies. Just as clearly, it does not appear to apply where all premiums were paid before that date. When some were paid before this date and some after, things are not so clear. It would not be a good practice to subject a customer to this possibility if it can be avoided by not involving a nonnatural person. Finally, there is no doubt that the rule applies to annuity contracts purchased today.

## Withdrawals

When money is withdrawn from an annuity, as either a partial withdrawal or partial surrender, there is income tax to be considered. There also may be a 10% penalty tax for a premature distribution in some instances. In addition, there may be a surrender charge applicable. The applicability and workings of the surrender charge are discussed in Chapter 8. But since the surrender charge and particularly the penalty tax are sometimes confused, we mention the surrender charge here. If the surrender charge applies because the amount surrendered is in excess of the surrender-charge-free amount permitted under the contract and because the applicable surrender charge period has not run, the charge will be levied against the amount withdrawn. This has no effect on whether the penalty tax applies, except that it applies only to the amount of withdrawal included in income for the year.

Before we consider the penalty tax further, let us look at taxation of the withdrawal itself. If the annuity was entered into after August 13, 1982, the current rule referred to as the "interest first" rule applies. If the contract was entered into before August 14, 1982, the old rule referred to as the "cost recovery rule" applies. Since the old rule is more favorable when there are withdrawals, an important point is to attempt to preserve its applicability when changes, particularly tax-free exchanges, are made to old contracts. We will look at this point later in this chapter.

Under the interest first rule, amounts received are taxable as income to the extent that the cash value of the contract immediately before the partial withdrawal or surrender exceeds the investment in the contract.[5] The investment in the contract, paid with previously taxed money, is then received without tax. Thus, all interest and earnings are distributed before any of the investment in the contract. As a result, when an annuity owner makes a series of withdrawals, the withdrawals are fully taxable until all of the interest and earnings have been distributed.

Under the cost recovery rule, the owner receives first whatever investment in the contract was paid before August 14, 1982, which has been taxed previously, on a tax-free basis. Withdrawals of amounts that are the investment in the contract continue on a tax-free basis until that entire amount has been recovered. Interest and earnings are taxed only after the recovery of the investment (cost) paid before the 1982 date.[6]

The reason that this portion of the law was changed was to limit the tax advantages of deferred annuities to long range investment purposes. Congress was persuaded that the advantage of tax deferral of buildup in values of annuities should not be coupled with the further advantage of the ability to withdraw at will with no tax payable until all of the investment in the contract had first been withdrawn. Other savings and investment products did not enjoy both of these advantages. (But note that partial surrenders of the cash values of life insurance generally still are governed by the cost recovery rule.)

An annuity entered into before August 14, 1982, may have some of its premiums paid before the rule change and some of them afterward. In such a case, amounts withdrawn are allocable first to investments made prior to August 14, 1982, then to income from those investments, then to income from investments made after August 13, and finally to investments in the contract made after August 13.[7] In other words, the sequence is tax-free, then fully taxed, then fully taxed, and then tax-free.

A related consideration has to do with when an annuity, subject to the cost recovery rule, is involved in a tax-free exchange under Internal Revenue Code Section 1035 (the provisions of which we will take up shortly). Such a replacement contract succeeds to the status of the surrendered contract, for purposes of determining when amounts are to be considered invested in the contract and for computing the taxability of any withdrawals.[8] Investment in the replacement contract is considered made on, before or after August 13, 1982 to the same extent the investment was made on, before or after August 13 in the replaced contract.

## Premature Distributions

With respect to nonqualified annuities, the 10% penalty is applied to that portion of the distribution or withdrawal that is includable in income. If there is a substantial distribution, e.g., $50,000, and only a portion of it is subject to tax, e.g., $30,000, then the penalty applies to the $30,000 and amounts to $3,000. Of course, the $30,000 also is taxed at the taxpayer's marginal rate for the year of the distribution. When an annuity owner takes relatively smaller withdrawals, it may be the case that all of the amount withdrawn in a particular year is subject to the penalty tax because all of the withdrawal is allocable to interest and earnings and none to the investment in the contract.

In addition to distributions from qualified plans, tax sheltered annuities, "eligible" 457 plans, and IRAs, the nonqualified annuity penalty tax does not apply to a distribution:

1. made on or after the taxpayer reaches age 59½;
2. attributable to the taxpayer's disability;
3. allocable to investment in the contract before August 14, 1982, including earnings on pre-August 14 investment;
4. made after the death of the annuity holder;
5. made under an immediate annuity contract;
6. made from an annuity purchased and held by an employer upon the termination of a qualified retirement plan;

7. under a qualified funding asset (i.e., any annuity contract which is purchased as a result of a liability to pay for damages which resulted from physical injury or sickness); or

8. that is part of a series of substantially equal periodic payments made (not less frequently than annually) for the life or life expectancy of the taxpayer or the joint lives or joint life expectancies of the taxpayer and his designated beneficiary.[9]

When the interest first rule and the 10% penalty became law, it did not take practitioners long to reason that if their customers bought several annuities, instead of just one, they could ameliorate some of the effects of the new rules by taking substantial or complete surrenders from one of them, leaving the others accumulating interest and earnings. Then, only part of the money would be subject to tax and the penalty, and the rest of the money could be recovered without tax or penalty. Since that was not the intention of the changes in the law, there is a further provision that all annuity contracts entered into after October 21, 1988, which are issued by the same company to the same policyholder during any calendar year, will be treated as one annuity contract for purposes of determining the amount of any distribution that is includable in income.[10] Again, this provision does not apply to qualified retirement plans, TSAs, IRAs, "eligible" 457 plans, and immediate annuities.

Before leaving this discussion of premature distributions, it is helpful to remember that qualified retirement plans have their own rules with respect to premature distributions as do IRAs, TSAs, and "eligible" 457 plans. These rules are discussed in Chapter 11.

## Section 1035 Exchanges

Variable annuity owners sometimes want to "trade in" their contracts for newer ones because of interest rates on the guaranteed account, because of the availability of new optional benefits, because of services or types of investments available with a new contract, because of insurance company solvency concerns (although this is a lesser consideration for variable annuities than for fixed annuities), and for other reasons. As noted earlier in this book, it is the position of regulators that exchanges of one variable annuity for another rarely is justified. That is because the advantages of new contracts often do not outweigh the costs, particularly the imposition of new surrender charge periods. However, there are times when exchanges are justified and there are numerous times when exchanges of life insurance policies and fixed annuities for variable annuities can be justified.

The reason the owner of a life insurance policy or annuity contract would want to make an exchange, instead of merely cashing in one contract and purchasing another, is so that there will be no taxable event at the time of the exchange. That is, there will be no inclusion of income subject to income tax. Tax-free exchanges of annuity and life insurance contracts are controlled by Internal Revenue Code Section 1035. That section says that the following exchanges may be made without current income taxation:

1. an annuity contract for another annuity contract;
2. a life insurance policy for an annuity contract;
3. an endowment contract for an annuity contract;
4. a life insurance policy for another life insurance policy;
5. a life insurance policy for an endowment contract; and
6. an endowment contract for an endowment contract that will begin making payments no later than payments would have commenced under the old contract.

Note that there is no provision for exchanging an annuity contract for a life insurance policy. Generally, there can be no exchange that postpones further the event of taxation with respect to the contract. Note also that the two provisions involving endowment contracts have been reduced in significance because current Internal Revenue Code definitions of life insurance make new endowment policies difficult to design. Here, again, we should point out that IRC Section 1035 does not apply to qualified retirement plans, IRAs, "eligible" 457 plans, and TSAs, which have their own rollover provisions.

If an annuity is exchanged for another annuity, both contracts must be payable to the same person or persons to qualify under IRC Section 1035.[11] The new contract can be issued by the same company or a different company.[12] Not withstanding the language referring to "an" annuity in these cases, there are rulings approving of exchange of one annuity for two annuities issued by the same company and for two annuities for one annuity in the same or different companies.[13]

After an IRC Section 1035 exchange, the cost basis (what has been referred to here as the investment in the annuity contract) of the new contract usually is the same as the old one. And in applicable cases, the cost recovery rule has been preserved, as discussed earlier in this chapter. The cost basis will not be the same if the annuity owner has received some cash in connection with the exchange. In that event, any gain, is recognized for income tax purposes.[14]

Further, if the exchanged contract has a loan outstanding, the situation may be complicated.[15] Since annuities usually do not have loans (partial withdrawals generally have been used instead), they are not a big issue. However, loans against life insurance policies can be an imposing problem. If a loan is merely erased during the exchange, the cash value securing the loan is considered to have been distributed and may result in a gain subject to current income tax. One should proceed cautiously when considering an exchange involving a life insurance policy with a large loan outstanding.

## Complete and Partial Surrenders

When an annuity owner surrenders the annuity in full, and does not elect to take payout provisions (to be discussed shortly), the owner must include in income for the year the difference between what was received and the contract's cost basis (or investment in the contract).

In most instances, the cost basis is the premiums paid; however, there will be reductions in the basis for any distributions that have not been included in income. For example, if the owner has taken partial withdrawals or surrenders, some of which were not includable in income because of operation of the cost recovery rule or because all of the interest and earnings had been distributed first under the interest first rule, the cost basis will be reduced by the amount of the nonincludable distributions. Also, if the annuity contract is one that has paid dividends, the dividends are considered return of premiums. The return of premium is not subject to tax but it reduces the cost basis or investment in the contract. Once the cost basis of the contract has been determined, the full surrender is taxed under the cost recovery rule.[16] The gain is ordinary income, not capital gain.

## Sale of an Annuity

Since an annuity is a piece of property, it can be sold. Generally, when there is a sale, the owner is taxed in the same way as when there has been a complete surrender. If the sale occurs after the owner has begun payout provisions (which we will take up next) the cost basis is adjusted for those amounts that have been received but were not includable in income. Apparently, if the sale has resulted in a loss, because the sale proceeds are less than the cost basis, the owner will have realized an ordinary loss. Such losses generally may not be deducted by individuals who entered into the annuity contract for personal reasons but may be claimed in connection with the owner's trade or business or in a transaction entered into for profit.[17] If the new owner elects to take payout provisions, the payments will be taxed in the same way they would have been had the original owner retained the contract, except that they will be calculated with the new owner's life expectancy, etc. If the new owner is a corporation or other nonnatural person, those provisions will apply to annual increases in the contract values.

## Taxation of Payouts

As discussed in Chapter 7, a variable annuity owner may elect a fixed payout or a variable payout, with a number of options available with either of the two. Income taxation of the payout depends on which of the two has been selected although the principles involved are quite similar. The basic rule is that the purchaser is to receive the investment in the contract in equal tax-free installments over the payment period. The rest of the amount received each year is included in gross income. Thus, each payment is taxable in part and tax-free in part.

### *Fixed Payout*

With respect to a fixed payout, the determination of what portion is taxed and what portion is not taxed is made using an exclusion ratio, which may be expressed as a fraction or as a percentage. It is arrived at by dividing the investment in the contract by the expected return. The exclusion ratio, so calculated, is applied to each annuity payment to find the portion that is excludable; then, the balance is includable in the year it is received.[18]

To illustrate, let us use an uncomplicated example: a single life (a male), age 65, with no term certain or refund feature. Let us suppose that the life income is $750 per month, $9,000 per year, and that the investment in the contract is $100,000. The numerator for the exclusion ratio is the $100,000 investment in the contract; the denominator is found by multiplying the annual return of $9,000 by 20, the unisex expected return multiple at age 65 in Table V of the IRS actuarial tables for taxing annuities; that figure is $180,000. When $100,000 is divided by $180,000, the result is 55.55%, the percentage of each year's payment that is excludable from income, approximately $5,000. The remainder, $4,000, is received as previously taxed income. However, it is likely that there is a limit to the number of years the $4,000 is not subject to tax.

If our example had been a fixed period or fixed amount, the denominator would be found by multiplying the annual return by the known number of years and months. The division of the investment in the contract by that expected return would result in a percentage of each year's payment that would be excludable from income, with the balance of the yearly payment includable.

In the case of joint life annuities, there are IRS actuarial tables indicating expectancy multiples; here, it depends on whether the payments will continue to the second annuitant (joint and survivor) or end when the first of the joint annuitants dies. When there is a term certain guarantee or a refund to a beneficiary, there are tables that establish percentage depending on the age of the annuitant. The applicable percentage is applied as a reduction in the investment in the contract.

### *Variable Payout*

When there is variable payout, the amount to be paid out each year is not known at the beginning. Therefore, it is the excludable portion that is calculated. This is done by dividing the investment in the contract by the expected return multiple in Table V.[19] Continuing with the same example as above under the fixed payout, $100,000 divided by 20 is $5,000. In our example of a presumed $9,000 payout, at least in the first year, $5,000 of the amount is excludable and $4,000 is includable. Of course, this is simply an example—keep in mind that it is unlikely that fixed payouts and variable payouts would be the same even in the first year. For that reason, it is probable that the difference in the way the two types of payouts are taxed should not be a significant factor in the decision of whether to elect a fixed or a variable payout.

The single life unisex table, Table V, was used in our example because the unisex tables must be used if the investment in the contract includes investments (premiums) made after June 30, 1986. If there are no investments in the contract after that date, sex-distinct tables are used.[20] (One transitional rule allows for an election to use the unisex tables even where there have been no investments in the contract after June 30, 1986. Another provides for an election in some situations to have separate calculations when there have been investments made both before and after the June 30 date.).[21]

How long the annual amount excludable may continue to be excluded is dependent on the annuity starting date, the first day of the first period for which an annuity payment is received.[22] If the annuity starting date is after December 31, 1986, amounts are excluded until the total investment in the contract has been received; after that no amounts are excludable from income and all amounts received are includable.[23] On the other hand, if the annuity starting date was before January 1, 1987, the exclusions continue so that the person receiving the annuity has the same amounts excluded from income throughout the entire payment period, not withstanding the fact that the full investment in the contract already has been received.

## Death of an Owner

The death of an annuity owner has both income and estate tax ramifications. Let us consider the income tax aspects first. When the owner dies before the entire interest in the contract has been paid out, certain distributions must be made. The distributions are a matter of tax policy; they are intended to prevent deferral of income tax on the gains in an annuity contract for years into the future by passing ownership from person to person but not taking taxable distributions.

In order for annuities issued after January 18, 1985 to receive the favorable treatment of deferral of tax on accumulations and spreading of tax on payouts, they must contain two provisions. First, if any owner dies after the annuity starting date but before the entire interest has been distributed, the remaining portion must be distributed at least as rapidly as under the method of distribution used by the owner at the time of death. Second, if the owner dies before the annuity starting date, the entire interest in the contract must be distributed within the five years following the owner's death.[24] Where there are joint owners of an annuity issued after April 22, 1987, the distribution requirements are applied when the first joint owner dies.[25] When a portion of the owner's interest is to be distributed to a designated beneficiary over the beneficiary's life (or over a period not extending beyond the life expectancy of the beneficiary) and the distribution to the beneficiary begins within one year following the owner's death, that portion is treated as distributed on the day the distribution begins.

When the designated beneficiary is the surviving spouse of the owner, there are special rules. When the spouse, as the designated beneficiary, becomes the new owner, she can take the place of the former owner.[26] If the annuity was still in the accumulation stage at the death of the original owner, the spouse can continue in that stage. She can add to the annuity if it is a flexible premium type. If the annuity was in the payout stage, the payout would continue according to the terms of the payout provisions. That is, if the provision was for the payout to continue for the remainder of 10 years, for example, then the payments would continue in that fashion. If the annuitant had outlived any guarantee period, payments would cease.

When the owner of an annuity issued after April 22, 1987 is a corporation or other nonnatural person, the primary annuitant is treated as the owner for purposes of applying the distribution rules taking effect at the death of the owner.[27] These distribution requirements are another factor when considering an exchange of an old contract. If a contract issued after January 18, 1985 is received in exchange for one issued before that date, it is considered a new contract and, as a result, subject to the distribution requirements.

The preceding distribution rules apply when the owner dies first or when the annuitant and owner are the same person. Although the majority of nonqualified annuities have the same person as owner and annuitant, sometimes they are different. In our discussion of education funding, there could have been an occasion where, for example, a grandparent could have been the owner while a child or grandchild was the annuitant.

When the annuitant dies first or the annuitant and owner dies, the death benefit as defined in the contract (see the discussion of death benefits in Chapter 7) is paid to the designated beneficiary. If the owner who is not the annuitant dies first, there may be a different death benefit payable. For example, one of the enhanced death benefit provisions may be in effect at the death of the annuitant or annuitant and owner. But merely the accumulated contract values at the death of the owner may be paid when the owner dies before the annuitant.

Whichever amount is paid at death, the amount is subject to federal income tax essentially the same as when the owner surrenders the contract prior to the annuity starting date. The gain in value over the investment in the contract is taxed as ordinary income in the year it is received. There is no exclusion from income tax as provided to life insurance death benefits. The beneficiary of death benefits does have one way to spread the tax. If the beneficiary elects within 60 days, he may apply the benefits under an installment or life income option. In that event, the payments are taxed under the payout provisions applicable to annuity owners described earlier in this chapter.[28]

## Federal Estate Tax

As we have seen throughout this book, the tax of the most concern with respect to annuities is the income tax. We have discussed deferral of tax during the time values are accumulated; we have looked at the taxation of withdrawals, including when penalties are applicable; and we have gone into the taxation connected with surrendering the contract or electing to take a fixed or variable payout of the contract values. All of these are important. But there are two other taxes that can be important at times.

The first of these is the federal estate tax. Annuities are property and usually are a part of the estates of people who die while owning them. If someone has been particularly successful at setting aside money and selecting funds that perform well, the contract value of the annuity will be substantial. It can add significantly to the other assets in the person's estate—the personal residence and any other real property, the values in qualified retirement plans, life insurance owned, other savings and investments, and, perhaps, an interest in a small business.

People often are complacent about the estate tax since it seems to take a significant amount of assets for an estate tax to be payable. Some of the complacence is understandable. Unless there are assets of more than $1,000,000, perhaps much more, after deduction of debts and funeral expenses, there is no tax because of the unified credit unless some of the credit has been used earlier to avoid gift tax. An estate has a credit to be deducted from the estate tax that would be due. Because, according to current law, the amount of the credit increases over the years, 2004 to 2009, the amount of assets that can be passed without estate tax rises from $1,500,000 to $3,500,000. In 2010, there is no estate tax; in 2011, the amount that may be passed without tax becomes $1,000,000 from then on. Few expect to see the law stay as it is and many expect there to be some estate tax after 2010.

A married individual can leave all of the assets to a spouse and have no taxable estate because of the unlimited marital deduction. But for many people, this would be short-sighted. If a person leaves all assets to a spouse, the spouse's estate will be subject to a sizable tax at the time of death. If the assets left continue to appreciate, as all hope they will, the tax is that much more before the remaining assets are available to children. It would have been better for the first spouse to leave at least the amount covered by the unified credit to children, with income going to the surviving spouse. Then, the second estate will be smaller by the unified credit covered amount. In these days of high divorce rates, it may be shortsighted to rely too much on the marital deduction. In fact, estate planning today often involves two or more families and must be done with care and deftness.

Another point to remember is what the estate tax rate is likely to be when it is assessed. Although the rates go from 18% to 55%, few estates will be taxed at the lowest rates. That is because of the way the calculation is made. The tax is calculated and then the unified credit is subtracted. This means that where the full unified credit is available, the first amount taxed is the amount above $1,000,000 to $3,500,000, depending on the year of death. For all intents and purposes, the minimum rate is somewhere between 41 and 45% in these cases. That makes the stakes high indeed. Anyone close to having an estate tax liability needs to engage in estate planning that will minimize, to the extent practicable, the estate tax to be paid by both spouses' estates.

A variable annuity in the accumulation phase will have a death benefit payable to a beneficiary, as discussed in Chapter 7 and earlier in this chapter. When the owner and annuitant dies, the value of the annuity, presumably the death benefit, is included in his estate.[29] When an annuitant who is not the owner dies, there is a payment to a beneficiary but the annuitant had no interest to be included in his estate. When an owner who is not the annuitant dies, the value of the annuity is what is referred to as replacement cost, the amount that it would cost to purchase a comparable annuity contract at the time of the owner's death.[30]

When an annuity is in the payout phase, the death benefit in the contract usually no longer is applicable. And the remaining value of the annuity depends on what type of payout provisions are operating. If a life income with no term certain or refund is in effect, nothing would be paid to a beneficiary and, for that reason, nothing would be includable in the owner's estate. Where there is a fixed period or fixed amount option selected, and all payments have not yet been received, the value of the unpaid installments would be includable. Similarly, where there is a life income with a period certain in effect, and the annuitant-owner dies before the period certain has run, the value of the unpaid installments is includable.[31] The value to be included is the present value of the payments; that is, interest that would have been earned over the remaining period is subtracted from the total of the remaining installments.

When two people use a joint and survivor annuity payout, and one of the two dies, the remaining value to be paid out is the amount, if any, that would be includable. The remaining value is the replacement value, the amount the same insurance company would charge for a single life annuity at the age of the surviving joint annuitant at the time of the death of the first.[32] However, two factors affect how much and whether that is actually includable. If both people had contributed to the purchase of the annuity, only that amount purchased by the decedent would be includable.[33] Also, if the two are a married couple, the remaining value is eligible for the marital deduction.[34] This would mean that none of the value is includable in the taxable estate of the decedent. If the two are not a married couple, the marital deduction is not available. Some joint and survivor payouts also have term certain provisions, applicable when both annuitants die before a period of years has run. In that case, any remaining value would be includable in the estate of the second to die.

Survivor benefits attributable to employer contributions in qualified retirement plans have been treated in a variety of ways for federal estate tax purposes over the years. Benefits paid to the estates of decedents dying after 1953 and before 1983 had a complete exclusion from estate tax. More recently, there was an exclusion of up to $100,000 for the estates of decedents dying after 1982 and before 1985. However, estates of decedents dying after 1984 have no exclusion.[35] Note that under certain circumstances the pre-1984 exclusion may have been preserved. There also are no exclusions for other types of plans such as IRAs and TSAs, although the effective dates of some of the changes are somewhat different.

## Federal Gift Tax

Making gifts during lifetime is an often used estate planning technique. Most property given away no longer will be in the estate of someone who dies after the gifts are made. But someone cannot simply give away everything just before death, thereby avoiding estate tax, because there will be gift tax to pay when the property is given away.

The federal estate and gift taxes are part of a unified system but unified credits applicable to estates and to gifts diverge beginning in 2004. The amount of assets that may be passed by gift, without gift tax, remains at $1,000,000. The gift tax does not end, even for one year, as does the estate tax. Estate tax and gift tax rates are the same, except for 2010, not withstanding the fact that the applicable unified credits differ. Lifetime gifts subject to the gift tax are taken into account when determining the size of the taxable estate of a decedent. In effect, if gifts have been made, and all or a portion of the unified credit applied so that less or no tax was paid at the time of the gifts, that portion of the unified credit is used up and not available to reduce the estate tax. Over the years, some people have elected not to apply the unified credit when they make gifts so that it can be retained for use when the estate tax is paid. In such cases, the property given away is out of the eventual estate and so is the cash used to pay the gift tax. With significantly larger unified credits applicable to estate taxes, it may be that many more people will choose to use the available gift tax unified credit instead of foregoing its use.

Outright gifts to other persons are subject to an annual exclusion of $11,000 (in 2005, as indexed) per recipient. A parent could give $11,000 to each of his five adult children; if both parents agree to "split" a gift, the amount can be doubled without gift tax,[36] to a total of $22,000 (in 2005, as indexed) per child per year. The amount of this annual exclusion will be indexed in future years.

For parents in normal health, this is an extremely valuable estate planning technique. Only gifts of a present interest are eligible for the annual exclusion. A present interest gift is one that the recipient can have immediate enjoyment and control. In contrast, a gift of a future interest is one where the right to use the property is at some point in the future. Gifts of a future interest usually are those given in trust with restrictions being placed on immediate control and enjoyment. Outright gifts are of a present interest.

The gift tax also has an unlimited marital deduction. That is, gifts made to a spouse are deducted from the gifts made for a year and, therefore, not subject to the gift tax.[37] As a result, an estate owner does not need to be overly concerned about transfers of property to a spouse where the transfers may be seen to be gifts. In fact, they may be gifts but not subject to tax because of the marital deduction.

Gifts to a qualified charity generally are deducted from other gifts made for the year and not subject to gift tax. Several types of charitable trusts are discussed in Chapter 11. Generally, no charitable deduction from the gift tax is allowed for the lead interest (in a charitable lead trust) unless the payments to the charity are made as a guaranteed annuity or as a fixed percentage of the property's fair market value. Further, no charitable deduction is available for a remainder interest in a trust unless the trust qualifies as a charitable remainder annuity trust, a charitable remainder unitrust, or a pooled income fund.[38] A gift tax charitable deduction is allowed for a charitable gift annuity (where the gift is made in exchange for an annuity to be paid by the charity) if the value of the gift exceeds the value of the annuity, and the annuity is payable out of the general funds of the charity.[39]

## Annuities as Gifts

We have discussed the gift tax and need now to look at when a gift can arise with respect to the purchase of an annuity. When a parent or grandparent pays the premium on an annuity owned by a child or grandchild, a gift of the premium has been made.[40] So long as the premium is $11,000 or less (in 2005, as indexed), the annual exclusion applies. The gift of the premium on a single premium annuity probably would exceed the exclusion, however. If the donor does not want to pay any gift tax or apply a portion of the unified credit, the arrangement should be structured to stay within the annual exclusion, noting that the annual amount that may be excluded is $22,000 (in 2005, as indexed) when a split gift with the donor's spouse is possible.

When a person wants to enter into a joint and survivor annuity with someone else, there is the potential for a gift, presuming that the first person is the source of all or most of the premiums. If the person retains the right to change the other joint annuitant, the gift will not have been completed. But that is not the usual situation with joint and survivor annuities. When it is an immediate annuity, it usually is issued on the basis of the two people involved and, therefore, is irrevocable. When it is a deferred annuity, both owners usually have joint rights. If the two joint annuitants are married to each other, the fact that there may be a gift is not important because of the unlimited marital deduction. If the two are not married, then there is likely to be a gift at the time the person who provides the money for premiums no longer retains the right to make changes without the consent of the other person.[41]

When there is a single life annuity with a period certain guarantee, a gift will arise if the beneficiary is named irrevocably. That is the case in spite of the fact that the beneficiary may not ever receive anything because the annuitant lives beyond the period certain. Obviously, this can be avoided by leaving the beneficiary designation revocable, which is the usual practice.

The owner of an annuity can make an assignment of the contract; this is a gift and will be subject to gift tax[42] unless the value of the contract is within the annual exclusion or the assignee is the spouse of the owner. Perhaps more serious is the income tax consideration if the annuity was issued after April 22, 1987. The donor of the gift of the annuity is treated as having received the contract value less the investment in the contract,[43] the same income tax result as if the person had surrendered the contract. This goes beyond the gift tax considerations. About the only positive impact of such a situation is the fact that the donee of the gift will receive a higher income tax basis in the contract than he would have received if this special provision did not apply. This means that if the new owner of the contract decides to surrender it later, there will be less gain since the original owner had already been subject to tax for the gain that had occurred prior to the gift.

When an annuity is given to another person as a gift, the value of the gift depends on several factors. If it is given immediately after the purchase, the value is the price paid by the donor; that is, it is the amount of the premium paid, single premium, for example. If the gift is made after some increases in values have occurred, the gift value is the replacement cost, that is, the premium required to purchase a similar contract from the same issuer. When one person purchases a joint and survivor annuity naming himself and another person as joint annuitants, the gift value is the cost of the joint and survivor contract, less the cost of a single life annuity for the person who supplied the cash for the purchase. Note that if the two people are spouses, any gift is subject to the unlimited marital deduction.[44]

## Planning Considerations

As we have seen, there are numerous considerations involving who owns an annuity, who the annuitant or annuitants are, and who the beneficiary is. These considerations can involve income and gift taxes and can impact any estate tax that eventually may be payable. Most attention is given to income tax—the deductibility of current contributions to IRAs, SEPs, TSAs, "eligible" 457 plans, and qualified retirement plans; the deferral of current income tax while the values in the contract accumulate; and when and how much income tax may be payable when withdrawals from the contract are made. In addition, most people have at least a notion that income tax can be spread out when a life income option, fixed or variable, is elected later in life. There usually is at least some recognition that annuities may be includable in estates for estate tax purposes. Relatively little attention is given to the gift tax aspects of transferring annuities or naming beneficiaries.

Yet, it is important to avoid gift tax involvement where possible. For example, when an annuity owner names a child as beneficiary for sentimental reasons, there will be a gift tax consideration should the owner die during the accumulation period. The situation could have been avoided by naming the spouse as beneficiary. More than that, if the spouse had been named beneficiary, that spouse might have benefited a great deal by being able to continue the annuity and the income tax deferral of accumulations of values inside the annuity.

There are a number of instances where similar considerations could enter the picture. The important point is that a valuable service that can be given to someone who purchases an annuity is to coordinate ownership and beneficiary designations with other financial and estate planning provisions. There are so many choices to be made at the beginning (not the least of which is the selection of variable accounts) but these ownership and beneficiary considerations should be given due weight.

## Chapter Endnotes

1. See generally IRC Sec. 72.
2. IRC Sec. 72(u).
3. IRC Sec. 72(u)(2).
4. IRC Sec. 72(u)(1).
5. IRC Secs. 72(e)(2), 72(e)(3).
6. IRC Sec. 72(e)(5)(B).
7. Rev. Rul. 85-159, 1985-2 CB 29.
8. Rev. Rul 85-159, 1985-2 CB 29; Let. Rul. 9442030.
9. IRC Sec. 72(q)(2).
10. IRC Sec. 72(e)(11).
11. Treas. Reg. §1.1035-1.
12. Rev. Rul. 68-235, 1968-1 CB 360; Rev. Rul. 72-358, 1972-2 CB 473.
13. Let. Rul. 9644016; Let. Rul. 199937042.
14. Treas. Reg. §1.1031(b)-1(a).
15. Treas. Reg. §1.1031(b)-1(c).
16. IRC Sec. 72(e)(5)(E).
17. IRC Sec. 165.
18. IRC Sec. 72(b)(1).
19. Treas. Reg. §1.72-2(b)(3).
20. Treas. Reg. §§1.72-5(a), 1.72-5(b).
21. Treas. Reg. §1.72-9.
22. IRC Sec. 72(c)(4); Treas. Reg. §1.72-4(b).
23. IRC Sec. 72(b)(2).
24. IRC Sec. 72(s)(1).
25. Tax Reform Act of 1986, P.L. 99-514, Sec. 1826(b)(2).
26. IRC Sec. 72(s)(3).
27. IRC Sec. 72(s)(6).
28. IRC Sec. 72(h); Treas. Reg. §§1.72-11(a), 1.72-11(e).
29. IRC Secs. 2033, 2039; Treas. Reg. §20.2039-1(d).
30. IRC Sec. 2031, Treas. Reg. §20.2031-1(b).
31. IRC Secs. 2033, 2039.

32. Treas. Reg. §20.2031-8.
33. IRC Sec. 2039.
34. IRC Sec. 2056.
35. IRC Sec. 2039, as prior to and altered by The Tax Equity and Fiscal Responsibility Act of 1982, P.L. 97-248, and The Deficit Reduction Act of 1984, P.L. 98-369. Note that under certain circumstances the pre-1984 exclusion may have been preserved.
36. IRC Sec. 2513.
37. IRC Sec. 2523(a).
38. IRC Sec. 2522.
39. IRC Sec. 2522(a); See Treas. Reg. §1.1011-2(c) Ex. 8.
40. See Treas. Reg. §25.2511-1(h)(8).
41. Treas. Reg. §25.2511-1.
42. Treas. Reg. §25.2511-1(h)(8).
43. IRC Sec. 72(e)(4)(C).
44. Treas. Reg. §25.2512-6.

# Appendix A

## Actuarial Tables for Taxing Annuities

Some of the tables used for taxing annuities appear on the following pages. Included here are unisex Tables V, VI, VIA, and VII. The gender-based tables are to be used if the investment in the contract does not include a post-June 30, 1986 investment in the contract.[1] The unisex tables are to be used if the investment in the contract does include a post-June 30, 1986 investment in the contract.

However, even if there is no investment in the contract after June 30, 1986, an annuitant receiving annuity payments after June 30, 1986 (regardless of when they first began) may elect to treat his entire investment in the contract as post-June 30, 1986 and apply Tables V-VII. This election may be made for any taxable year in which such amounts are received by the taxpayer; it is irrevocable and applies with respect to all amounts the taxpayer receives as an annuity under the contract in the taxable year for which the election is made or in any subsequent tax year.

If investment in the contract includes both a pre-July 1986 investment and a post-June 1986 investment, an election may be made to make separate computations with respect to each portion of the aggregate investment in the contract using with respect to each portion the tables applicable to it. The amount excludable is the sum of the amounts determined under the separate computations. However, the election is not available (i.e., the entire investment must be treated as post-June 1986 investment) if the annuity starting date is after June 30, 1986 and the contract provides an option (whether or not it is exercised) to receive amounts under the contract other than in the form of a life annuity.[2]

Treasury regulations extend some of the tables to higher and lower ages, but the partial tables contained here are adequate for all practical purposes. The multiples in Tables V, VI, and VIA need not be adjusted for monthly payments. For quarterly, semi-annual or annual payments, they must be adjusted according to the Frequency of Payment Adjustment Table, below. Table VII multiples, giving the percentage value of refund features, are never adjusted.

All tables are entered with the age of the annuitant at his or her birthday nearest the annuity starting date.

## Frequency of Payment Adjustment Table

| If the number of whole months from the annuity starting date to the first payment date is | 0-1 | 2 | 3 | 4 | 5 | 6 | 7 | 8 | 9 | 10 | 11 | 12 |
|---|---|---|---|---|---|---|---|---|---|---|---|---|
| And payments under the contract are to be made: | | | | | | | | | | | | |
| Annually | +0.5 | +0.4 | +0.3 | +0.2 | +0.1 | 0 | 0 | -0.1 | -0.2 | -0.3 | -0.4 | -0.5 |
| Semiannually | + .2 | + .1 | 0 | 0 | - .1 | - .2 | .... | .... | .... | .... | .... | .... |
| Quarterly | + .1 | 0 | - .1 | .... | .... | .... | .... | .... | .... | .... | .... | .... |

Example. Ed Black bought an annuity contract on January 1 which provides him with an *annual* payment of $4,000 payable on December 31st of each year. His age on birthday nearest the annuity starting date (January 1) is 66. The multiple from Table V for male age 66, is 19.2. This multiple must be adjusted for annual payment by subtracting .5 (19.2 - .5 = 18.7). Thus, his total expected return is $74,800 (18.7 x $4,000).[3]

## Endnotes

1. See Treas. Reg. §1.72-9. Tthe gender-based tables are also reproduced in Appendix A in *Tax Facts on Insurance & Employee Benefits* and in Appendix A in *The Annuity Handbook*, both of which are published by The National Underwriter Company, Cincinnati, OH, 1-800-543-0874..
2. Treas. Reg. §1.72-6(d).
3. See Treas. Reg. §1.72-5(a)(2).

## Table V — Ordinary Life Annuities — One Life — Expected Return Multiples

| Age | Multiple | Age | Multiple | Age | Multiple |
|---|---|---|---|---|---|
| 5 | 76.6 | 42 | 40.6 | 79 | 10.0 |
| 6 | 75.6 | 43 | 39.6 | 80 | 9.5 |
| 7 | 74.7 | 44 | 38.7 | 81 | 8.9 |
| 8 | 73.7 | 45 | 37.7 | 82 | 8.4 |
| 9 | 72.7 | 46 | 36.8 | 63 | 7.9 |
| 10 | 71.7 | 47 | 35.9 | 84 | 7.4 |
| 11 | 70.7 | 48 | 34.9 | 85 | 6.9 |
| 12 | 69.7 | 49 | 34.0 | 86 | 6.5 |
| 13 | 68.8 | 50 | 33.1 | 87 | 6.1 |
| 14 | 67.8 | 51 | 32.2 | 88 | 5.7 |
| 15 | 66.8 | 52 | 31.3 | 89 | 5.3 |
| 16 | 65.8 | 53 | 30.4 | 90 | 5.0 |
| 17 | 64.8 | 54 | 29.5 | 91 | 4.7 |
| 18 | 63.9 | 55 | 28.6 | 92 | 4.4 |
| 19 | 62.9 | 56 | 27.7 | 93 | 4.1 |
| 20 | 61.9 | 57 | 26.8 | 94 | 3.9 |
| 21 | 60.9 | 58 | 25.9 | 95 | 3.7 |
| 22 | 59.9 | 59 | 25.0 | 96 | 3.4 |
| 23 | 59.0 | 60 | 24.2 | 97 | 3.2 |
| 24 | 58.0 | 61 | 23.3 | 98 | 3.0 |
| 25 | 57.0 | 62 | 22.5 | 99 | 2.8 |
| 26 | 56.0 | 63 | 21.6 | 100 | 2.7 |
| 27 | 55.1 | 64 | 20.8 | 101 | 2.5 |
| 28 | 54.1 | 65 | 20.0 | 102 | 2.3 |
| 29 | 53.1 | 66 | 19.2 | 103 | 2.1 |
| 30 | 52.2 | 67 | 18.4 | 104 | 1.9 |
| 31 | 51.2 | 68 | 17.6 | 105 | 1.8 |
| 32 | 50.2 | 69 | 16.8 | 106 | 1.6 |
| 33 | 49.3 | 70 | 16.0 | 107 | 1.4 |
| 34 | 48.3 | 71 | 15.3 | 108 | 1.3 |
| 35 | 47.3 | 72 | 14.6 | 109 | 1.1 |
| 36 | 46.4 | 73 | 13.9 | 110 | 1.0 |
| 37 | 45.4 | 74 | 13.2 | 111 | .9 |
| 38 | 44.4 | 75 | 12.5 | 112 | .8 |
| 39 | 43.5 | 76 | 11.9 | 113 | .7 |
| 40 | 42.5 | 77 | 11.2 | 114 | .6 |
| 41 | 41.5 | 78 | 10.6 | 115 | .5 |

## Table VI — Ordinary Joint Life and Last Survivor Annuities — Two Lives — Expected Return Multiples

| AGES | 35 | 36 | 37 | 38 | 39 | 40 | 41 | 42 | 43 | 44 | 45 | 46 | 47 | 48 | 49 | 50 |
|---|---|---|---|---|---|---|---|---|---|---|---|---|---|---|---|---|
| 35 | 54.0 | ... | ... | ... | ... | ... | ... | ... | ... | ... | ... | ... | ... | ... | ... | ... |
| 36 | 53.5 | 53.0 | ... | ... | ... | ... | ... | ... | ... | ... | ... | ... | ... | ... | ... | ... |
| 37 | 53.0 | 52.5 | 52.0 | ... | ... | ... | ... | ... | ... | ... | ... | ... | ... | ... | ... | ... |
| 38 | 52.6 | 52.0 | 51.5 | 51.0 | ... | ... | ... | ... | ... | ... | ... | ... | ... | ... | ... | ... |
| 39 | 52.2 | 51.6 | 51.0 | 50.5 | 50.0 | ... | ... | ... | ... | ... | ... | ... | ... | ... | ... | ... |
| 40 | 51.8 | 51.2 | 50.6 | 50.0 | 49.5 | 49.0 | ... | ... | ... | ... | ... | ... | ... | ... | ... | ... |
| 41 | 51.4 | 50.8 | 50.2 | 49.6 | 49.1 | 48.5 | 48.0 | ... | ... | ... | ... | ... | ... | ... | ... | ... |
| 42 | 51.1 | 50.4 | 49.8 | 49.2 | 48.6 | 48.1 | 47.5 | 47.0 | ... | ... | ... | ... | ... | ... | ... | ... |
| 43 | 50.8 | 50.1 | 49.5 | 48.8 | 48.2 | 47.6 | 47.1 | 46.6 | 46.0 | ... | ... | ... | ... | ... | ... | ... |
| 44 | 50.5 | 49.8 | 49.1 | 48.5 | 47.8 | 47.2 | 46.7 | 46.1 | 45.6 | 45.1 | ... | ... | ... | ... | ... | ... |
| 45 | 50.2 | 49.5 | 48.8 | 48.1 | 47.5 | 46.9 | 46.3 | 45.7 | 45.1 | 44.6 | 44.1 | ... | ... | ... | ... | ... |
| 46 | 50.0 | 49.2 | 48.5 | 47.8 | 47.2 | 46.5 | 45.9 | 45.3 | 44.7 | 44.1 | 43.6 | 43.1 | ... | ... | ... | ... |
| 47 | 49.7 | 49.0 | 48.3 | 47.5 | 46.8 | 46.2 | 45.5 | 44.9 | 44.3 | 43.7 | 43.2 | 42.6 | 42.1 | ... | ... | ... |
| 48 | 49.5 | 48.8 | 48.0 | 47.3 | 46.6 | 45.9 | 45.2 | 44.5 | 43.9 | 43.3 | 42.7 | 42.2 | 41.7 | 41.2 | ... | ... |
| 49 | 49.3 | 48.5 | 47.8 | 47.0 | 46.3 | 45.6 | 44.9 | 44.2 | 43.6 | 42.9 | 42.3 | 41.8 | 41.2 | 40.7 | 40.2 | ... |
| 50 | 49.2 | 48.4 | 47.6 | 46.8 | 46.0 | 45.3 | 44.6 | 43.9 | 43.2 | 42.6 | 42.0 | 41.4 | 40.8 | 40.2 | 39.7 | 39.2 |
| 51 | 49.0 | 48.2 | 47.4 | 46.6 | 45.8 | 45.1 | 44.3 | 43.6 | 42.9 | 42.2 | 41.6 | 41.0 | 40.4 | 39.8 | 39.3 | 38.7 |
| 52 | 48.8 | 48.0 | 47.2 | 46.4 | 45.6 | 44.8 | 44.1 | 43.3 | 42.6 | 41.9 | 41.3 | 40.6 | 40.0 | 39.4 | 38.8 | 38.3 |
| 53 | 48.7 | 47.9 | 47.0 | 46.2 | 45.4 | 44.6 | 43.9 | 43.1 | 42.4 | 41.7 | 41.0 | 40.3 | 39.7 | 39.0 | 38.4 | 37.9 |
| 54 | 48.6 | 47.7 | 46.9 | 46.0 | 45.2 | 44.4 | 43.6 | 42.9 | 42.1 | 41.4 | 40.7 | 40.0 | 39.3 | 38.7 | 38.1 | 37.5 |
| 55 | 48.5 | 47.6 | 46.7 | 45.9 | 45.1 | 44.2 | 43.4 | 42.7 | 41.9 | 41.2 | 40.4 | 39.7 | 39.0 | 38.4 | 37.7 | 37.1 |
| 56 | 48.3 | 47.5 | 46.6 | 45.8 | 44.9 | 44.1 | 43.3 | 42.5 | 41.7 | 40.9 | 40.2 | 39.5 | 38.7 | 38.1 | 37.4 | 36.8 |
| 57 | 48.3 | 47.4 | 46.5 | 45.6 | 44.8 | 43.9 | 43.1 | 42.3 | 41.5 | 40.7 | 40.0 | 39.2 | 38.5 | 37.8 | 37.1 | 36.4 |
| 58 | 48.2 | 47.3 | 46.4 | 45.5 | 44.7 | 43.8 | 43.0 | 42.1 | 41.3 | 40.5 | 39.7 | 39.0 | 38.2 | 37.5 | 36.8 | 36.1 |
| 59 | 48.1 | 47.2 | 46.3 | 45.4 | 44.5 | 43.7 | 42.8 | 42.0 | 41.2 | 40.4 | 39.6 | 38.8 | 38.0 | 37.3 | 36.6 | 35.9 |
| 60 | 48.0 | 47.1 | 46.2 | 45.3 | 44.4 | 43.6 | 42.7 | 41.9 | 41.0 | 40.2 | 39.4 | 38.6 | 37.8 | 37.1 | 36.3 | 35.6 |
| 61 | 47.9 | 47.0 | 46.1 | 45.2 | 44.3 | 43.5 | 42.6 | 41.7 | 40.9 | 40.0 | 39.2 | 38.4 | 37.6 | 36.9 | 36.1 | 35.4 |
| 62 | 47.9 | 47.0 | 46.0 | 45.1 | 44.2 | 43.4 | 42.5 | 41.6 | 40.8 | 39.9 | 39.1 | 38.3 | 37.5 | 36.7 | 35.9 | 35.1 |
| 63 | 47.8 | 46.9 | 46.0 | 45.1 | 44.2 | 43.3 | 42.4 | 41.5 | 40.6 | 39.8 | 38.9 | 38.1 | 37.3 | 36.5 | 35.7 | 34.9 |
| 64 | 47.8 | 46.8 | 45.9 | 45.0 | 44.1 | 43.2 | 42.3 | 41.4 | 40.5 | 39.7 | 38.8 | 38.0 | 37.2 | 36.3 | 35.5 | 34.8 |
| 65 | 47.7 | 46.8 | 45.9 | 44.9 | 44.0 | 43.1 | 42.2 | 41.3 | 40.4 | 39.6 | 38.7 | 37.9 | 37.0 | 36.2 | 35.4 | 34.6 |
| 66 | 47.7 | 46.7 | 45.8 | 44.9 | 44.0 | 43.1 | 42.2 | 41.3 | 40.4 | 39.5 | 38.6 | 37.8 | 36.9 | 36.1 | 35.2 | 34.4 |
| 67 | 47.6 | 46.7 | 45.8 | 44.8 | 43.9 | 43.0 | 42.1 | 41.2 | 40.3 | 39.4 | 38.5 | 37.7 | 36.8 | 36.0 | 35.1 | 34.3 |
| 68 | 47.6 | 46.7 | 45.7 | 44.8 | 43.9 | 42.9 | 42.0 | 41.1 | 40.2 | 39.3 | 38.4 | 37.6 | 36.7 | 35.8 | 35.0 | 34.2 |
| 69 | 47.6 | 46.6 | 45.7 | 44.8 | 43.8 | 42.9 | 42.0 | 41.1 | 40.2 | 39.3 | 38.4 | 37.5 | 36.6 | 35.7 | 34.9 | 34.1 |
| 70 | 47.5 | 46.6 | 45.7 | 44.7 | 43.8 | 42.9 | 41.9 | 41.0 | 40.1 | 39.2 | 38.3 | 37.4 | 36.5 | 35.7 | 34.8 | 34.0 |
| 71 | 47.5 | 46.6 | 45.6 | 44.7 | 43.8 | 42.8 | 41.9 | 41.0 | 40.1 | 39.1 | 38.2 | 37.3 | 36.5 | 35.6 | 34.7 | 33.9 |
| 72 | 47.5 | 46.6 | 45.6 | 44.7 | 43.7 | 42.8 | 41.9 | 40.9 | 40.0 | 39.1 | 38.2 | 37.3 | 36.4 | 35.5 | 34.6 | 33.8 |
| 73 | 47.5 | 46.5 | 45.6 | 44.7 | 43.7 | 42.8 | 41.8 | 40.9 | 40.0 | 39.0 | 38.1 | 37.2 | 36.3 | 35.4 | 34.6 | 33.7 |
| 74 | 47.5 | 46.5 | 45.6 | 44.7 | 43.7 | 42.7 | 41.8 | 40.9 | 39.9 | 39.0 | 38.1 | 37.2 | 36.3 | 35.4 | 34.5 | 33.6 |
| 75 | 47.4 | 46.5 | 45.5 | 44.7 | 43.6 | 42.7 | 41.8 | 40.8 | 39.9 | 39.0 | 38.1 | 37.1 | 36.2 | 35.3 | 34.5 | 33.6 |
| 76 | 47.4 | 46.5 | 45.5 | 44.7 | 43.6 | 42.7 | 41.7 | 40.8 | 39.9 | 38.9 | 38.0 | 37.1 | 36.2 | 35.3 | 34.4 | 33.5 |
| 77 | 47.4 | 46.5 | 45.5 | 44.7 | 43.6 | 42.7 | 41.7 | 40.8 | 39.8 | 38.9 | 38.0 | 37.1 | 36.2 | 35.3 | 34.4 | 33.5 |
| 78 | 47.4 | 46.4 | 45.5 | 44.5 | 43.6 | 42.6 | 41.7 | 40.7 | 39.8 | 38.9 | 38.0 | 37.0 | 36.1 | 35.2 | 34.3 | 33.4 |
| 79 | 47.4 | 46.4 | 45.5 | 44.5 | 43.6 | 42.6 | 41.7 | 40.7 | 39.8 | 38.9 | 37.9 | 37.0 | 36.1 | 35.2 | 34.3 | 33.4 |
| 80 | 47.4 | 46.4 | 45.5 | 44.5 | 43.6 | 42.6 | 41.7 | 40.7 | 39.8 | 38.8 | 37.9 | 37.0 | 36.1 | 35.2 | 34.2 | 33.4 |
| 81 | 47.4 | 46.4 | 45.5 | 44.5 | 43.5 | 42.6 | 41.6 | 40.7 | 39.8 | 38.8 | 37.9 | 37.0 | 36.0 | 35.1 | 34.2 | 33.3 |
| 82 | 47.4 | 46.4 | 45.4 | 44.5 | 43.5 | 42.6 | 41.6 | 40.7 | 39.7 | 38.8 | 37.9 | 36.9 | 36.0 | 35.1 | 34.2 | 33.3 |
| 83 | 47.4 | 46.4 | 45.4 | 44.5 | 43.5 | 42.6 | 41.6 | 40.7 | 39.7 | 38.8 | 37.9 | 36.9 | 36.0 | 35.1 | 34.2 | 33.3 |
| 84 | 47.4 | 46.4 | 45.4 | 44.5 | 43.5 | 42.6 | 41.6 | 40.7 | 39.7 | 38.8 | 37.8 | 36.9 | 36.0 | 35.0 | 34.1 | 33.2 |
| 85 | 47.4 | 46.4 | 45.4 | 44.5 | 43.5 | 42.6 | 41.6 | 40.7 | 39.7 | 38.8 | 37.8 | 36.9 | 36.0 | 35.0 | 34.1 | 33.2 |
| 86 | 47.3 | 46.4 | 45.4 | 44.5 | 43.5 | 42.5 | 41.6 | 40.6 | 39.7 | 38.8 | 37.8 | 36.9 | 36.0 | 35.0 | 34.1 | 33.2 |
| 87 | 47.3 | 46.4 | 45.4 | 44.5 | 43.5 | 42.5 | 41.6 | 40.6 | 39.7 | 38.7 | 37.8 | 36.9 | 35.9 | 35.0 | 34.1 | 33.2 |
| 88 | 47.3 | 46.4 | 45.4 | 44.5 | 43.5 | 42.5 | 41.6 | 40.6 | 39.7 | 38.7 | 37.8 | 36.9 | 35.9 | 35.0 | 34.1 | 33.2 |
| 89 | 47.3 | 46.4 | 45.4 | 44.4 | 43.5 | 42.5 | 41.6 | 40.6 | 39.7 | 38.7 | 37.8 | 36.9 | 35.9 | 35.0 | 34.1 | 33.2 |
| 90 | 47.3 | 46.4 | 45.4 | 44.4 | 43.5 | 42.5 | 41.6 | 40.6 | 39.7 | 38.7 | 37.8 | 36.9 | 35.9 | 35.0 | 34.1 | 33.2 |

**Table VI — Ordinary Joint Life and Last Survivor Annuities — Two Lives — Expected Return Multiples**

| AGES | 51 | 52 | 53 | 54 | 55 | 56 | 57 | 58 | 59 | 60 | 61 | 62 | 63 | 64 | 65 | 66 |
|---|---|---|---|---|---|---|---|---|---|---|---|---|---|---|---|---|
| 51 | 38.2 | ... | ... | ... | ... | ... | ... | ... | ... | ... | ... | ... | ... | ... | ... | ... |
| 52 | 37.8 | 37.3 | ... | ... | ... | ... | ... | ... | ... | ... | ... | ... | ... | ... | ... | ... |
| 53 | 37.3 | 36.8 | 36.3 | ... | ... | ... | ... | ... | ... | ... | ... | ... | ... | ... | ... | ... |
| 54 | 36.9 | 36.4 | 35.8 | 35.3 | ... | ... | ... | ... | ... | ... | ... | ... | ... | ... | ... | ... |
| 55 | 36.5 | 55.9 | 35.4 | 34.9 | 34.4 | ... | ... | ... | ... | ... | ... | ... | ... | ... | ... | ... |
| 56 | 36.1 | 35.6 | 35.0 | 34.4 | 33.9 | 33.4 | ... | ... | ... | ... | ... | ... | ... | ... | ... | ... |
| 57 | 35.8 | 35.2 | 34.6 | 34.0 | 33.5 | 33.0 | 32.5 | ... | ... | ... | ... | ... | ... | ... | ... | ... |
| 58 | 35.5 | 34.8 | 34.2 | 33.6 | 33.1 | 32.5 | 32.0 | 31.5 | ... | ... | ... | ... | ... | ... | ... | ... |
| 59 | 35.2 | 34.5 | 33.9 | 33.3 | 32.7 | 32.1 | 31.6 | 31.1 | 30.6 | ... | ... | ... | ... | ... | ... | ... |
| 60 | 34.9 | 34.2 | 33.6 | 32.9 | 32.3 | 31.7 | 31.2 | 30.6 | 30.1 | 29.7 | ... | ... | ... | ... | ... | ... |
| 61 | 34.6 | 33.9 | 33.3 | 32.6 | 32.0 | 31.4 | 30.8 | 30.2 | 29.7 | 29.2 | 28.7 | ... | ... | ... | ... | ... |
| 62 | 34.4 | 33.7 | 33.0 | 32.3 | 31.7 | 31.0 | 30.4 | 29.9 | 29.3 | 28.8 | 28.3 | 27.8 | ... | ... | ... | ... |
| 63 | 34.2 | 33.5 | 32.7 | 32.0 | 31.4 | 30.7 | 30.1 | 29.5 | 28.9 | 28.4 | 27.8 | 27.3 | 26.9 | ... | ... | ... |
| 64 | 34.0 | 33.2 | 32.5 | 31.8 | 31.1 | 30.4 | 29.8 | 29.2 | 28.6 | 28.0 | 27.4 | 26.9 | 26.4 | 25.9 | ... | ... |
| 65 | 33.8 | 33.0 | 32.3 | 31.6 | 30.9 | 30.2 | 29.5 | 28.9 | 28.2 | 27.6 | 27.1 | 26.5 | 26.0 | 25.5 | 25.0 | ... |
| 66 | 33.6 | 32.9 | 32.1 | 31.4 | 30.6 | 29.9 | 29.2 | 28.6 | 27.9 | 27.3 | 26.7 | 26.1 | 25.6 | 25.1 | 24.6 | 24.1 |
| 67 | 33.5 | 32.7 | 31.9 | 31.2 | 30.4 | 29.7 | 29.0 | 28.3 | 27.6 | 27.0 | 26.4 | 25.8 | 25.2 | 24.7 | 24.2 | 23.7 |
| 68 | 33.4 | 32.5 | 31.8 | 31.0 | 30.2 | 29.5 | 28.8 | 28.1 | 27.4 | 26.7 | 26.1 | 25.5 | 24.9 | 24.3 | 23.8 | 23.3 |
| 69 | 33.2 | 32.4 | 31.6 | 30.8 | 30.1 | 29.3 | 28.6 | 27.8 | 27.1 | 26.5 | 25.8 | 25.2 | 24.6 | 24.0 | 23.4 | 22.9 |
| 70 | 33.1 | 32.3 | 31.5 | 30.7 | 29.9 | 29.1 | 28.4 | 27.6 | 26.9 | 26.2 | 25.6 | 24.9 | 24.3 | 23.7 | 23.1 | 22.5 |
| 71 | 33.0 | 32.2 | 31.4 | 30.5 | 29.7 | 29.0 | 28.2 | 27.5 | 26.7 | 26.0 | 25.3 | 24.7 | 24.0 | 23.4 | 22.8 | 22.2 |
| 72 | 32.9 | 32.1 | 31.2 | 30.4 | 29.6 | 28.8 | 28.1 | 27.3 | 26.5 | 25.8 | 25.1 | 24.4 | 23.8 | 23.1 | 22.5 | 21.9 |
| 73 | 32.8 | 32.0 | 31.1 | 30.3 | 29.5 | 28.7 | 27.9 | 27.1 | 26.4 | 25.6 | 24.9 | 24.2 | 23.5 | 22.9 | 22.2 | 21.6 |
| 74 | 32.8 | 31.9 | 31.1 | 30.2 | 29.4 | 28.6 | 27.8 | 27.0 | 26.2 | 25.5 | 24.7 | 24.0 | 23.3 | 22.7 | 22.0 | 21.4 |
| 75 | 32.7 | 31.8 | 31.0 | 30.1 | 29.3 | 28.5 | 27.7 | 26.9 | 26.1 | 25.3 | 24.6 | 23.8 | 23.1 | 22.4 | 21.8 | 21.1 |
| 76 | 32.6 | 31.8 | 30.9 | 30.1 | 29.2 | 28.4 | 27.6 | 26.8 | 26.0 | 25.2 | 24.4 | 23.7 | 23.0 | 22.3 | 21.6 | 20.9 |
| 77 | 32.6 | 31.7 | 30.8 | 30.0 | 29.1 | 28.3 | 27.5 | 26.7 | 25.9 | 25.1 | 24.3 | 23.6 | 22.8 | 22.1 | 21.4 | 20.7 |
| 78 | 32.5 | 31.7 | 30.8 | 29.9 | 29.1 | 28.2 | 27.4 | 26.6 | 25.8 | 25.0 | 24.2 | 23.4 | 22.7 | 21.9 | 21.2 | 20.5 |
| 79 | 32.5 | 31.6 | 30.7 | 29.9 | 29.0 | 28.2 | 27.3 | 26.5 | 25.7 | 24.9 | 24.1 | 23.3 | 22.6 | 21.8 | 21.1 | 20.4 |
| 80 | 32.5 | 31.6 | 30.7 | 29.8 | 29.0 | 28.1 | 27.3 | 26.4 | 25.6 | 24.8 | 24.0 | 23.2 | 22.4 | 21.7 | 21.0 | 20.2 |
| 81 | 32.4 | 31.5 | 30.7 | 29.8 | 28.9 | 28.1 | 27.2 | 26.4 | 25.5 | 24.7 | 23.9 | 23.1 | 22.3 | 21.6 | 20.8 | 20.1 |
| 82 | 32.4 | 31.5 | 30.6 | 29.7 | 28.9 | 28.0 | 27.2 | 26.3 | 25.5 | 24.6 | 23.8 | 23.0 | 22.3 | 21.5 | 20.7 | 20.0 |
| 83 | 32.4 | 31.5 | 30.6 | 29.7 | 28.8 | 28.0 | 27.1 | 26.3 | 25.4 | 24.6 | 23.8 | 23.0 | 22.2 | 21.4 | 20.6 | 19.9 |
| 84 | 32.3 | 31.4 | 30.6 | 29.7 | 28.8 | 27.9 | 27.1 | 26.2 | 25.4 | 24.5 | 23.7 | 22.9 | 22.1 | 21.3 | 20.5 | 19.8 |
| 85 | 32.3 | 31.4 | 30.5 | 29.6 | 28.8 | 27.9 | 27.0 | 26.2 | 25.3 | 24.5 | 23.7 | 22.8 | 22.0 | 21.3 | 20.5 | 19.7 |
| 86 | 32.3 | 31.4 | 30.5 | 29.6 | 28.7 | 27.9 | 27.0 | 26.1 | 25.3 | 24.5 | 23.6 | 22.8 | 22.0 | 21.2 | 20.4 | 19.6 |
| 87 | 32.3 | 31.4 | 30.5 | 29.6 | 28.7 | 27.8 | 27.0 | 26.1 | 25.3 | 24.4 | 23.6 | 22.8 | 21.9 | 21.1 | 20.4 | 19.6 |
| 88 | 32.3 | 31.4 | 30.5 | 29.6 | 28.7 | 27.8 | 27.0 | 26.1 | 25.2 | 24.4 | 23.5 | 22.7 | 21.9 | 21.1 | 20.3 | 19.5 |
| 89 | 32.3 | 31.4 | 30.5 | 29.6 | 28.7 | 27.8 | 26.9 | 26.1 | 25.2 | 24.4 | 23.5 | 22.7 | 21.9 | 21.1 | 20.3 | 19.5 |
| 90 | 32.3 | 31.3 | 30.5 | 29.5 | 28.7 | 27.8 | 26.9 | 26.1 | 25.2 | 24.3 | 23.5 | 22.7 | 21.8 | 21.0 | 20.2 | 19.4 |

**Table VI — Ordinary Joint Life and Last Survivor Annuities — Two Lives — Expected Return Multiples**

| AGES | 67 | 68 | 69 | 70 | 71 | 72 | 73 | 74 | 75 | 76 | 77 | 78 | 79 | 80 | 81 | 82 |
|---|---|---|---|---|---|---|---|---|---|---|---|---|---|---|---|---|
| 67 | 23.2 | ... | ... | ... | ... | ... | ... | ... | ... | ... | ... | ... | ... | ... | ... | ... |
| 68 | 22.8 | 22.3 | ... | ... | ... | ... | ... | ... | ... | ... | ... | ... | ... | ... | ... | ... |
| 69 | 22.4 | 21.9 | 21.5 | ... | ... | ... | ... | ... | ... | ... | ... | ... | ... | ... | ... | ... |
| 70 | 22.0 | 21.5 | 21.1 | 20.6 | ... | ... | ... | ... | ... | ... | ... | ... | ... | ... | ... | ... |
| 71 | 21.7 | 21.2 | 20.7 | 20.2 | 19.8 | ... | ... | ... | ... | ... | ... | ... | ... | ... | ... | ... |
| 72 | 21.3 | 20.8 | 20.3 | 19.8 | 19.4 | 18.9 | ... | ... | ... | ... | ... | ... | ... | ... | ... | ... |
| 73 | 21.0 | 20.5 | 20.0 | 19.4 | 19.0 | 18.5 | 18.1 | ... | ... | ... | ... | ... | ... | ... | ... | ... |
| 74 | 20.8 | 20.2 | 19.6 | 19.1 | 18.6 | 18.2 | 17.7 | 17.3 | ... | ... | ... | ... | ... | ... | ... | ... |
| 75 | 20.5 | 19.9 | 19.3 | 18.8 | 18.3 | 17.8 | 17.3 | 16.9 | 16.5 | ... | ... | ... | ... | ... | ... | ... |
| 76 | 20.3 | 19.7 | 19.1 | 18.5 | 18.0 | 17.5 | 17.0 | 16.5 | 16.1 | 15.7 | ... | ... | ... | ... | ... | ... |
| 77 | 20.1 | 19.4 | 18.8 | 18.3 | 17.7 | 17.2 | 16.7 | 16.2 | 15.8 | 15.4 | 15.0 | ... | ... | ... | ... | ... |
| 78 | 19.9 | 19.2 | 18.6 | 18.0 | 17.5 | 16.9 | 16.4 | 15.9 | 15.4 | 15.0 | 14.6 | 14.2 | ... | ... | ... | ... |
| 79 | 19.7 | 19.0 | 18.4 | 17.8 | 17.2 | 16.7 | 16.1 | 15.6 | 15.1 | 14.7 | 14.3 | 13.9 | 13.5 | ... | ... | ... |
| 80 | 19.5 | 18.9 | 18.2 | 17.6 | 17.0 | 16.4 | 15.9 | 15.4 | 14.9 | 14.4 | 14.0 | 13.5 | 13.2 | 12.8 | ... | ... |
| 81 | 19.4 | 18.7 | 18.1 | 17.4 | 16.8 | 16.2 | 15.7 | 15.1 | 14.6 | 14.1 | 13.7 | 13.2 | 12.8 | 12.5 | 12.1 | ... |
| 82 | 19.3 | 18.6 | 17.9 | 17.3 | 16.6 | 16.0 | 15.5 | 14.9 | 14.4 | 13.9 | 13.4 | 13.0 | 12.5 | 12.2 | 11.8 | 11.5 |
| 83 | 19.2 | 18.5 | 17.8 | 17.1 | 16.5 | 15.9 | 15.3 | 14.7 | 14.2 | 13.7 | 13.2 | 12.7 | 12.3 | 11.9 | 11.5 | 11.1 |
| 84 | 19.1 | 18.4 | 17.7 | 17.0 | 16.3 | 15.7 | 15.1 | 14.5 | 14.0 | 13.5 | 13.0 | 12.5 | 12.0 | 11.6 | 11.2 | 10.9 |
| 85 | 19.0 | 18.3 | 17.6 | 16.9 | 16.2 | 15.6 | 15.0 | 14.4 | 13.8 | 13.3 | 12.8 | 12.3 | 11.8 | 11.4 | 11.0 | 10.6 |
| 86 | 18.9 | 18.2 | 17.5 | 16.8 | 16.1 | 15.5 | 14.8 | 14.2 | 13.7 | 13.1 | 12.6 | 12.1 | 11.6 | 11.2 | 10.8 | 10.4 |
| 87 | 18.8 | 18.1 | 17.4 | 16.7 | 16.0 | 15.4 | 14.7 | 14.1 | 13.5 | 13.0 | 12.4 | 11.9 | 11.4 | 11.0 | 10.6 | 10.1 |
| 88 | 18.8 | 18.0 | 17.3 | 16.6 | 15.9 | 15.3 | 14.6 | 14.0 | 13.4 | 12.8 | 12.3 | 11.8 | 11.3 | 10.8 | 10.4 | 10.0 |
| 89 | 18.7 | 18.0 | 17.2 | 16.5 | 15.8 | 15.2 | 14.5 | 13.9 | 13.3 | 12.7 | 12.2 | 11.6 | 11.1 | 10.7 | 10.2 | 9.8 |
| 90 | 18.7 | 17.9 | 17.2 | 16.5 | 15.8 | 15.1 | 14.5 | 13.8 | 13.2 | 12.6 | 12.1 | 11.5 | 11.0 | 10.5 | 10.1 | 9.6 |

**Table VI — Ordinary Joint Life and Last Survivor Annuities — Two Lives — Expected Return Multiples**

| AGES | 83 | 84 | 85 | 86 | 87 | 88 | 89 | 90 |
|---|---|---|---|---|---|---|---|---|
| 83 | 10.8 | ... | ... | ... | ... | ... | ... | ... |
| 84 | 10.5 | 10.2 | ... | ... | ... | ... | ... | ... |
| 85 | 10.2 | 9.9 | 9.6 | ... | ... | ... | ... | ... |
| 86 | 10.0 | 9.7 | 9.3 | 9.1 | ... | ... | ... | ... |
| 87 | 9.8 | 9.4 | 9.1 | 8.8 | 8.5 | ... | ... | ... |
| 88 | 9.6 | 9.2 | 8.9 | 8.6 | 8.3 | 8.0 | ... | ... |
| 89 | 9.4 | 9.0 | 8.7 | 8.3 | 8.1 | 7.8 | 7.5 | ... |
| 90 | 9.2 | 8.8 | 8.5 | 8.2 | 7.9 | 7.6 | 7.3 | 7.1 |

**Table VIA — Annuities for Joint Life Only — Two Lives — Expected Return Multiples**

| AGES | 35 | 36 | 37 | 38 | 39 | 40 | 41 | 42 | 43 | 44 | 45 | 46 | 47 | 48 | 49 | 50 |
|---|---|---|---|---|---|---|---|---|---|---|---|---|---|---|---|---|
| 35 | 40.7 | ... | ... | ... | ... | ... | ... | ... | ... | ... | ... | ... | ... | ... | ... | ... |
| 36 | 40.2 | 39.7 | ... | ... | ... | ... | ... | ... | ... | ... | ... | ... | ... | ... | ... | ... |
| 37 | 39.7 | 39.3 | 38.8 | ... | ... | ... | ... | ... | ... | ... | ... | ... | ... | ... | ... | ... |
| 38 | 39.2 | 38.7 | 38.3 | 37.9 | ... | ... | ... | ... | ... | ... | ... | ... | ... | ... | ... | ... |
| 39 | 38.6 | 38.2 | 37.8 | 37.4 | 36.9 | ... | ... | ... | ... | ... | ... | ... | ... | ... | ... | ... |
| 40 | 38.0 | 37.7 | 37.3 | 36.9 | 36.4 | 36.0 | ... | ... | ... | ... | ... | ... | ... | ... | ... | ... |
| 41 | 37.4 | 37.1 | 36.7 | 36.3 | 35.9 | 35.5 | 35.1 | ... | ... | ... | ... | ... | ... | ... | ... | ... |
| 42 | 36.8 | 36.5 | 36.2 | 35.8 | 35.4 | 35.0 | 34.6 | 34.1 | ... | ... | ... | ... | ... | ... | ... | ... |
| 43 | 36.2 | 35.9 | 35.6 | 35.2 | 34.9 | 34.5 | 34.1 | 33.7 | 33.2 | ... | ... | ... | ... | ... | ... | ... |
| 44 | 35.5 | 35.2 | 34.9 | 34.6 | 34.3 | 34.0 | 33.6 | 33.2 | 32.8 | 32.3 | ... | ... | ... | ... | ... | ... |
| 45 | 34.8 | 34.6 | 34.3 | 34.0 | 33.7 | 33.4 | 33.0 | 32.7 | 32.3 | 31.8 | 31.4 | ... | ... | ... | ... | ... |
| 46 | 34.1 | 33.9 | 33.7 | 33.4 | 33.1 | 32.8 | 32.5 | 32.1 | 31.8 | 31.4 | 30.9 | 30.3 | ... | ... | ... | ... |
| 47 | 33.4 | 33.2 | 33.0 | 32.8 | 32.5 | 32.2 | 31.9 | 31.6 | 31.2 | 30.8 | 30.5 | 30.0 | 29.6 | ... | ... | ... |
| 48 | 32.7 | 32.5 | 32.3 | 32.1 | 31.8 | 31.6 | 31.3 | 31.0 | 30.7 | 30.3 | 30.0 | 29.6 | 29.2 | 28.7 | ... | ... |
| 49 | 32.0 | 31.8 | 31.6 | 31.4 | 31.2 | 30.9 | 30.7 | 30.4 | 30.1 | 29.8 | 29.4 | 29.1 | 28.7 | 28.3 | 27.9 | ... |
| 50 | 31.3 | 31.1 | 30.9 | 30.7 | 30.5 | 30.3 | 30.0 | 29.8 | 29.5 | 29.2 | 28.9 | 28.5 | 28.2 | 27.4 | 27.4 | 27.0 |
| 51 | 30.5 | 30.4 | 30.2 | 30.0 | 29.8 | 29.6 | 29.4 | 29.2 | 28.9 | 28.6 | 28.3 | 28.0 | 27.7 | 27.3 | 26.9 | 26.5 |
| 52 | 29.7 | 29.6 | 29.5 | 29.3 | 29.1 | 28.9 | 28.7 | 28.5 | 28.3 | 28.0 | 27.7 | 27.4 | 27.1 | 26.8 | 26.5 | 26.1 |
| 53 | 29.0 | 28.9 | 28.7 | 28.6 | 28.4 | 28.2 | 28.1 | 27.9 | 27.6 | 27.4 | 27.1 | 26.9 | 26.6 | 26.3 | 25.9 | 25.6 |
| 54 | 28.2 | 28.1 | 28.0 | 27.8 | 27.7 | 27.5 | 27.4 | 27.2 | 27.0 | 26.8 | 26.5 | 26.3 | 26.0 | 25.7 | 25.4 | 25.1 |
| 55 | 27.4 | 27.3 | 27.2 | 27.1 | 27.0 | 26.8 | 26.7 | 26.5 | 26.3 | 26.1 | 25.9 | 25.7 | 25.4 | 25.1 | 24.9 | 24.6 |
| 56 | 26.7 | 26.6 | 26.5 | 26.3 | 26.2 | 26.1 | 26.0 | 25.8 | 25.6 | 25.4 | 25.2 | 25.0 | 24.8 | 24.6 | 24.3 | 24.0 |
| 57 | 25.9 | 25.8 | 25.7 | 25.6 | 25.3 | 25.4 | 25.2 | 25.1 | 24.9 | 24.8 | 24.6 | 24.4 | 24.2 | 24.0 | 23.7 | 23.5 |
| 58 | 25.1 | 25.0 | 24.9 | 24.8 | 24.7 | 24.6 | 24.5 | 24.4 | 24.2 | 24.1 | 23.9 | 23.7 | 23.5 | 23.3 | 23.1 | 22.9 |
| 59 | 24.3 | 24.2 | 24.1 | 24.1 | 24.0 | 23.9 | 23.8 | 23.6 | 23.3 | 23.4 | 23.2 | 23.1 | 22.9 | 22.7 | 22.5 | 22.3 |
| 60 | 23.5 | 23.4 | 23.4 | 23.3 | 23.2 | 23.1 | 23.0 | 22.9 | 22.8 | 22.7 | 22.5 | 22.4 | 22.2 | 22.1 | 21.9 | 21.7 |
| 61 | 22.7 | 22.6 | 22.6 | 22.5 | 22.4 | 22.4 | 22.3 | 22.2 | 22.1 | 22.0 | 21.8 | 21.7 | 21.6 | 21.4 | 21.2 | 21.1 |
| 62 | 21.9 | 21.9 | 21.8 | 21.7 | 21.7 | 21.6 | 21.5 | 21.4 | 21.3 | 21.2 | 21.1 | 21.0 | 20.9 | 20.7 | 20.6 | 20.4 |
| 63 | 21.1 | 21.1 | 21.0 | 21.0 | 20.9 | 20.8 | 20.8 | 20.7 | 20.6 | 20.5 | 20.4 | 20.3 | 20.2 | 20.1 | 19.9 | 19.8 |
| 64 | 20.3 | 20.3 | 20.2 | 20.2 | 20.1 | 20.1 | 20.0 | 20.0 | 19.9 | 19.8 | 19.7 | 19.6 | 19.5 | 19.4 | 19.3 | 19.1 |
| 65 | 19.6 | 19.5 | 19.5 | 19.4 | 19.4 | 19.3 | 19.3 | 19.2 | 19.1 | 19.1 | 19.0 | 18.9 | 18.8 | 18.7 | 18.6 | 18.5 |
| 66 | 18.8 | 18.8 | 18.7 | 18.7 | 18.6 | 18.6 | 18.5 | 18.5 | 18.4 | 18.4 | 18.3 | 18.2 | 18.1 | 18.0 | 17.9 | 17.8 |
| 67 | 18.0 | 18.0 | 18.0 | 17.9 | 17.9 | 17.9 | 17.8 | 17.8 | 17.7 | 17.6 | 17.6 | 17.5 | 17.4 | 17.3 | 17.3 | 17.2 |
| 68 | 17.3 | 17.3 | 17.2 | 17.2 | 17.2 | 17.1 | 17.1 | 17.0 | 17.0 | 16.9 | 16.9 | 16.8 | 16.7 | 16.7 | 16.6 | 16.5 |
| 69 | 16.5 | 16.5 | 16.5 | 16.5 | 16.4 | 16.4 | 16.4 | 16.3 | 16.3 | 16.2 | 16.2 | 16.1 | 16.1 | 16.0 | 15.9 | 15.8 |
| 70 | 15.8 | 15.8 | 15.8 | 15.7 | 15.7 | 15.7 | 15.6 | 15.6 | 15.6 | 15.5 | 15.5 | 15.4 | 15.4 | 15.3 | 15.3 | 15.2 |
| 71 | 15.1 | 15.1 | 15.1 | 15.0 | 15.0 | 15.0 | 15.0 | 14.9 | 14.9 | 14.9 | 14.8 | 14.8 | 14.7 | 14.7 | 14.6 | 14.5 |
| 72 | 14.4 | 14.4 | 14.4 | 14.3 | 14.3 | 14.3 | 14.3 | 14.2 | 14.2 | 14.2 | 14.1 | 14.1 | 14.1 | 14.0 | 14.0 | 13.9 |
| 73 | 13.7 | 13.7 | 13.7 | 13.7 | 13.7 | 13.6 | 13.6 | 13.6 | 13.6 | 13.5 | 13.5 | 13.5 | 13.4 | 13.4 | 13.3 | 13.3 |
| 74 | 13.1 | 13.0 | 13.0 | 13.0 | 13.0 | 13.0 | 13.0 | 12.9 | 12.9 | 12.9 | 12.8 | 12.8 | 12.8 | 12.7 | 12.7 | 12.7 |
| 75 | 12.4 | 12.4 | 12.4 | 12.4 | 12.3 | 12.3 | 12.3 | 12.3 | 12.3 | 12.2 | 12.2 | 12.2 | 12.2 | 12.1 | 12.1 | 12.1 |
| 76 | 11.8 | 11.8 | 11.7 | 11.7 | 11.7 | 11.7 | 11.7 | 11.7 | 11.6 | 11.6 | 11.6 | 11.6 | 11.6 | 11.5 | 11.5 | 11.5 |
| 77 | 11.1 | 11.1 | 11.1 | 11.1 | 11.1 | 11.1 | 11.1 | 11.1 | 11.0 | 11.0 | 11.0 | 11.0 | 11.0 | 10.9 | 10.9 | 10.9 |
| 78 | 10.5 | 10.5 | 10.5 | 10.5 | 10.5 | 10.5 | 10.5 | 10.5 | 10.5 | 10.4 | 10.4 | 10.4 | 10.4 | 10.4 | 10.3 | 10.3 |
| 79 | 10.0 | 10.0 | 9.9 | 9.9 | 9.9 | 9.9 | 9.9 | 9.9 | 9.9 | 9.9 | 9.9 | 9.8 | 9.8 | 9.8 | 9.8 | 9.8 |
| 80 | 9.4 | 9.4 | 9.4 | 9.4 | 9.4 | 9.4 | 9.4 | 9.3 | 9.3 | 9.3 | 9.3 | 9.3 | 9.3 | 9.3 | 9.2 | 9.2 |
| 81 | 8.9 | 8.8 | 8.8 | 8.8 | 8.8 | 8.8 | 8.8 | 8.8 | 8.8 | 8.8 | 8.8 | 8.8 | 8.7 | 8.7 | 8.7 | 8.7 |
| 82 | 8.3 | 8.3 | 8.3 | 8.3 | 8.3 | 8.3 | 8.3 | 8.3 | 8.3 | 8.3 | 8.3 | 8.2 | 8.2 | 8.2 | 8.2 | 8.2 |
| 83 | 7.8 | 7.8 | 7.8 | 7.8 | 7.8 | 7.8 | 7.8 | 7.8 | 7.6 | 7.8 | 7.8 | 7.8 | 7.7 | 7.7 | 7.7 | 7.7 |
| 84 | 7.3 | 7.3 | 7.3 | 7.3 | 7.3 | 7.3 | 7.3 | 7.3 | 7.3 | 7.3 | 7.3 | 7.3 | 7.3 | 7.3 | 7.3 | 7.2 |
| 85 | 6.9 | 6.9 | 6.9 | 6.9 | 6.9 | 6.9 | 6.9 | 6.9 | 6.9 | 6.9 | 6.8 | 6.8 | 6.8 | 6.8 | 6.8 | 6.8 |
| 86 | 6.5 | 6.5 | 6.5 | 6.5 | 6.4 | 6.4 | 6.4 | 6.4 | 6.4 | 6.4 | 6.4 | 6.4 | 6.4 | 6.4 | 6.4 | 6.4 |
| 87 | 6.1 | 6.0 | 6.0 | 6.0 | 6.0 | 6.0 | 6.0 | 6.0 | 6.0 | 6.0 | 6.0 | 6.0 | 6.0 | 6.0 | 6.0 | 6.0 |
| 88 | 5.7 | 5.7 | 5.7 | 5.7 | 5.7 | 5.7 | 5.7 | 5.6 | 5.6 | 5.6 | 5.6 | 5.6 | 5.6 | 5.6 | 5.6 | 5.6 |
| 89 | 5.3 | 5.3 | 5.3 | 5.3 | 5.3 | 5.3 | 5.3 | 5.3 | 5.3 | 5.3 | 5.3 | 5.3 | 5.3 | 5.3 | 5.3 | 5.3 |
| 90 | 5.0 | 5.0 | 5.0 | 5.0 | 5.0 | 5.0 | 5.0 | 5.0 | 5.0 | 5.0 | 5.0 | 4.9 | 4.9 | 4.9 | 4.9 | 4.9 |

**(Table VIA continues on the following page.)**

**Table VIA — Annuities for Joint Life Only — Two Lives — Expected Return Multiples**

| AGES | 51 | 52 | 53 | 54 | 55 | 56 | 57 | 58 | 59 | 60 | 61 | 62 | 63 | 64 | 65 | 66 |
|---|---|---|---|---|---|---|---|---|---|---|---|---|---|---|---|---|
| 51 | 26.1 | ... | ... | ... | ... | ... | ... | ... | ... | ... | ... | ... | ... | ... | ... | ... |
| 52 | 25.7 | 25.3 | ... | ... | ... | ... | ... | ... | ... | ... | ... | ... | ... | ... | ... | ... |
| 53 | 25.2 | 24.8 | 24.4 | ... | ... | ... | ... | ... | ... | ... | ... | ... | ... | ... | ... | ... |
| 54 | 24.7 | 24.4 | 24.0 | 23.6 | ... | ... | ... | ... | ... | ... | ... | ... | ... | ... | ... | ... |
| 55 | 24.2 | 23.9 | 23.5 | 23.2 | 22.7 | ... | ... | ... | ... | ... | ... | ... | ... | ... | ... | ... |
| 56 | 23.7 | 23.4 | 23.1 | 22.7 | 22.3 | 21.9 | ... | ... | ... | ... | ... | ... | ... | ... | ... | ... |
| 57 | 23.2 | 22.9 | 22.6 | 22.2 | 21.9 | 21.5 | 21.1 | ... | ... | ... | ... | ... | ... | ... | ... | ... |
| 58 | 22.6 | 22.4 | 22.1 | 21.7 | 21.4 | 21.1 | 20.7 | 20.3 | ... | ... | ... | ... | ... | ... | ... | ... |
| 59 | 22.1 | 21.8 | 21.5 | 21.2 | 20.9 | 20.6 | 20.3 | 19.9 | 19.5 | ... | ... | ... | ... | ... | ... | ... |
| 60 | 21.5 | 21.2 | 21.0 | 20.7 | 20.4 | 20.1 | 19.8 | 19.5 | 19.1 | 18.7 | ... | ... | ... | ... | ... | ... |
| 61 | 20.9 | 20.6 | 20.4 | 20.2 | 19.9 | 19.6 | 19.3 | 19.0 | 18.7 | 18.3 | 17.9 | ... | ... | ... | ... | ... |
| 62 | 20.2 | 20.0 | 19.8 | 19.6 | 19.4 | 19.1 | 18.8 | 18.5 | 18.2 | 17.9 | 17.5 | 17.1 | ... | ... | ... | ... |
| 63 | 19.6 | 19.4 | 19.2 | 19.0 | 18.8 | 18.6 | 18.3 | 18.0 | 17.7 | 17.4 | 17.1 | 16.8 | 16.4 | ... | ... | ... |
| 64 | 19.0 | 18.8 | 18.6 | 18.5 | 18.3 | 18.0 | 17.8 | 17.5 | 17.3 | 17.0 | 16.7 | 16.3 | 16.0 | 15.6 | ... | ... |
| 65 | 18.3 | 18.2 | 18.0 | 17.9 | 17.7 | 17.5 | 17.3 | 17.0 | 16.8 | 16.5 | 16.2 | 15.9 | 15.6 | 15.3 | 14.9 | ... |
| 66 | 17.7 | 17.6 | 17.4 | 17.3 | 17.1 | 16.9 | 16.7 | 16.5 | 16.3 | 16.0 | 15.8 | 15.5 | 15.2 | 14.9 | 14.5 | 14.2 |
| 67 | 17.1 | 16.9 | 16.8 | 16.7 | 16.5 | 16.3 | 16.2 | 16.0 | 15.8 | 15.5 | 15.3 | 15.0 | 14.7 | 14.5 | 14.1 | 13.8 |
| 68 | 16.4 | 16.3 | 16.2 | 16.1 | 15.9 | 15.8 | 15.6 | 15.4 | 15.2 | 15.0 | 14.8 | 14.6 | 14.3 | 14.0 | 13.7 | 13.4 |
| 69 | 15.8 | 15.7 | 15.6 | 15.4 | 15.3 | 15.2 | 15.0 | 14.9 | 14.7 | 14.5 | 14.3 | 14.1 | 13.9 | 13.6 | 13.3 | 13.1 |
| 70 | 15.1 | 15.0 | 14.9 | 14.8 | 14.7 | 14.6 | 14.5 | 14.3 | 14.2 | 14.0 | 13.8 | 13.6 | 13.4 | 13.2 | 12.9 | 12.6 |
| 71 | 14.5 | 14.4 | 14.3 | 14.2 | 14.1 | 14.0 | 13.9 | 13.8 | 13.6 | 13.5 | 13.3 | 13.1 | 12.9 | 12.7 | 12.5 | 12.2 |
| 72 | 13.8 | 13.8 | 13.7 | 13.6 | 13.5 | 13.4 | 13.3 | 13.2 | 13.1 | 12.9 | 12.8 | 12.6 | 12.4 | 12.3 | 12.0 | 11.8 |
| 73 | 13.2 | 13.2 | 13.1 | 13.0 | 13.0 | 12.9 | 12.8 | 12.7 | 12.5 | 12.4 | 12.3 | 12.1 | 12.0 | 11.8 | 11.6 | 11.4 |
| 74 | 12.6 | 12.6 | 12.5 | 12.4 | 12.4 | 12.3 | 12.2 | 12.1 | 12.0 | 11.9 | 11.8 | 11.6 | 11.5 | 11.3 | 11.2 | 11.0 |
| 75 | 12.0 | 12.0 | 11.9 | 11.9 | 11.8 | 11.7 | 11.7 | 11.6 | 11.5 | 11.4 | 11.3 | 11.1 | 11.0 | 10.9 | 10.7 | 10.5 |
| 76 | 11.4 | 11.4 | 11.3 | 11.3 | 11.2 | 11.2 | 11.1 | 11.0 | 10.9 | 10.9 | 10.8 | 10.6 | 10.5 | 10.4 | 10.3 | 10.1 |
| 77 | 10.8 | 10.8 | 10.8 | 10.7 | 10.7 | 10.6 | 10.6 | 10.5 | 10.4 | 10.3 | 10.3 | 10.2 | 10.0 | 9.9 | 9.8 | 9.7 |
| 78 | 10.3 | 10.2 | 10.2 | 10.2 | 10.1 | 10.1 | 10.0 | 10.0 | 9.9 | 9.8 | 9.8 | 9.7 | 9.6 | 9.5 | 9.4 | 9.2 |
| 79 | 9.7 | 9.7 | 9.7 | 9.6 | 9.6 | 9.6 | 9.5 | 9.5 | 9.4 | 9.3 | 9.3 | 9.2 | 9.1 | 9.0 | 8.9 | 8.8 |
| 80 | 9.2 | 9.2 | 9.1 | 9.1 | 9.1 | 9.0 | 9.0 | 9.0 | 8.9 | 8.9 | 8.8 | 8.7 | 8.7 | 8.6 | 8.5 | 8.4 |
| 81 | 8.7 | 8.7 | 8.6 | 8.6 | 8.6 | 8.5 | 8.5 | 8.5 | 8.4 | 8.4 | 8.3 | 8.3 | 8.2 | 8.1 | 8.0 | 8.0 |
| 82 | 8.2 | 8.2 | 8.1 | 8.1 | 8.1 | 8.1 | 8.0 | 8.0 | 8.0 | 7.9 | 7.9 | 7.8 | 7.8 | 7.7 | 7.6 | 7.5 |
| 83 | 7.7 | 7.7 | 7.7 | 7.6 | 7.6 | 7.6 | 7.6 | 7.5 | 7.5 | 7.5 | 7.4 | 7.4 | 7.3 | 7.3 | 7.2 | 7.1 |
| 84 | 7.2 | 7.2 | 7.2 | 7.2 | 7.2 | 7.1 | 7.1 | 7.1 | 7.1 | 7.0 | 7.0 | 7.0 | 6.9 | 6.9 | 6.8 | 6.7 |
| 85 | 6.8 | 6.8 | 6.8 | 6.7 | 6.7 | 6.7 | 6.7 | 6.7 | 6.6 | 6.6 | 6.6 | 6.5 | 6.5 | 6.5 | 6.4 | 6.4 |
| 86 | 6.4 | 6.4 | 6.3 | 6.3 | 6.3 | 6.3 | 6.3 | 6.3 | 6.2 | 6.2 | 6.2 | 6.2 | 6.1 | 6.1 | 6.0 | 6.0 |
| 87 | 6.0 | 6.0 | 6.0 | 5.9 | 5.9 | 5.9 | 5.9 | 5.9 | 5.9 | 5.8 | 5.8 | 5.8 | 5.8 | 5.7 | 5.7 | 5.6 |
| 88 | 5.6 | 5.6 | 5.6 | 5.6 | 5.6 | 5.5 | 5.5 | 5.5 | 5.5 | 5.5 | 5.5 | 5.4 | 5.4 | 5.4 | 5.3 | 5.3 |
| 89 | 5.2 | 5.2 | 5.2 | 5.2 | 5.2 | 5.2 | 5.2 | 5.2 | 5.2 | 5.1 | 5.1 | 5.1 | 5.1 | 5.1 | 5.0 | 5.0 |
| 90 | 4.9 | 4.9 | 4.9 | 4.9 | 4.9 | 4.9 | 4.9 | 4.9 | 4.9 | 4.8 | 4.8 | 4.8 | 4.8 | 4.8 | 4.7 | 4.7 |

**Table VIA — Annuities for Joint Life Only — Two Lives — Expected Return Multiples**

| AGES | 67 | 68 | 69 | 70 | 71 | 72 | 73 | 74 | 75 | 76 | 77 | 78 | 79 | 80 | 81 | 82 |
|---|---|---|---|---|---|---|---|---|---|---|---|---|---|---|---|---|
| 67 | 13.5 | ... | ... | ... | ... | ... | ... | ... | ... | ... | ... | ... | ... | ... | ... | ... |
| 68 | 13.1 | 12.8 | ... | ... | ... | ... | ... | ... | ... | ... | ... | ... | ... | ... | ... | ... |
| 69 | 12.8 | 12.5 | 12.1 | ... | ... | ... | ... | ... | ... | ... | ... | ... | ... | ... | ... | ... |
| 70 | 12.4 | 12.1 | 11.8 | 11.5 | ... | ... | ... | ... | ... | ... | ... | ... | ... | ... | ... | ... |
| 71 | 12.0 | 11.7 | 11.4 | 11.2 | 10.9 | ... | ... | ... | ... | ... | ... | ... | ... | ... | ... | ... |
| 72 | 11.6 | 11.4 | 11.1 | 10.8 | 10.5 | 10.2 | ... | ... | ... | ... | ... | ... | ... | ... | ... | ... |
| 73 | 11.2 | 11.0 | 10.7 | 10.5 | 10.2 | 9.9 | 9.7 | ... | ... | ... | ... | ... | ... | ... | ... | ... |
| 74 | 10.8 | 10.6 | 10.4 | 10.1 | 9.9 | 9.6 | 9.4 | 9.1 | ... | ... | ... | ... | ... | ... | ... | ... |
| 75 | 10.4 | 10.2 | 10.0 | 9.8 | 9.5 | 9.3 | 9.1 | 8.8 | 8.6 | ... | ... | ... | ... | ... | ... | ... |
| 76 | 9.9 | 9.8 | 9.6 | 9.4 | 9.2 | 9.0 | 8.8 | 8.5 | 8.3 | 8.0 | ... | ... | ... | ... | ... | ... |
| 77 | 9.5 | 9.4 | 9.2 | 9.0 | 8.8 | 8.6 | 8.4 | 8.2 | 8.0 | 7.8 | 7.5 | ... | ... | ... | ... | ... |
| 78 | 9.1 | 9.0 | 8.8 | 8.7 | 8.5 | 8.3 | 8.1 | 7.9 | 7.7 | 7.5 | 7.3 | 7.0 | ... | ... | ... | ... |
| 79 | 8.7 | 8.6 | 8.4 | 8.3 | 8.1 | 8.0 | 7.8 | 7.6 | 7.4 | 7.2 | 7.0 | 6.8 | 6.6 | ... | ... | ... |
| 80 | 8.3 | 8.2 | 8.0 | 7.9 | 7.8 | 7.6 | 7.5 | 7.3 | 7.1 | 6.9 | 6.8 | 6.6 | 6.3 | 6.1 | ... | ... |
| 81 | 7.9 | 7.9 | 7.7 | 7.5 | 7.4 | 7.3 | 7.1 | 7.0 | 6.8 | 6.7 | 6.5 | 6.3 | 6.1 | 5.9 | 5.7 | ... |
| 82 | 7.5 | 7.4 | 7.3 | 7.2 | 7.1 | 6.9 | 6.6 | 6.7 | 6.5 | 6.4 | 6.2 | 6.0 | 5.9 | 5.7 | 5.5 | 5.3 |
| 83 | 7.1 | 7.0 | 6.9 | 6.8 | 6.7 | 6.6 | 6.5 | 6.4 | 6.2 | 6.1 | 5.9 | 5.8 | 5.6 | 5.5 | 5.3 | 5.1 |
| 84 | 6.7 | 6.6 | 6.5 | 6.4 | 6.4 | 6.3 | 6.2 | 6.0 | 5.9 | 5.8 | 5.7 | 5.5 | 5.4 | 5.2 | 5.1 | 4.9 |
| 85 | 6.3 | 6.2 | 6.2 | 6.1 | 6.0 | 5.9 | 5.8 | 5.7 | 5.6 | 5.5 | 5.4 | 5.3 | 5.2 | 5.0 | 4.9 | 4.7 |
| 86 | 5.9 | 5.9 | 5.8 | 5.8 | 5.7 | 5.6 | 5.5 | 5.4 | 5.4 | 5.3 | 5.1 | 5.0 | 4.9 | 4.8 | 4.7 | 4.5 |
| 87 | 5.6 | 5.6 | 5.5 | 5.4 | 5.4 | 5.3 | 5.2 | 5.2 | 5.1 | 5.0 | 4.9 | 4.8 | 4.7 | 4.6 | 4.4 | 4.3 |
| 88 | 5.3 | 5.2 | 5.2 | 5.1 | 5.1 | 5.0 | 5.0 | 4.9 | 4.8 | 4.7 | 4.6 | 4.5 | 4.4 | 4.3 | 4.2 | 4.1 |
| 89 | 5.0 | 4.9 | 4.9 | 4.8 | 4.8 | 4.7 | 4.7 | 4.6 | 4.5 | 4.5 | 4.4 | 4.3 | 4.2 | 4.1 | 4.0 | 3.9 |
| 90 | 4.7 | 4.6 | 4.6 | 4.6 | 4.5 | 4.5 | 4.4 | 4.4 | 4.3 | 4.2 | 4.2 | 4.1 | 4.0 | 3.9 | 3.8 | 3.8 |

| AGES | 83 | 84 | 85 | 86 | 87 | 88 | 89 | 90 |
|---|---|---|---|---|---|---|---|---|
| 83 | 4.9 | ... | ... | ... | ... | ... | ... | ... |
| 84 | 4.7 | 4.6 | ... | ... | ... | ... | ... | ... |
| 85 | 4.6 | 4.4 | 4.2 | ... | ... | ... | ... | ... |
| 86 | 4.4 | 4.2 | 4.1 | 3.9 | ... | ... | ... | ... |
| 87 | 4.2 | 4.1 | 3.9 | 3.8 | 3.6 | ... | ... | ... |
| 88 | 4.0 | 3.9 | 3.8 | 3.6 | 3.5 | 3.4 | ... | ... |
| 89 | 3.8 | 3.7 | 3.6 | 3.5 | 3.4 | 3.2 | 3.1 | ... |
| 90 | 3.7 | 3.5 | 3.4 | 3.3 | 3.2 | 3.1 | 3.0 | 2.9 |

## Table VII — Percent Value of Refund Feature
### Duration of Guaranteed Amount

| Age | 1 Yr. | 2 Yrs. | 3 Yrs. | 4 Yrs. | 5 Yrs. | 6 Yrs. | 7 Yrs. | 8 Yrs. | 9 Yrs. | 10 Yrs. | 11 Yrs. | 12 Yrs. | 13 Yrs. | 14 Yrs. | 15 Yrs. | 16 Yrs. | 17 Yrs. | 18 Yrs. | 19 Yrs. | 20 Yrs. |
|---|---|---|---|---|---|---|---|---|---|---|---|---|---|---|---|---|---|---|---|---|
| 19 | ... | ... | ... | ... | ... | ... | ... | ... | ... | ... | ... | ... | ... | ... | ... | ... | ... | ... | ... | ... |
| 20 | ... | ... | ... | ... | ... | ... | ... | ... | ... | ... | ... | ... | ... | ... | ... | ... | ... | ... | ... | 1 |
| 21 | ... | ... | ... | ... | ... | ... | ... | ... | ... | ... | ... | ... | ... | ... | ... | ... | ... | ... | ... | 1 |
| 22 | ... | ... | ... | ... | ... | ... | ... | ... | ... | ... | ... | ... | ... | ... | ... | ... | ... | ... | ... | 1 |
| 23 | ... | ... | ... | ... | ... | ... | ... | ... | ... | ... | ... | ... | ... | ... | ... | ... | ... | 1 | 1 | 1 |
| 24 | ... | ... | ... | ... | ... | ... | ... | ... | ... | ... | ... | ... | ... | ... | ... | ... | ... | 1 | 1 | 1 |
| 25 | ... | ... | ... | ... | ... | ... | ... | ... | ... | ... | ... | ... | ... | ... | ... | ... | 1 | 1 | 1 | 1 |
| 26 | ... | ... | ... | ... | ... | ... | ... | ... | ... | ... | ... | ... | ... | ... | ... | ... | 1 | 1 | 1 | 1 |
| 27 | ... | ... | ... | ... | ... | ... | ... | ... | ... | ... | ... | ... | ... | ... | ... | 1 | 1 | 1 | 1 | 1 |
| 28 | ... | ... | ... | ... | ... | ... | ... | ... | ... | ... | ... | ... | ... | ... | 1 | 1 | 1 | 1 | 1 | 1 |
| 29 | ... | ... | ... | ... | ... | ... | ... | ... | ... | ... | ... | ... | ... | ... | 1 | 1 | 1 | 1 | 1 | 1 |
| 30 | ... | ... | ... | ... | ... | ... | ... | ... | ... | ... | ... | ... | ... | 1 | 1 | 1 | 1 | 1 | 1 | 1 |
| 31 | ... | ... | ... | ... | ... | ... | ... | ... | ... | ... | ... | ... | ... | 1 | 1 | 1 | 1 | 1 | 1 | 1 |
| 32 | ... | ... | ... | ... | ... | ... | ... | ... | ... | ... | ... | ... | ... | 1 | 1 | 1 | 1 | 1 | 1 | 1 |
| 33 | ... | ... | ... | ... | ... | ... | ... | ... | ... | ... | ... | ... | 1 | 1 | 1 | 1 | 1 | 1 | 1 | 1 |
| 34 | ... | ... | ... | ... | ... | ... | ... | ... | ... | ... | ... | 1 | 1 | 1 | 1 | 1 | 1 | 1 | 1 | 1 |
| 35 | ... | ... | ... | ... | ... | ... | ... | ... | ... | ... | ... | 1 | 1 | 1 | 1 | 1 | 1 | 1 | 1 | 1 |
| 36 | ... | ... | ... | ... | ... | ... | ... | ... | ... | ... | 1 | 1 | 1 | 1 | 1 | 1 | 1 | 1 | 1 | 1 |
| 37 | ... | ... | ... | ... | ... | ... | ... | ... | ... | 1 | 1 | 1 | 1 | 1 | 1 | 1 | 1 | 1 | 1 | 1 |
| 38 | ... | ... | ... | ... | ... | ... | ... | ... | ... | 1 | 1 | 1 | 1 | 1 | 1 | 1 | 1 | 1 | 1 | 2 |
| 39 | ... | ... | ... | ... | ... | ... | ... | ... | 1 | 1 | 1 | 1 | 1 | 1 | 1 | 1 | 1 | 1 | 2 | 2 |
| 40 | ... | ... | ... | ... | ... | ... | ... | 1 | 1 | 1 | 1 | 1 | 1 | 1 | 1 | 1 | 1 | 2 | 2 | 2 |
| 41 | ... | ... | ... | ... | ... | ... | ... | 1 | 1 | 1 | 1 | 1 | 1 | 1 | 1 | 1 | 2 | 2 | 2 | 2 |
| 42 | ... | ... | ... | ... | ... | ... | 1 | 1 | 1 | 1 | 1 | 1 | 1 | 1 | 1 | 2 | 2 | 2 | 2 | 2 |
| 43 | ... | ... | ... | ... | ... | ... | 1 | 1 | 1 | 1 | 1 | 1 | 1 | 1 | 2 | 2 | 2 | 2 | 2 | 3 |
| 44 | ... | | | ... | ... | 1 | 1 | 1 | 1 | 1 | 1 | 1 | 1 | 2 | 2 | 2 | 2 | 2 | 3 | 3 |
| 45 | ... | ... | ... | ... | ... | 1 | 1 | 1 | 1 | 1 | 1 | 1 | 2 | 2 | 2 | 2 | 2 | 3 | 3 | 3 |
| 46 | ... | ... | ... | ... | 1 | 1 | 1 | 1 | 1 | 1 | 1 | 2 | 2 | 2 | 2 | 2 | 3 | 3 | 3 | 3 |
| 47 | ... | ... | ... | ... | 1 | 1 | 1 | 1 | 1 | 1 | 1 | 2 | 2 | 2 | 2 | 2 | 3 | 3 | 3 | 4 |
| 48 | ... | ... | ... | ... | 1 | 1 | 1 | 1 | 1 | 1 | 2 | 2 | 2 | 2 | 2 | 3 | 3 | 3 | 4 | 4 |
| 49 | ... | ... | ... | 1 | 1 | 1 | 1 | 1 | 1 | 2 | 2 | 2 | 2 | 2 | 3 | 3 | 3 | 4 | 4 | 4 |
| 50 | ... | ... | ... | 1 | 1 | 1 | 1 | 1 | 1 | 2 | 2 | 2 | 2 | 3 | 3 | 3 | 3 | 4 | 4 | 5 |
| 51 | ... | ... | ... | 1 | 1 | 1 | 1 | 1 | 2 | 2 | 2 | 2 | 3 | 3 | 3 | 3 | 4 | 4 | 4 | 5 |
| 52 | ... | ... | ... | 1 | 1 | 1 | 1 | 1 | 2 | 2 | 2 | 2 | 3 | 3 | 3 | 4 | 4 | 5 | 5 | 5 |
| 53 | ... | ... | 1 | 1 | 1 | 1 | 1 | 2 | 2 | 2 | 2 | 3 | 3 | 3 | 4 | 4 | 5 | 5 | 5 | 6 |
| 54 | ... | ... | 1 | 1 | 1 | 1 | 1 | 2 | 2 | 2 | 3 | 3 | 3 | 4 | 4 | 4 | 5 | 5 | 6 | 7 |
| 55 | ... | ... | 1 | 1 | 1 | 1 | 2 | 2 | 2 | 2 | 3 | 3 | 4 | 4 | 4 | 5 | 5 | 6 | 7 | 7 |
| 56 | ... | ... | 1 | 1 | 1 | 1 | 2 | 2 | 2 | 3 | 3 | 3 | 4 | 4 | 5 | 5 | 6 | 7 | 7 | 8 |
| 57 | ... | ... | 1 | 1 | 1 | 2 | 2 | 2 | 3 | 3 | 3 | 4 | 4 | 5 | 5 | 6 | 6 | 7 | 8 | 9 |
| 58 | ... | 1 | 1 | 1 | 1 | 2 | 2 | 2 | 3 | 3 | 4 | 4 | 5 | 5 | 6 | 6 | 7 | 8 | 9 | 9 |
| 59 | ... | 1 | 1 | 1 | 1 | 2 | 2 | 3 | 3 | 4 | 4 | 5 | 5 | 6 | 6 | 7 | 8 | 9 | 9 | 10 |
| 60 | ... | 1 | 1 | 1 | 2 | 2 | 2 | 3 | 3 | 4 | 4 | 5 | 6 | 6 | 7 | 8 | 9 | 10 | 10 | 11 |
| 61 | ... | 1 | 1 | 1 | 2 | 2 | 3 | 3 | 4 | 4 | 5 | 6 | 6 | 7 | 8 | 9 | 10 | 10 | 11 | 13 |
| 62 | ... | 1 | 1 | 2 | 2 | 2 | 3 | 4 | 4 | 5 | 5 | 6 | 7 | 8 | 9 | 10 | 11 | 12 | 13 | 14 |
| 63 | ... | 1 | 1 | 2 | 2 | 3 | 3 | 4 | 5 | 5 | 6 | 7 | 8 | 9 | 10 | 11 | 12 | 13 | 14 | 15 |
| 64 | ... | 1 | 1 | 2 | 2 | 3 | 4 | 4 | 5 | 6 | 7 | 8 | 8 | 9 | 10 | 12 | 13 | 14 | 15 | 17 |
| 65 | ... | 1 | 2 | 2 | 3 | 3 | 4 | 5 | 6 | 6 | 7 | 8 | 9 | 10 | 12 | 13 | 14 | 15 | 17 | 18 |
| 66 | 1 | 1 | 2 | 2 | 3 | 4 | 5 | 5 | 6 | 7 | 8 | 9 | 10 | 12 | 13 | 14 | 15 | 17 | 18 | 20 |
| 67 | 1 | 1 | 2 | 3 | 3 | 4 | 5 | 6 | 7 | 8 | 9 | 10 | 11 | 13 | 14 | 15 | 17 | 18 | 20 | 22 |
| 68 | 1 | 1 | 2 | 3 | 4 | 5 | 6 | 7 | 8 | 9 | 10 | 11 | 13 | 14 | 15 | 17 | 19 | 20 | 22 | 24 |
| 69 | 1 | 1 | 2 | 3 | 4 | 5 | 6 | 7 | 8 | 10 | 11 | 12 | 14 | 15 | 17 | 19 | 20 | 22 | 24 | 26 |
| 70 | 1 | 2 | 3 | 4 | 5 | 6 | 7 | 8 | 9 | 11 | 12 | 14 | 15 | 17 | 19 | 20 | 22 | 24 | 26 | 28 |
| 71 | 1 | 2 | 3 | 4 | 5 | 6 | 8 | 9 | 10 | 12 | 13 | 15 | 17 | 18 | 20 | 22 | 24 | 26 | 28 | 30 |
| 72 | 1 | 2 | 3 | 4 | 6 | 7 | 8 | 10 | 11 | 13 | 15 | 17 | 18 | 20 | 22 | 24 | 26 | 28 | 30 | 32 |
| 73 | 1 | 2 | 4 | 5 | 6 | 8 | 9 | 11 | 13 | 14 | 16 | 18 | 20 | 22 | 24 | 26 | 28 | 31 | 33 | 35 |
| 74 | 1 | 3 | 4 | 5 | 7 | 9 | 10 | 12 | 14 | 16 | 18 | 20 | 22 | 24 | 26 | 28 | 31 | 33 | 35 | 37 |
| 75 | 1 | 3 | 4 | 6 | 8 | 9 | 11 | 13 | 15 | 17 | 19 | 22 | 24 | 26 | 28 | 31 | 33 | 35 | 38 | 40 |
| 76 | 2 | 3 | 5 | 7 | 9 | 10 | 12 | 15 | 17 | 19 | 21 | 24 | 26 | 28 | 31 | 33 | 36 | 38 | 40 | 43 |
| 77 | 2 | 4 | 5 | 7 | 9 | 12 | 14 | 16 | 18 | 21 | 23 | 26 | 28 | 31 | 33 | 36 | 38 | 41 | 43 | 45 |
| 78 | 2 | 4 | 6 | 8 | 10 | 13 | 15 | 18 | 20 | 23 | 25 | 28 | 31 | 33 | 36 | 38 | 41 | 43 | 46 | 48 |
| 79 | 2 | 4 | 7 | 9 | 11 | 14 | 17 | 19 | 22 | 25 | 28 | 30 | 33 | 36 | 38 | 41 | 44 | 46 | 48 | 51 |
| 80 | 2 | 5 | 7 | 10 | 13 | 15 | 18 | 21 | 24 | 27 | 30 | 33 | 36 | 38 | 41 | 44 | 46 | 49 | 51 | 53 |
| 81 | 3 | 5 | 8 | 11 | 14 | 17 | 20 | 23 | 26 | 29 | 32 | 35 | 38 | 41 | 44 | 47 | 48 | 51 | 54 | 56 |
| 82 | 3 | 6 | 9 | 12 | 15 | 19 | 22 | 25 | 28 | 32 | 35 | 38 | 41 | 44 | 47 | 49 | 52 | 54 | 56 | 58 |
| 83 | 3 | 7 | 10 | 13 | 17 | 20 | 24 | 27 | 31 | 34 | 38 | 41 | 44 | 47 | 49 | 52 | 54 | 57 | 59 | 61 |
| 84 | 4 | 7 | 11 | 15 | 19 | 22 | 26 | 30 | 33 | 37 | 40 | 44 | 47 | 49 | 52 | 55 | 57 | 59 | 61 | 63 |
| 85 | 4 | 8 | 12 | 16 | 20 | 24 | 28 | 32 | 36 | 40 | 43 | 46 | 49 | 52 | 55 | 57 | 59 | 62 | 63 | 65 |
| 86 | 4 | 9 | 13 | 18 | 22 | 27 | 31 | 35 | 39 | 42 | 46 | 49 | 52 | 55 | 57 | 60 | 62 | 64 | 66 | 67 |
| 87 | 5 | 10 | 15 | 20 | 24 | 29 | 33 | 37 | 41 | 45 | 48 | 52 | 55 | 57 | 60 | 62 | 64 | 66 | 68 | 69 |
| 88 | 5 | 11 | 16 | 21 | 26 | 31 | 36 | 40 | 44 | 48 | 51 | 54 | 57 | 60 | 62 | 64 | 66 | 68 | 70 | 71 |
| 89 | 6 | 12 | 18 | 23 | 28 | 33 | 38 | 43 | 47 | 50 | 54 | 57 | 60 | 62 | 65 | 67 | 68 | 70 | 72 | 73 |
| 90 | 7 | 13 | 19 | 25 | 31 | 36 | 41 | 45 | 49 | 53 | 56 | 59 | 62 | 64 | 67 | 69 | 70 | 72 | 74 | 75 |

## Table VII — Percent Value of Refund Feature
### Duration of Guaranteed Amount

| Age | 21 Yrs. | 22 Yrs. | 23 Yrs. | 24 Yrs. | 25 Yrs. | 26 Yrs. | 27 Yrs. | 28 Yrs. | 29 Yrs. | 30 Yrs. | 31 Yrs. | 32 Yrs. | 33 Yrs. | 34 Yrs. | 35 Yrs. | 36 Yrs. | 37 Yrs. | 38 Yrs. | 39 Yrs. | 40 Yrs. |
|---|---|---|---|---|---|---|---|---|---|---|---|---|---|---|---|---|---|---|---|---|
| 5 | ... | ... | ... | ... | ... | ... | ... | ... | ... | ... | ... | 1 | 1 | 1 | 1 | 1 | 1 | 1 | 1 | 1 |
| 6 | ... | ... | ... | ... | ... | ... | ... | ... | ... | ... | ... | 1 | 1 | 1 | 1 | 1 | 1 | 1 | 1 | 1 |
| 7 | ... | ... | ... | ... | ... | ... | ... | ... | ... | ... | 1 | 1 | 1 | 1 | 1 | 1 | 1 | 1 | 1 | 1 |
| 8 | ... | ... | ... | ... | ... | ... | ... | ... | ... | 1 | 1 | 1 | 1 | 1 | 1 | 1 | 1 | 1 | 1 | 1 |
| 9 | ... | ... | ... | ... | ... | ... | ... | ... | ... | 1 | 1 | 1 | 1 | 1 | 1 | 1 | 1 | 1 | 1 | 1 |
| 10 | ... | ... | ... | ... | ... | ... | ... | 1 | 1 | 1 | 1 | 1 | 1 | 1 | 1 | 1 | 1 | 1 | 1 | 1 |
| 11 | ... | ... | ... | ... | ... | ... | 1 | 1 | 1 | 1 | 1 | 1 | 1 | 1 | 1 | 1 | 1 | 1 | 1 | 1 |
| 12 | ... | ... | ... | ... | ... | ... | 1 | 1 | 1 | 1 | 1 | 1 | 1 | 1 | 1 | 1 | 1 | 1 | 1 | 1 |
| 13 | ... | ... | ... | ... | ... | 1 | 1 | 1 | 1 | 1 | 1 | 1 | 1 | 1 | 1 | 1 | 1 | 1 | 1 | 1 |
| 14 | ... | ... | ... | ... | 1 | 1 | 1 | 1 | 1 | 1 | 1 | 1 | 1 | 1 | 1 | 1 | 1 | 1 | 1 | 1 |
| 15 | ... | ... | ... | 1 | 1 | 1 | 1 | 1 | 1 | 1 | 1 | 1 | 1 | 1 | 1 | 1 | 1 | 1 | 1 | 1 |
| 16 | ... | ... | 1 | 1 | 1 | 1 | 1 | 1 | 1 | 1 | 1 | 1 | 1 | 1 | 1 | 1 | 1 | 1 | 1 | 1 |
| 17 | ... | ... | 1 | 1 | 1 | 1 | 1 | 1 | 1 | 1 | 1 | 1 | 1 | 1 | 1 | 1 | 1 | 1 | 1 | 1 |
| 18 | ... | 1 | 1 | 1 | 1 | 1 | 1 | 1 | 1 | 1 | 1 | 1 | 1 | 1 | 1 | 1 | 1 | 1 | 1 | 2 |
| 19 | 1 | 1 | 1 | 1 | 1 | 1 | 1 | 1 | 1 | 1 | 1 | 1 | 1 | 1 | 1 | 1 | 1 | 1 | 2 | 2 |
| 20 | 1 | 1 | 1 | 1 | 1 | 1 | 1 | 1 | 1 | 1 | 1 | 1 | 1 | 1 | 1 | 1 | 1 | 2 | 2 | 2 |
| 21 | 1 | 1 | 1 | 1 | 1 | 1 | 1 | 1 | 1 | 1 | 1 | 1 | 1 | 1 | 1 | 1 | 2 | 2 | 2 | 2 |
| 22 | 1 | 1 | 1 | 1 | 1 | 1 | 1 | 1 | 1 | 1 | 1 | 1 | 1 | 1 | 1 | 2 | 2 | 2 | 2 | 2 |
| 23 | 1 | 1 | 1 | 1 | 1 | 1 | 1 | 1 | 1 | 1 | 1 | 1 | 1 | 2 | 2 | 2 | 2 | 2 | 2 | 2 |
| 24 | 1 | 1 | 1 | 1 | 1 | 1 | 1 | 1 | 1 | 1 | 1 | 1 | 2 | 2 | 2 | 2 | 2 | 2 | 2 | 2 |
| 25 | 1 | 1 | 1 | 1 | 1 | 1 | 1 | 1 | 1 | 1 | 1 | 2 | 2 | 2 | 2 | 2 | 2 | 2 | 2 | 3 |
| 26 | 1 | 1 | 1 | 1 | 1 | 1 | 1 | 1 | 1 | 1 | 2 | 2 | 2 | 2 | 2 | 2 | 2 | 2 | 3 | 3 |
| 27 | 1 | 1 | 1 | 1 | 1 | 1 | 1 | 1 | 1 | 2 | 2 | 2 | 2 | 2 | 2 | 2 | 2 | 3 | 3 | 3 |
| 28 | 1 | 1 | 1 | 1 | 1 | 1 | 1 | 1 | 2 | 2 | 2 | 2 | 2 | 2 | 2 | 2 | 3 | 3 | 3 | 3 |
| 29 | 1 | 1 | 1 | 1 | 1 | 1 | 1 | 2 | 2 | 2 | 2 | 2 | 2 | 2 | 2 | 3 | 3 | 3 | 3 | 4 |
| 30 | 1 | 1 | 1 | 1 | 1 | 1 | 2 | 2 | 2 | 2 | 2 | 2 | 2 | 3 | 3 | 3 | 3 | 3 | 4 | 4 |
| 31 | 1 | 1 | 1 | 1 | 1 | 2 | 2 | 2 | 2 | 2 | 2 | 2 | 3 | 3 | 3 | 3 | 3 | 4 | 4 | 4 |
| 32 | 1 | 1 | 1 | 1 | 2 | 2 | 2 | 2 | 2 | 2 | 2 | 3 | 3 | 3 | 3 | 3 | 4 | 4 | 4 | 5 |
| 33 | 1 | 1 | 1 | 2 | 2 | 2 | 2 | 2 | 2 | 2 | 3 | 3 | 3 | 3 | 3 | 4 | 4 | 4 | 5 | 5 |
| 34 | 1 | 1 | 2 | 2 | 2 | 2 | 2 | 2 | 2 | 3 | 3 | 3 | 3 | 3 | 4 | 4 | 4 | 5 | 5 | 5 |
| 35 | 1 | 2 | 2 | 2 | 2 | 2 | 2 | 2 | 3 | 3 | 3 | 3 | 3 | 4 | 4 | 4 | 5 | 5 | 5 | 6 |
| 36 | 2 | 2 | 2 | 2 | 2 | 2 | 2 | 3 | 3 | 3 | 3 | 4 | 4 | 4 | 4 | 5 | 5 | 5 | 6 | 6 |
| 37 | 2 | 2 | 2 | 2 | 2 | 2 | 3 | 3 | 3 | 3 | 4 | 4 | 4 | 4 | 5 | 5 | 6 | 6 | 6 | 7 |
| 38 | 2 | 2 | 2 | 2 | 2 | 3 | 3 | 3 | 3 | 4 | 4 | 4 | 5 | 5 | 5 | 6 | 6 | 7 | 7 | 8 |
| 39 | 2 | 2 | 2 | 2 | 3 | 3 | 3 | 3 | 4 | 4 | 4 | 5 | 5 | 5 | 6 | 6 | 7 | 7 | 8 | 8 |
| 40 | 2 | 2 | 3 | 3 | 3 | 3 | 3 | 4 | 4 | 4 | 5 | 5 | 5 | 6 | 6 | 7 | 7 | 8 | 8 | 9 |
| 41 | 2 | 3 | 3 | 3 | 3 | 3 | 4 | 4 | 4 | 5 | 5 | 5 | 6 | 6 | 7 | 7 | 8 | 9 | 9 | 10 |
| 42 | 3 | 3 | 3 | 3 | 3 | 4 | 4 | 4 | 5 | 5 | 6 | 6 | 6 | 7 | 7 | 8 | 9 | 9 | 10 | 11 |
| 43 | 3 | 3 | 3 | 4 | 4 | 4 | 4 | 5 | 5 | 6 | 6 | 7 | 7 | 8 | 8 | 9 | 9 | 10 | 11 | 12 |
| 44 | 3 | 3 | 4 | 4 | 4 | 4 | 5 | 5 | 6 | 6 | 7 | 7 | 8 | 8 | 9 | 10 | 10 | 11 | 12 | 13 |
| 45 | 3 | 4 | 4 | 4 | 5 | 5 | 5 | 6 | 6 | 7 | 7 | 8 | 8 | 9 | 10 | 10 | 11 | 12 | 13 | 14 |
| 46 | 4 | 4 | 4 | 5 | 5 | 5 | 6 | 6 | 7 | 7 | 8 | 9 | 9 | 10 | 11 | 11 | 12 | 13 | 14 | 15 |
| 47 | 4 | 4 | 5 | 5 | 5 | 6 | 6 | 7 | 7 | 8 | 9 | 9 | 10 | 11 | 12 | 12 | 13 | 14 | 15 | 16 |
| 48 | 4 | 5 | 5 | 5 | 6 | 6 | 7 | 7 | 8 | 9 | 9 | 10 | 11 | 12 | 13 | 14 | 15 | 16 | 17 | 18 |
| 49 | 5 | 5 | 5 | 6 | 6 | 7 | 8 | 8 | 9 | 10 | 10 | 11 | 12 | 13 | 14 | 15 | 16 | 17 | 18 | 19 |
| 50 | 5 | 5 | 6 | 6 | 7 | 8 | 8 | 9 | 10 | 10 | 11 | 12 | 13 | 14 | 15 | 16 | 17 | 18 | 20 | 21 |
| 51 | 5 | 6 | 6 | 7 | 8 | 8 | 9 | 10 | 11 | 11 | 12 | 13 | 14 | 15 | 16 | 17 | 19 | 20 | 21 | 22 |
| 52 | 6 | 7 | 7 | 8 | 8 | 9 | 10 | 11 | 11 | 12 | 13 | 14 | 15 | 17 | 18 | 19 | 20 | 21 | 23 | 24 |
| 53 | 7 | 7 | 8 | 8 | 9 | 10 | 11 | 12 | 13 | 14 | 15 | 16 | 17 | 18 | 19 | 20 | 22 | 23 | 24 | 26 |
| 54 | 7 | 8 | 8 | 9 | 10 | 11 | 12 | 13 | 14 | 15 | 16 | 17 | 18 | 19 | 21 | 22 | 23 | 25 | 26 | 28 |
| 55 | 8 | 9 | 9 | 10 | 11 | 12 | 13 | 14 | 15 | 16 | 17 | 18 | 20 | 21 | 22 | 24 | 25 | 27 | 28 | 30 |
| 56 | 9 | 9 | 10 | 11 | 12 | 13 | 14 | 15 | 16 | 18 | 19 | 20 | 21 | 23 | 24 | 26 | 27 | 29 | 30 | 32 |
| 57 | 9 | 10 | 11 | 12 | 13 | 14 | 15 | 17 | 18 | 19 | 20 | 22 | 23 | 25 | 26 | 28 | 29 | 31 | 32 | 34 |
| 58 | 10 | 11 | 12 | 13 | 14 | 16 | 17 | 18 | 19 | 21 | 22 | 24 | 25 | 27 | 28 | 30 | 31 | 33 | 34 | 36 |
| 59 | 11 | 12 | 13 | 15 | 16 | 17 | 18 | 20 | 21 | 22 | 24 | 25 | 27 | 28 | 30 | 32 | 33 | 35 | 36 | 38 |
| 60 | 12 | 14 | 15 | 16 | 17 | 19 | 20 | 21 | 23 | 24 | 26 | 27 | 29 | 31 | 32 | 34 | 35 | 37 | 38 | 40 |
| 61 | 14 | 15 | 16 | 17 | 19 | 20 | 22 | 23 | 25 | 26 | 28 | 29 | 31 | 33 | 34 | 36 | 37 | 39 | 40 | 42 |
| 62 | 15 | 16 | 18 | 19 | 20 | 22 | 23 | 25 | 27 | 28 | 30 | 32 | 33 | 35 | 36 | 38 | 40 | 41 | 42 | 44 |
| 63 | 16 | 18 | 19 | 21 | 22 | 24 | 25 | 27 | 29 | 30 | 32 | 34 | 35 | 37 | 39 | 40 | 42 | 43 | 45 | 46 |
| 64 | 18 | 19 | 21 | 23 | 24 | 26 | 28 | 29 | 31 | 33 | 34 | 36 | 38 | 39 | 41 | 42 | 44 | 45 | 47 | 48 |
| 65 | 20 | 21 | 23 | 25 | 26 | 28 | 30 | 31 | 33 | 35 | 37 | 38 | 40 | 42 | 43 | 45 | 46 | 47 | 49 | 50 |
| 66 | 21 | 23 | 25 | 27 | 28 | 30 | 32 | 34 | 35 | 37 | 39 | 41 | 42 | 44 | 45 | 47 | 48 | 50 | 51 | 52 |
| 67 | 23 | 25 | 27 | 29 | 31 | 32 | 34 | 36 | 38 | 40 | 41 | 43 | 45 | 46 | 48 | 49 | 50 | 52 | 53 | 54 |
| 68 | 25 | 27 | 29 | 31 | 33 | 35 | 37 | 38 | 40 | 42 | 44 | 45 | 47 | 48 | 50 | 51 | 52 | 54 | 55 | 56 |
| 69 | 28 | 29 | 31 | 33 | 35 | 37 | 39 | 41 | 43 | 44 | 46 | 48 | 49 | 51 | 52 | 53 | 54 | 56 | 57 | 58 |
| 70 | 30 | 32 | 34 | 36 | 38 | 40 | 42 | 43 | 45 | 47 | 48 | 50 | 51 | 53 | 54 | 55 | 57 | 58 | 59 | 60 |
| 71 | 32 | 34 | 36 | 38 | 40 | 42 | 44 | 46 | 47 | 49 | 51 | 52 | 54 | 55 | 56 | 57 | 59 | 60 | 61 | 62 |
| 72 | 35 | 37 | 39 | 41 | 43 | 45 | 46 | 48 | 50 | 51 | 53 | 54 | 56 | 57 | 58 | 59 | 60 | 62 | 62 | 63 |
| 73 | 37 | 39 | 41 | 43 | 45 | 47 | 49 | 51 | 52 | 54 | 55 | 57 | 58 | 59 | 60 | 61 | 62 | 63 | 64 | 65 |
| 74 | 40 | 42 | 44 | 46 | 48 | 50 | 51 | 53 | 54 | 56 | 57 | 59 | 60 | 61 | 62 | 63 | 64 | 65 | 66 | 67 |
| 75 | 42 | 44 | 46 | 48 | 50 | 52 | 54 | 55 | 57 | 58 | 59 | 61 | 62 | 63 | 64 | 65 | 66 | 67 | 68 | 69 |
| 76 | 45 | 47 | 49 | 51 | 53 | 54 | 56 | 58 | 59 | 60 | 62 | 63 | 64 | 65 | 66 | 67 | 68 | 69 | 69 | 70 |
| 77 | 47 | 50 | 51 | 53 | 55 | 57 | 58 | 60 | 61 | 62 | 64 | 65 | 66 | 67 | 68 | 69 | 70 | 70 | 71 | 72 |
| 78 | 50 | 52 | 54 | 56 | 57 | 59 | 61 | 62 | 63 | 64 | 66 | 67 | 68 | 69 | 70 | 70 | 71 | 72 | 73 | 73 |
| 79 | 53 | 55 | 56 | 58 | 60 | 61 | 63 | 64 | 65 | 66 | 67 | 68 | 69 | 70 | 71 | 72 | 73 | 73 | 74 | 75 |
| 80 | 55 | 57 | 59 | 60 | 62 | 63 | 65 | 66 | 67 | 68 | 69 | 70 | 71 | 72 | 73 | 74 | 74 | 75 | 76 | 76 |
| 81 | 58 | 59 | 61 | 63 | 64 | 66 | 67 | 68 | 69 | 70 | 71 | 72 | 73 | 74 | 74 | 75 | 76 | 76 | 77 | 78 |
| 82 | 60 | 62 | 63 | 65 | 66 | 68 | 69 | 70 | 71 | 72 | 73 | 74 | 74 | 75 | 76 | 77 | 77 | 78 | 78 | 79 |
| 83 | 62 | 64 | 66 | 67 | 68 | 70 | 71 | 72 | 73 | 74 | 74 | 75 | 76 | 77 | 77 | 78 | 79 | 79 | 80 | 80 |
| 84 | 65 | 66 | 68 | 69 | 70 | 71 | 72 | 73 | 74 | 75 | 76 | 77 | 77 | 78 | 79 | 79 | 80 | 80 | 81 | 81 |
| 85 | 67 | 68 | 70 | 71 | 72 | 73 | 74 | 75 | 76 | 77 | 78 | 78 | 79 | 79 | 80 | 81 | 81 | 82 | 82 | 83 |
| 86 | 69 | 70 | 72 | 73 | 74 | 75 | 76 | 77 | 77 | 78 | 79 | 80 | 80 | 81 | 81 | 82 | 82 | 83 | 83 | 84 |
| 87 | 71 | 72 | 73 | 75 | 76 | 76 | 77 | 78 | 79 | 80 | 80 | 81 | 81 | 82 | 83 | 83 | 83 | 84 | 84 | 85 |
| 88 | 73 | 74 | 75 | 76 | 77 | 78 | 79 | 80 | 80 | 81 | 82 | 82 | 83 | 83 | 84 | 84 | 85 | 85 | 85 | 86 |
| 89 | 74 | 76 | 77 | 78 | 79 | 79 | 80 | 81 | 81 | 82 | 83 | 83 | 84 | 84 | 85 | 85 | 85 | 86 | 86 | 87 |
| 90 | 76 | 77 | 78 | 79 | 80 | 81 | 81 | 82 | 83 | 83 | 84 | 84 | 85 | 85 | 86 | 86 | 86 | 87 | 87 | 87 |

# Index


## A

Account and balance summaries........106-107
Account rebalancing, automatic ..........76, 143
Account transfer fee....................................164
Accounts
  Guaranteed interest..........................136-137
    selection of variable, see "variable accounts"
    transfers among...........................142-143
  variable, see "variable accounts"
Accumulation units.............................131-132
Allocation
  asset......................................97, 98-100, 108
  investment.......................6-7, 74-75, 76, 77
  premium.......................................11, 74, 76
Annual variable annuity sales ........................9
Annuities as gifts .........................210, 230-231
Annuitizing (also see "payouts"and "payout options")..................12, 16-17, 25, 27-28, 29, 31, 83-84, 146-150
Asset allocation ...............97, 98-100, 108, 142
Asset allocation model..........................98-100
Automatic account rebalancing ................143
Averaging,
  dollar cost..................61, 71-73, 95-97, 108

## B

Bonds
  callable....................................................180
  convertible...............................................180
  debentures...............................................180
  municipal...............................182-183, 187
  secured ...................................................180
Bonus annuities...................123-124, 150-151
Broker/dealers
  compliance meetings.............................117
  continuing education ............................118
  field offices.....................................118-120
  products ..................................................112
  registration ............................112, 114-115
  sales literature.................................120-121

## C

Certificates of deposit (CD).......................189
Charges and fees
  account transfer fee ...............................164
  comparisons and customer
    value..........................................167-168
  contract fee ............................................160
  interest margin in guaranteed
    accounts....................................160-161
  investment advisory fee ..........160, 162-163
Charges and fees (cont'd)
  investment management fee...........162-163
  mortality and expense (M & E)
    charge.........................................161-162
  optional benefits....................................163
  reasonableness standard ................159-160
  sales load.................................159-160, 165
  surrender charge........144, 145-146, 164-166
Charitable gifts ...................................210-211
Charitable trusts .................................211-212
Code of ethics, RIA ............................116-117
College expenses................63, 66-69, 206-210
Commission rates
  asset-based......................172, 173-174, 175
  fixed annuities................................173-174
  premiums........................172, 173-174, 175
Compensation
  manager................................................ 173
  producer.................................................172
Contract exchanges ............................123-124
Contract fee ............................................... 160
Control
  changing investments for ...........61, 76, 143
  maintaining........................................61, 76
  timing income taxes ..........................51, 76
Convenient to purchase variable
  annuities .................................................8-9
Cost of Delay ....................................61, 69-71
Coverdell Educational Savings.............67, 207
Credits
  Hope Scholarship ............................66, 207
  Lifetime Learning .......................66, 67, 207
Customer satisfaction,
  achieving.....................................93-94, 109

## D

Death benefit, regular,
  enhanced .......................61, 81-82, 139, 141
Death of annuity owner,
  income taxation .............................224-225
Deferral of income tax during
  accumulation.............................1, 61, 73-74, 224-225, 231
Deferred compensation plans .......90, 204, 205
Delivery of contract..................................125
Disclosure, required...................................113
Distribution rules, qualified
  plan .........................................194, 199-200
Distributions, income
  taxation of..............................221, 224-225
Diversification of investments.........5, 6, 8, 16, 25, 27, 29, 32, 61, 79

Dollar cost averaging among
accounts..........................61, 71-73, 143-144
Dollar cost averaging........................61, 71-73,
95-97, 108, 143-144

## E

Education expenses.............61, 66-69,206-210
Eisenhower generation ................................26
Employer retirement
plans................................21-23, 27, 32, 201
Equity-indexed annuity ......................152-154
Estate taxation of annuities ................226-228
Ethical practices..................................125-126
Exchanges, contract.............................123-124
Expectations for future, customer ..............94
Expense benchmarks, NAVA......................158

## F

Features, product, see "product features"
Fixed payout ..................................1, 5, 12, 147
529 plans...............................................67, 208
401(k) plans.................................196, 200, 201
403 (b) plans .................................65, 202-203
457 plans .......................................67, 203-204
Futures contracts........................................183

## G

Generation X................................................26
Generation Y ...............................................26
Gift taxation of annuities...................228-229
Gifts of annuities .........................210, 230-231
Group annuities
pricing.............................................166-167
types ......................................................154
Guaranteed interest
accounts .........................61, 80, 86, 136-137
Guaranteed living
benefits...........................61, 82-83, 139-141
Guaranteed minimum accumulation
benefit.......................................82, 139-140
Guaranteed minimum income
benefit.............................................82, 140
Guaranteed minimum withdrawal
benefit.......................................82, 140-141
Guarantees, using in sales.......................80-83

## H

Hedge funds........................................187-188
Histories, performance ...............................100
Hope Scholarship Credit ..............................66
Households, composition of...................18-19

## I

Illustrations, sales...............................106, 122
Immediate variable annuity.......................150
Income taxation of annuities
death of annuity owner .................224-225
Income taxation of annuities (cont'd)
deferral during
accumulations ...................224-225, 231
distributions ...........................221, 224-225
payouts...........................................222-224
premature
distributions................216-217, 218-219
sale of an annuity...........................221-222
surrenders ..............................................221
withdrawals ...................................216-218
Income, maximizing (also see
"payout options")....................30-31, 83-84
Indexed annuity, equity.......................152-154
Individual Retirement Account
(Annuity) IRA
contributions ..................62-66, 198-199
Coverdell educational
account....................................67, 207
deductible IRAs................62, 63, 67, 198
distributions .........................67, 199-200
market, as a..............................27-28, 32
Roth IRAs .................62, 63, 67, 198, 199
Inheritances, investing..................................86
Insurance company ratings.................101-103
Investment advisory fee ......................162-163
Investment allocation ..............6-7, 75, 76, 97,
98-100, 108, 142
Investment diversification ..............5, 6, 8, 61,
79, 132-135
Investment management fee...............162-163
Investment selection.......................6-7, 65, 68,
71, 72, 97,98-101, 105, 142
Investors, mutual fund.........6, 15-16, 183-185
IRA, see "Individual Retirement Account
(Annuity) IRA"
Issue age, annuity.......................................131

## L

Large, one-time amounts,
handling........................................61, 86-87
Licensing
insurance and annuity............111-113, 116
securities..........................................114-115
Life income options .............................88, 148
Lifetime Learning Credit .............................66
Limited partnerships...........................187-188

## M

Maintaining purchasing
power........................4-5, 8, 9-10, 13, 61, 78
Market research
analyzing data......................................42-43
conducting research ...............................39
designing survey.................................40-42
Market timing, limiting .....................124-125
Market value adjustment ...................151-152

Market, annuities as primary ........................36
Market, annuities as supplementary....................................35-36
Market, joining organizations ................43-44
Marketing and sales support (see Chapter 5 generally)
Maturity age, annuity ................................131
Maximizing income (also see "payout options") ....................30-31, 83-84
Mortality and expense (M&E) charge.............................................161-162
Mutual fund investors..........6, 15-16, 183-185
Mutual funds, compared with variable annuities ...........................183-186

## N

NASDAQ ...................................................180
National Association of Securities Dealers (NASD) ..................111, 113, 114, 115-116, 117, 119, 120-123, 125, 159
Nonqualified retirement plans ...........204-205
North American Securities Administrators Association (NASAA) ............114-115, 117

## O

Options to buy or sell ................................183

## P

Payout options
- fixed amount............................1, 5, 12, 147
- fixed period ..............................5, 8, 12, 147
- joint and survivor ..........................148-149
- life income (annuitization) ............147, 148

Payout options (continued)
- life income with period certain .............148
- variable payouts.........................12, 149-150

Payouts and life insurance......................61, 88
Payouts, income taxation of
- fixed ..............................................222-223
- variable ..........................................223-224

Penalty tax perspective...........................84-85
Pension plans.....................................191-192
Performance histories ................................100
Population segments ..............................26-27
Premature distributions, income taxation of
- annuities......................216-217, 218-219
- qualified plans...........................199, 201

Premium allocation .....................................11
Premium tax...............................................166
Premiums, allocation to accounts..............142
Premiums, minimum requirements ................................130-131
Presentation, building sales..........................56
Pricing, annuity ..................157, 159, 166-167
Producer compensation.............................172
Product features
- accumulation units .........................131-132
- death benefit..................17, 28, 29, 138-139
- dollar cost averaging among accounts ...............................72, 143-144
- enhanced death benefits...........72, 139, 141
- guaranteed interest accounts.......61, 80, 86, 136-137
- guaranteed living benefits............62, 82-83, 139, 141
- issue age.................................................131
- maturity age ...........................................131
- minimum premiums .....................130-131
- payout options, see "payout options"
- surrender charges....................144, 164-166
- transfers among accounts ...........60, 73, 80, 86, 142-143
- used in sales process, features.........108-109
- variable accounts, see "variable accounts"
- waiver of surrender charges ...........145-146
- withdrawals ................60, 74, 77, 80, 82, 83, 144, 145, 151-152, 216-218

Profit sharing plans....................191, 192, 196
Profitable products ......173-174, 175, 176-177
Prospectus
- contents ..........................................103-105
- market timing disclosure................124-125
- presenting .......................................103-105

Purchasing power, maintaining............4, 5, 8, 9-10, 13, 61, 78
Purchasing variable annuities, convenience of........................................8-9

## Q

Qualified retirement plans............29, 191-198

## R

Ratings, insurance company...............101-103
Real estate as an investment................188-189
Real estate investment trusts (REIT) .........189
Rebalancing, automatic account.......................................76, 77, 143
Registered Investment Advisor (RIA).......................................114, 116-117
Required minimum distributions..............194
Research, market, see "market research"
Retirement income, composition of .................................20-25
Retirement plans
- nonqualified
  - executive equity plans....................89, 90
  - deferred compensation ..............204-205
  - supplemental ..............................204-205
- qualified
  - distribution rules...............194, 199-200

Retirement plans (cont'd)
qualified (cont'd)
401(k) plans........................196, 201-202
market, as ............................................29
pension ......................................191-192
profit sharing .....................191, 192, 196
required minimum distributions.......194
SIMPLE 401(k) plans ......67, 89, 196-197
Retirement, providing for ..................3-4, 5, 8
Risk disclosure
document.........................105-106, 119, 122
Roth IRA.....................................63, 64, 65, 67, 198, 199, 202

## S

Sale of annuity, income taxation of....221-222
Sales illustrations ................................106, 122
Sales literature
approval by broker/dealer...............120-121
filed with SEC.................................120-121
Sales load.....................................158-160, 165
Sales of property, investing
proceeds ....................................................32
Sales presentation, building..........................56
Sales process, tailoring ............................47-49
Sales, variable annuity annual ....................1-2
Saving what is needed for
future17, 24-25, 27-28, 29-30
Savings accounts .........................................189
Section 403(b) plans......................65, 202-203
Section 457 plans...........................67, 203-204
Section 529 plans ..................................67, 208
Securities Exchange
Commission (SEC)........116, 120, 122, 123, 124, 125, 158-160
Securities licensing .............................114-115
Securities Market Improvement
Act ..............................................158-160
Self employed persons
as market............................22, 27-28, 65
Seminar selling
design of seminar...............................53-54
sponsored ...........................................51-52
tips .....................................................49-50
SEP, see "Simplified Employee Pension"
Severance package, investing........................32
SIMPLE IRA .................................89, 200-201
Simplified Employee Pension
(SEP)..........................27-28, 65, 201-202
Social security benefits taxation,
effect of annuity on ............................61, 87
Social security trends .............................20-21
Standard of living, maintaining.............24-25
Stock
common .........................................179-180
preferred.........................................180, 187
Student loan interest....................................68
Suitability statement...........................121-123
Suitability supervision ................................123
Summaries, account and balance .......106-107
Supplemental retirement plans .............28-29, 60, 89-90, 204-205
Support, marketing and sales
(see Chapter 5 generally)
Surrender charge .........................144, 164-166
Surrenders, income taxation of annuity....221

## T

Target market characteristics..................37-39
Tax Sheltered Annuity (TSA)........65, 202-203
Tax, deferral of income ..............16-17, 27, 61, 73-74, 77, 84-85, 224-225, 231
Taxation of annuities
federal estate tax.............................226-228
federal gift tax ................................228-229
federal income tax, see "income
taxation of annuities"
Taxes, timing income .............................61, 77
Taxes, when to pay .............................7, 11, 12
Timing the market ............................61, 71, 95
Transfers among accounts ...............60, 73, 80, 86, 142-143
Treasury securities ..............................180-181

## U

Unit investment trusts.........................187-188

## V

Variable accounts
allocation of premiums..........................142
objectives and strategies .................132-134
selection of accounts ......................135, 142
types of accounts.............................132-134
Variable payout.............................12, 149-150
Voluntary benefits programs........................46

## W

Waiver of surrender charge.................145-146
Withdrawals
charge-free.......................................144-145
income taxation of..........................216-218
optional surrender benefits....................144
optional withdrawal provisions.............145
periodic withdrawal program................145
surrender charges....................144, 164-166
Wrap accounts, mutual fund .............186-187